Stephen & Jane

Christmas Day, 1931

THE PHILOSOPHY OF
THE GOOD LIFE

THE PHILOSOPHY OF
THE GOOD LIFE

BEING THE GIFFORD LECTURES DELIVERED
IN THE UNIVERSITY OF ST. ANDREWS, 1929-30

BY CHARLES GORE, D.D.

HON. D.D. EDIN. AND DURHAM, HON. D.C.L. OXFORD, HON. LL.D. CAMBRIDGE
AND BIRMINGHAM, PH.D. ATHENS, HON. FELLOW OF BALLIOL AND TRINITY
COLLEGES, OXFORD, AND FELLOW OF KING'S COLLEGE, LONDON

NEW YORK
CHARLES SCRIBNER'S SONS
1930

FIRST EDITION . . . 1930

171·16
G66p
186088 c·3

PRINTED IN GREAT BRITAIN

PREFACE

THE divisions of this book are entitled " chapters," but it will be plain to every reader that they are in fact the printed record of lectures—twelve lectures delivered during the winter of 1929–30 before the University of St. Andrews on the foundation of Lord Gifford ; and that I have not attempted to alter their character. The fact that they are lectures must be my excuse for some obvious repetitions, such as seemed to be necessary if what was to be said was to be made intelligible to an audience which did not consist entirely of the same persons on each occasion. It is also to be borne in mind that the lectures were intended to be intelligible to an audience not mainly consisting of expert philosophers. In the introductory lecture I have sufficiently explained the nature of the subject to be dealt with, and the special purpose of the lecturer.

Some years ago in *The Reconstruction of Belief* I published what was intended to be a systematic *apologia* for the Christian Faith. Nothing of the sort is attempted in this book. My subject is the idea of the good life as it is to be found in history. Half of the book consists of the historical survey ; after which I analyse the presuppositions both of the " idealist " and the more definitely " monotheist " presentations of the good life, and finally in the four last lectures

I endeavour to show the superior rationality of the " monotheist " presuppositions in their Christian form. Those who are disposed to agree with my reasonings will then be able to approach what are called the Christian " evidences " without any hostile prejudice.

I do not know that there is anything more that need be said by way of preface. But I must be allowed to express my cordial thanks to the University of St. Andrews—both professors, lecturers, and students—for the kindness with which they received me and for the happy weeks which I passed in their beautiful and historic city.

I owe a debt of gratitude to my neighbour the Rev. Christopher Cheshire for having read the lectures before they went to press and made a number of useful suggestions.

C. G.

27 Eaton Terrace,
    London, S.W.
        August, 1930.

CONTENTS

CHAPTER I

INTRODUCTORY

CHAPTER II

ZARATHUSTRA

CONTENTS

CHAPTER III

SIDDARTHA GOTAMA, THE BUDDHA

CHAPTER IV

THE TEACHERS OF ASIA

CHAPTER V

PLATONISM

CHAPTER VI

ISRAEL

CHAPTER VII

JESUS THE CHRIST

CHAPTER VIII

REFLECTION UPON THE HISTORICAL SURVEY

CHAPTER IX

THE CHRISTIAN IDEA OF GOD

CHAPTER X

THE CHRISTIAN IDEA OF HUMAN NATURE

CHAPTER XI

THE IDEA OF REVELATION

CONTENTS

CHAPTER XII

RATIONAL FAITH

CHAPTER I

§ 1

CALLED to the honourable post of a Gifford
Lecturer in this University of St. Andrews,
I have, of course, studied the Trust Disposition
and Settlement of the late Lord Gifford, or the
portion of it relevant to the lecturers, and
find myself able to correspond heartily with his
intentions.

First, he intended the lectures delivered under
his Trust Deed to have for their object " the
promoting, advancing, teaching and diffusing
the study of Natural Theology, in the widest
sense of that term, in other words, the knowledge
of God . . . the knowledge of His nature and
attributes, the knowledge of the relations which
men and the whole Universe bear to Him, the
knowledge of the nature and foundation of
Ethics and Morals, and of all the Obligations
and Duties thence arising."

Secondly, the lectures were to be the expression
of the free individual opinion of the lecturer,
whether his conclusions on the momentous
subject, or group of subjects, assigned to him
should turn out to be positive and constructive,
or negative and destructive, or purely sceptical.
He must speak as one bound by no formula or
standard of belief as constraining either himself

1

or his hearers. He must express simply the
ideas or conclusions arrived at in the exercise
of his own rational powers, and, of course, the
arguments or motives which had led him to
such ideas or conclusions, arguments or motives
which might lead other individual minds along
the same road to the same goal, whether of
affirmation, denial or doubt. So I interpret in
my own words Lord Gifford's fourth and fifth
requirements.

Thirdly, the lectures were to be " popular,"
in the sense, I suppose, that the lecturer, dealing
with a subject or group of subjects which is of
vital importance for every man, and taking it
for granted that those who listen to him would
be fairly educated men and women, capable of
following a philosophical train of thought, should
at the same time avoid as much as possible the
technical language which is commonly used
among philosophical and theological experts,
and should explain it where he is obliged to use
it, taking nothing for granted but the average
intelligence of the educated person. So I interpret Lord Gifford's sixth requirement—the
rest, which I have not noticed, concerning only
details of arrangement and in no way the substance of the lectures.

But I must notice one desire expressed by
Lord Gifford which, I am told, has been generally
ignored—that, besides giving public lectures,
the lecturer should also have personal contact
with those who attend his lectures, so that they
might have the opportunity to " heckle " him
with their personal questionings. I heartily

desire to correspond with the Founder's intention in this respect.[1]

The above requirements, then, I can accept with a hearty goodwill. The subject—whether there be something eternal behind this changing universe of things and persons, whether and in what sense there be a God or gods, and, if there be, of what sort is the divine nature and what is man's relation to it—is the fundamental problem of philosophy. I suppose it is unlikely that anyone who was asked for a description of your present lecturer would describe him as a philosopher. But if a " philosopher "—that is, a lover of wisdom—means a man whose spirit can find no rest unless he can gain and keep some " theory " or vision of the world of things and experiences, such as shall enable him to interpret its manifold phenomena as parts of one whole, and as expressive in some sort of one purpose, in which he himself is called to co-operate with will and intelligence—if that be the meaning of a philosopher, then, though defective knowledge and capacity may render me a poor specimen of the class, certainly I am a philosopher.

For though the vision or theory which I have gained or can hope to gain may be sadly imperfect—something seen " through a glass darkly " or " a scheme imperfectly comprehended "—yet I never could endure to desist from the philosophic quest. I never could tolerate with any degree of equanimity the idea

[1] The lectures as they stand in print have been a good deal altered from what was originally spoken (at least in detail) as a result in part of such personal contacts.

of keeping the findings of different fields of
thought or experience in separate mental compartments, paying no attention to their inconsistency.

Again, to pass to the second requirement
described above, in that quest I could never
endure to be otherwise than a free-thinker. I
mean by that that whatever obligation I may
have inherited or contracted to any traditional
system of belief or thought, I could never allow
it to blind me to anything which might seem
to be truth, whatever its origin, or to shackle me
so that I could not follow the light of reason
whithersoever it should lead.

I say this of myself with trembling, for
experience of life and of books leads one to feel
how very difficult it is to be really a free-thinker.
Orthodox theologians are supposed to be more
especially liable to become the slaves of illegitimate prejudice—to be men whose eyes are blinded
to unwelcome truths and who " reason in chains."
But, reading the books of men who have obviously
rebelled against every kind of orthodoxy, I seem
to see that even extreme reaction against
established opinion affords no kind of security
against prejudice. The rebels appear to find
it at least as hard to recognize the strong points
in the positions of their adversaries in debate as
do the orthodox. But recognizing the difficulty,
we must not give up the struggle to be fully
open-eyed to the light from whatever source it
comes, and we must, if we would be worthy of
the name of lovers of wisdom, pledge ourselves
solemnly and seriously to refuse no conclusion,

however unpalatable, which on serious consideration appears to be true.

It is of course the case that every man's
opinions in science, theology or morals have
owed in one way or another a vast deal to
authority, whether it be the authority of home
or class or nation, or of some church or organization, or of some individual, philosopher or poet
or prophet—whether, I may add, the authority
ultimately constrains him to obedience or drives
him to rebellion. When Dr. A. N. Whitehead
defines religion as " what the individual does
with his own solitariness," [1] he is expressing, no
doubt, a very important element in the higher
kinds of religion, but as a definition it is a paradox,
and indeed it is so one-sided as to be untrue.
Religion is also—and probably, if you consider it
as it appears in history, it is primarily—a social
fact ; and social influences have largely made
the religion and morality of any man what they
are. It is also true that, for a great number of
us, the opinions on religion and morals which
we have received from some kind of authority
continue to be accepted just as they are, so long
as they appear to work well and to satisfy the
requirements of experience, without much consideration of their grounds. But certainly no
one can put in any claim to share the philosophic
spirit, unless for him the whole subject-matter,
whether in religion or morality or in any other
department of life—unless the whole subject-
matter, received on whatever authority, has
been sifted in his own experience and thought,

[1] *Religion in the Making*, p. 6.

and has passed from being merely a tradition received to become a reasoned conviction of his own mind. For myself I can profess that in all that I am to say in these lectures I shall be speaking nothing more nor less than my own reasoned convictions, without regard to any constraining authority, social, ecclesiastical, or individual.

As for Lord Gifford's remaining requirement— that the lectures should be " popular "—I do resent and have always resented the tendency of philosophers and theologians to retire into some inner *enclave*, where they can talk a language intelligible only to themselves. For their subject—the meaning of the world we live in and the relation in which we stand to this meaning —is a subject of vital concern to all men, and those who profess to expound it ought at least to strive to express themselves in words which men and women of common intelligence can be expected to understand.

§ 2

My chosen subject, though it will be found to involve the whole topic of the nature of reality and the reason of man, is specially Moral Philosophy. My starting-point is to investigate the conception of the good life with its postulates, as mankind in general has understood it. For in any general review of mankind, especially where it has risen to any degree of civilization, we find this conception everywhere entertained. " The state," says Aristotle, in a phrase which endures and finds almost universal assent, " comes into existence for the sake of life, but it exists for the sake of the good life." [1]   As distinct from what the individual may find pleasant to his senses, or what he may find profitable to his acquisitive instinct, we find the sense of obligation, of duty, of responsibility and the distinction of right and wrong.   The dominance in the modern world of the conception of evolution has led men to the hypothesis that this sense of duty is nothing else at bottom than " the herd instinct," [2] so easily recognizable among animals, which subordinates the interest of the individual to that of the group, so that, according to this view, the undoubted authority of conscience is purely of social origin and requires to account for it no reference to any higher or supernatural power.   But I propose, to start with at least, to leave aside this question of the biological or psychological origin of the sense of duty and simply to examine in some detail the idea of the good life, just as we might examine the idea of beauty as it is found in developed man ;   I am proposing to act on the fundamental Aristotelian principle, which nevertheless will require justification, that the true nature of anything is then first apparent when it is fully developed.

I have just set side by side the idea of the

---

[1] *Pol.*, i, 2.

[2] Prof. G. Elliot Smith (*History of Man*, p. 255) declares that the evidence concerning primitive man " reveals no trace of the assembling of any ' herd ' other than the family group, either for self-defence or any other purpose."   " The primal horde . . . is fiction pure and simple.   ' The Herd Instinct ' belongs to the same category of misleading speculations."   This question I leave to the anthropologists.

good and the idea of the beautiful.[1] There are those, like Prof. Gilbert Murray, who—in his truly illuminating and noble book on the *Classical Tradition*—would identify the two. "I have never," he says, " been able to see, though people have tried to point it out to me for forty years, any real difference between the moral and the æsthetic." [2] Now, the two are indeed certainly akin. They are both intuitions rather than conclusions from reasoning. Also, I should admit that among the Greeks they were held very close together, the good and the beautiful being almost identified in the idea of τὸ καλόν—though where Plato would banish the poets, whose work he yet acknowledges to be beautiful, from his ideal state, in the interests of virtue, and speaks of the long-standing quarrel between them and the philosophers,[3] he is recognizing a broad distinction between the two ideas or kinds of men. Whatever authority, however, Murray may find for his identification, I feel sure we must reject it. Experience cries out against it. The great moral prophets and saints of history have not been especially æsthetic, and the great artists, the supreme experts in beauty, have not been in the main patterns of morality. For an individual to be wholly dominated by the sense of beauty is obviously not the same thing as to be on fire with the love of goodness. A nation also which is possessed with the idea

[1] On the trinity of values—goodness, beauty and truth—see App. Note, p. 30.

[2] He is following Shelley in this identification. *Cl. Trad. in Poetry*, p. 259.

[3] *Rep.*, x, 607.

of the good life, like the ancient people of
Israel, may be deficient in the æsthetic sense.
The two senses may no doubt be combined, but
they are different and even very often an-
tagonistic.

For our consideration, then, in these Lectures
I propose the idea of the good life. I do so,
first, because of the masterful intensity with
which the supreme obligation of the good, of
duty, as something quite distinct from the claim
of pleasure or profit, or even the requirement of
honour, has impressed itself upon the souls of
the men whom the world has agreed to call the
best. The founder of the philosophy of the
Stoics, Zeno, would distinguish the " impressions "
we receive by their intensity, holding that the
most intense impressions have the most right
to be considered representative of reality. There
are some, he said, so intense that they " seize us
by the hair of our head and drag us to consent."
Surely one of these is the impression of moral
duty as absolute. Some of us would remember
being deeply moved, when we began the study
of Plato, by Socrates' declaration [1] : " And this
is the point in which, as I think, I am superior
to men in general, and in which I might perhaps
fancy myself wiser than other men, that, whereas
I know but little of the world below, I do not
suppose that I know ; but I do know that injustice and disobedience to a better, whether
God or man, is evil and dishonourable, and I will
never fear or avoid a possible good [such as death]
rather than a certain evil [wrong-doing]. . . .

[1] *Apology*, 29.

Men of Athens, I honour and love you ; but I shall obey God rather than you." This means that for Socrates moral convictions are stronger than speculative opinions ; and though he may rank himself as singular in this respect, I think we should find the majority of men in agreement with him.

Of course, any such general statement needs qualification. There are in all civilizations a great many people who appear to have no clear ideal of life. I remember seeing, scratched upon the pavement of the Roman city of Timgad in Algeria by some ancient lounger, the words " Venari, lavari, ludere, ridere occ est vivere," [1] and though the precise occupations or amusements to be enumerated would vary in different states of civilization or different classes of society, the same apparent absence of anything worthy to be called an ideal of life is everywhere found in a great number of individuals. It is also of course lamentably true that men may sophisticate their consciences so as to profess, and even believe themselves, to be following some noble ideal while their underlying motive is self-interest or vanity. The light that is in them has become darkness. It is true again that, instead of seeking to form moral convictions of their own, most men are content to live by the standard of public opinion ; and that public opinion is constantly in the wrong, and the social tradition of a community may be corrupt and corrupting is undeniable.

Once more, in modification of the idea of

[1] To hunt, to bathe, to gamble, to laugh, that is to live.

moral certitude, it must be admitted that even
for the best men there remains a region of
moral problems, where different duties seem
to collide, which are fairly insoluble. But when
all these considerations are allowed their full
force, and the variety of actual moral standards
among individuals and nations and epochs is
fully kept in view, it still, I contend, remains
true that the honest, candid man of all nations
and civilizations can more easily and securely
arrive at certitude as to what he ought to do,
and can more easily and securely distinguish
the trustworthy moral guide from the clever
sophist, than he can arrive at certitude by
abstract argument or distinguish false from true
in the region of philosophy.

Again, if you pass from thinking of the
individual to thinking of societies of men, there
is more reliance to be put on their moral ideals
than on almost any other part of their heritage;
and more value is to be attached to these ideals
than to the arguments by which they are tradi-
tionally defended. For the moral ideals professed by a nation, even when notoriously the
majority of its members fall very far short
of them or hardly attempt to follow them,
probably represent the convictions of the best
minds which have been at work among them;
and moral, like æsthetic, ideals are felt, rather
than reasoned, and are mostly derived from some
prophetic teacher.[1]

[1] There is a noticeable phrase in Plato's *Republic* (382 E),
where Adeimantus is represented as assenting to Socrates' dogmatic statement of God's essential goodness as something which

For this reason, then, I set myself to examine the range and nature of this masterful conviction of the claim of the good among the great teachers of men and their followers.

Secondly, I do so because I cannot but think that this is the best way to restore respect for philosophy. It can hardly be denied—it is acknowledged by our philosophers themselves [1]— that while intelligent mankind pays the highest respect to science, which indeed it cannot but do, considering what science has accomplished in the last hundred years, and even though the respect paid to it has recently been deeply tinged both with dismay and bewilderment, yet it pays very little attention to the philosophers, such as it would pay if their speculations " mattered " to the practical man. And the chaotic condition of philosophy goes far to justify this attitude. It was a like scepticism about the value of current philosophizing which led to Socrates' successful attempt to bring philosophy down from the clouds into the

becomes evident to him when Socrates asserts it. " So I myself think, now you say so." This represents the average human attitude towards the great moral prophets of mankind. Ordinary men accept their teaching as true, in virtue of a responsive assent of their own consciences, though by themselves they would never have thought of it.

[1] See, e.g., Collingwood's *Speculum Mentis*, pp. 278, 281; cf. pp. 34, 286: " Most people regard philosophy as the acme of futility, the abstraction of abstractions." . . . " The philosophers have lost touch with the people so egregiously that it is hardly worth while insisting on the point. . . . All alike are asking what use they are in the world." Cf. A. N. Whitehead, *Process and Reality*, p. 218: " The combined influence of these allied errors has been to reduce philosophy to a negligible influence in the formation of contemporary modes of thought."

common life of man and to lead it to become
moral philosophy—the enquiry into the good
life and into its grounds. That is a subject in
which every decent man must be profoundly
interested and one on which he starts with a
great deal of knowledge based on experience
and a more or less trained faculty of judgment.
Thus moral philosophy can be made truly human
and popular and is the best introduction to
metaphysical thinking. Moreover, in a demo-
cratic and journalistic age, where everything is
being put to the vote and judged by majorities,
it is an extraordinarily valuable study, because
it teaches us, in the most forcible way imaginable,
that the great issues are not decided by majorities
—that it is small minorities, who seemed to their
contemporaries to be fighting a desperate battle
with their backs against the wall, who again
and again have won the day in the later judgment and common sense of mankind.

Thirdly, there is surely a very special reason
why we give a first place in importance to moral
philosophy in the present age. We may be very
clever to-day, and we may have a right to
denounce as misleaders, or to ignore, the prophets
and teachers of the Victorian age. Speaking as
a person who was well advanced in years when the
great queen died, I do not feel that the current
indictment of the Victorians is unjust, at least
in some respects. But the thought of the present
age, if it is full of curiosity and of variety, is also
full of confusion ; and the confusion is nowhere
so noticeable as in respect of morality. The
prophets of the Victorian age were in no respect

more short-sighted than in their constant assurances that agnosticism in respect of theology would not undermine the Christian moral standard. There were those who even then lifted their voices to express grave doubt of this assurance ; and certainly none of the Victorian assumptions has been found more unwarrantable. To-day, at least as conspicuously as orthodox theology, the accepted moral standard of Christian tradition is being assailed with contempt, with ridicule, and with indignant argument—not only the morality of sex, but also the whole idea of self-denial and the service of the weak by the strong. The current popular literature is demanding above all things free individual self-expression, unshackled by parental or ecclesiastical authority or by considerations of humility or charity.

But a great many serious people, who are by no means puritans, or persons distinguished for conservative orthodoxy, cannot but view the enthronement of free individual self-expression as an object of worship with the deepest dread. There is no doubt a sense in which " to save one's own soul," which, however understood, must be the aim of everyone, may be translated " to obtain for oneself free self-expression " ; but we feel that if this translation is to be justified, it must also be recognized that the self or soul, with all its multifarious ambitions and desires, as it is found at starting in all varieties of human beings, needs a great deal of chastisement and reconstruction before it can be safely set free.[1] It must die to live,

---

[1] See below, pp. 221 f.

as even Goethe acknowledged. Thus there are a great number of not specially conservative people who are seriously alarmed to-day at the moral outlook not only in this country. Surely, then, the needs of the moment suggest to would-be philosophers, distressed that their labours meet with so little attention from practical men, that they should devote themselves specially to the line of research and reflection along which not only notable distinction, but the attention and respect of common men, have been won in the past both in Scotland and England, as by Joseph Butler, and the glory of Germany who was by race a Scot, Immanuel Kant—the line of moral philosophy. James Martineau, Hastings Rashdall, and Dr. Sorley, who is still with us, are more recent examples. For we can depend upon it that moral standards, if they are to maintain themselves, imperatively need justification to the reason. They cannot survive as an unreasoned emotion or feeling.[1] In other words, the study of the good life as it has been preached and lived requires also anxious search into the validity of its presuppositions.

§ 3

My subject, then, is to be Moral Philosophy—the philosophy of the good life ; and my next step must be to explain the course of the argument which I intend to follow in these lectures, for whatever measure of originality a man may have consists largely in his approach to his

[1] See Rashdall, *Is Conscience an Emotion ?*, p. 5.

subject or the perspective in which he sees it.
So Montaigne and Pascal rightly defend themselves against the charge of not being original
because they are found to borrow the thoughts
and expressions of others. The old thought,
they said in self-defence, may have gained a quite
new meaning by being set in a new context
and development.[1] " Qu'on ne dise pas que je
n'ai rien dit de nouveau : la disposition des
matières est nouvelle ; quand on joue à la
paume, c'est une même balle dont joue l'un
et l'autre, mais l'un la place mieux." So Lessing
in his *Kleine Schriften* says : " The manner in
which one comes to a matter is as valuable and
even as instructive as the matter itself." In
this sense every honest thinker has some measure
of originality. In my own case, then, the philosophy which commands my respect is that which
has least the character of being abstract or *a
priori*, and which is most deeply rooted and
most securely verified in the actual experience
of mankind. I propose therefore to take my
stand first of all upon the ground of the moral
consciousness of men as shown in history.
Everywhere mankind appears—even the rudest
tribes—as having some sort of standard of a
good life—the life which is approved and which
binds man to his fellows, or conversely a life
the obligations of which he cannot ignore without
falling under obloquy and punishment. As has
already been said,[2] it has been often supposed
that the moral sense has its roots in this herd

[1] See Brunschvigg's *Pensées de Bl. Pasca* vol. i, pp. 33–4.
[2] See above, p. 7, and note.

instinct—that it is at bottom purely social, simply akin to what is to be found among the higher animals. But I am not proposing at present to consider its origin, only its most notable developments.

Thus in very early history we find that the idea of the good life is developed, perhaps for the first time on very distinct lines, in the teaching of the Iranian prophet Zarathustra : we find it taking other expressions in India and in the remoter East, as later in Arabia under the teaching of Muhammad. We are by tradition much more familiar with its very rich development in the poets and philosophers of Greece ; and on a strikingly different basis in the history of Israel and in the teaching of Jesus Christ. These developments occur quite independently of one another, save that what we find in the world of Islam may be described as an out-growth of Judaism, though on very distinctive lines ; and that which is most intimately bound up with European history, the teaching of Jesus Christ and of the Christian Church, is professedly based upon the foundations of Israel.

All these expressions of the conception of the good life for man will be passed under careful review. In almost all of them we shall find that they have outgrown the merely social sanction, in which the sense of moral obligation is commonly found to originate, in two directions. First, that the obligation of the individual to obey the tribal law has passed into the wider and deeper conception of the individual soul as holding within itself the witness to its own value and

2

end—a value and end which it is its highest duty
to realize in itself and to respect in other men,
and which are something much more than an
obligation to obey the tribe. Secondly, that
the sense of moral obligation has carried man
above himself and found its sanction and its
aim in the relation of man to the divine being;
though to this last tendency we shall find at
least in original Buddhism a marked exception.

When we have finished our review of the
actual developments among mankind of moral
practice and theory—which must necessarily
be a rather protracted survey—it will become
our business to analyse out as carefully as possible
the intellectual presuppositions of these various
types of morality which have actually prevailed,
and to consider whether they are intellectually
justifiable—whether they belong to the realm
of reality or of myth—whether they can be
brought into harmony to-day with the postulates
of human experience in other departments of
human experience, with art, with science, with
history—and can thus make a fresh claim to the
allegiance of mankind at large. For, if practical
moral certainty is to survive, it must become
an intellectual apprehension also and be found
consistent with the whole body of knowledge.
This is obviously a wide-ranging enquiry which
I can only hope to attempt in respect of its
main lines, and with the help of the consideration which will have emerged that (with the
exception of Buddhism) there is up to a certain
point a very remarkable agreement in principle
among all the prophets and teachers of the good

life, whom we shall have examined, with regard to the realities which they postulate behind the visible world of nature and man.

Since the origin of Christianity, or perhaps I should say since the first spread of Islam, there does not appear to have arisen any great teacher who has proclaimed a new moral way for man so as to command any wide or permanent allegiance ; but we shall of course have to take account of notable rebellions against all the moral standards appealing to ancient authority in different lands, and among these what will be most vividly in our eyes will be the rebellions in modern Europe against the Christian moral tradition. These rebellions are of two kinds. There are the rebels against the actual moral standard of Christianity, such as were Voltaire and Rousseau, and Goethe in a milder form, and in a much more revolutionary form Nietzsche and a good many contemporary writers. And there are the rebels who, claiming to retain the traditional moral standard in practice, believe that this can be done while placing it on a quite new basis of intellectual presupposition—such as are to be found among materialists, positivists and agnostics, and also among idealists.

But before embarking on this formidable enquiry into facts and principles, I want to say a word concerning the relation of philosophy to experience in general and to moral and religious experience in particular.[1]

---

[1] What follows is substantially a repetition of what I have said elsewhere, but I thought such repetition could not be avoided.

§ 4

Philosophy is a comparatively late-comer into human history. Mankind had accumulated a vast store of experience and verified in a rough-and-ready way, or rejected as worthless, a great number of instinctive assumptions and conjectures before the philosopher appears upon the scene. It had moved out in three directions.

(1) Impelled, first of all, by the instinct of self-preservation, both individual and tribal, it had moved out towards nature, including under that name all its living breeds, to appropriate its resources and to defend itself against the perils which threatened it.[1] In this process it had accumulated a vast store of experience and had reached instinctively a number of general notions, such as the notion of a prevailing order in nature which makes it relatively trustworthy, and concurrently the notion that there were among natural phenomena some which could not be reckoned upon or accounted for, and must be attributed to the arbitrary wills of spirits good or bad. Leaving the latter class of notion aside for the moment, we find ourselves tracing the development of civilization, with the various kinds of utilitarian science and the earlier forms of the æsthetic arts ; for the same instinctive pressure led man to find in nature not only the satisfaction of his demand for the sustenance of his physical life, but also the response to a

---

[1] " Since man first acquired the ability to examine the conditions of his existence, his first occupation has always been the conscious search for the means of safeguarding his own life."—Prof. Elliot Smith, *Human History*, p. 24.

hunger for beauty. The philosopher therefore
when he comes upon the scene finds the minds
of men preoccupied with convictions about the
solidity, reality and normal orderliness of nature,
and also with the conception of beauty and, we
may add, of truth, as things to be desired in
and for themselves. There is mixed up in these
convictions a vast amount of gross mistake,
of which the " wise man " may fairly easily
demonstrate the futility and gradually dispossess
the minds of his contemporaries. But the underlying assumptions remain solidly established,
as verified in constant experience.

(2) And all this time primitive man has been
moving out towards his fellow-men. He had
inherited from his animal ancestors a group
instinct which led him to live for his group
and sacrifice himself for it. Thus he distinguishes
men from animals, and deals with them differently
by the use of language as a vehicle of his thoughts
and intentions. Potentially they all seem to
have common interests, and the area of friendliness or fellowship extends, and within each unit
of human action organization takes place. Thus
we trace the development of human society
based upon certain postulates about human
nature which experience suggested and has
verified—without which human society could
not go on—such as freedom, duty and responsibility, and a widening sense of brotherhood among
men.

(3) Meanwhile, man is also found in history
(or in the discoveries which tell us something
certain about prehistoric man) to be moving

out in another direction—towards God or gods. The unaccountable features in the proceedings of nature suggested no doubt the activity of spirits good and bad whose wills might be influenced, like the wills of men, by gifts and persuasions ; and dead ancestors presented themselves in dreams and visitations, and inspired both terror and the hope of protection. The origins of religion are of course obscure,[1] but the enormous development of religion is apparent wherever the remains of an early civilization are discovered by the antiquarian, as well as when historical records or memories begin to appear. Everywhere we find man's greatest efforts and skill devoted to the building of temples, and the proper ordering of sacrifice and worship, while the priesthoods, which are supposed to possess the knowledge of the ways of the gods and to interpret them to men, are held in the highest honour. The question whether the amount of mere error which appears in the early traditions of religion is greater or grosser than appears in primitive ideas concerning nature and man need not here delay us. At any rate, the amount of gross error was immense.

But we witness also developments of morality and religion which are confessedly noble and pure—which almost everyone would acclaim to be on the highest level of human thought and achievement—and these developments carry

---

[1] I cannot but think that Prof. Elliot Smith's account of its origin is a great deal too simple to be at all plausible. " Simple explanations," says Dr. A. N. Whitehead truly, " are to be sought but distrusted."

with them the conception of the good life for
man as involving his relation to God, as much as
his relation to his fellow-men. We are not yet
considering whether the occupation of mankind
with religion is a rational occupation at all,
or whether the conception of the good life must
really be held to involve his fellowship with God.
We are only noting that in fact man's development has been in three and not two directions
—towards nature, towards man and towards
God—and that his instinctive movements in
these three directions have received such con-
firmation in experience as that when the philosophers begin to appear upon the scene they
have found already in possession among mankind
certain apparently ineradicable convictions about
nature, about man and also about the divine
being, with which the philosophers have been
compelled to deal, and which in fact they are
found to have dealt with in many different ways.
But while there are innumerable differences
among the philosophers in their attitude towards
common experience, there is one difference
which tends to divide them into two classes,
and it is this difference to which I wish to call
attention and on which I must dare to express
a personal judgment. The difference I am referring to is that between the predominantly
a priori or abstract philosophers and those predominantly experiential or *a posteriori*.[1]

[1] Any epistemology, i.e. any attempt to analyse experience
or knowledge, must recognize in it some sort of synthesis
between what is derived from sensations, over which the mind
has no control, and the action of the mind upon sensations.
Of what kind the synthesis is, and how the difference between

The East, especially India, is the home of the *a priori* thinking in a pre-eminent sense. It is there that we find that common experience, fundamentally derived through the senses, is most readily depreciated as delusion. But even if we confine ourselves to Europe, and to the main stream of philosophy which had its roots in Greek thinking, we still find the two types of philosophers in constant evidence and antagonism. If, leaving aside the child-like attempts of the early physicists to find the unitary principle in nature, we make our beginning with Socrates, we shall find him starting simply from one part of man's experience, his notion of the good to be pursued by man, and seeking to find some fundamental definition of virtue or the virtues by a sceptical analysis of common conceptions. He works on the solid basis of common experience. On the product of this analysis we find Plato rising higher and higher into the region of first principles and finally appearing (as in the *Timæus*) with a markedly dogmatic and *a priori* construction, but at the same time refusing to lose his hold on common experience. Aristotle is, we should agree, markedly experientialist on the whole and distrustful of the *a priori*. The Neo-Platonists, on the other hand, with whom Greek philosophy reaches its climax, are in the opposite extreme. When that extraordinary product of the dark ages, John the Scot (which

real knowledge and erroneous opinion is to be explained, has been one main problem of European philosophy since Plato's day. But I am not at present concerned with this problem. I am simply contrasting two classes of philosophers exhibiting two opposite mental characteristics.

designation you must, I fear, recognize as meaning John the Irishman, rather than an early
philosophical product of your own country [1])—
when that remarkable product of the ninth
century gave to the Catholic world his all-embrac-
ing philosophy it was a thorough-going Neo-
Platonism, barely interspersed with deferential
allusions to the Christian Scriptures, embodying
the *a priori* method in its extremest form, that
is, exhibiting a thorough confidence in the power
of the human reason to develop the universal
scheme of things out of its own self-contained
intuitions with the slenderest equipment of
actual knowledge. The great schoolmen, such
as St. Thomas Aquinas or Raymond Lull,
exhibit a very much greater deference alike to
the restrictive authority of Aristotle and to the
dogmatic requirements of the Church. But there
still remains in their vast products of thought
what seems to us a naïve belief in the capacity
of the human mind to perceive *a priori* what
must have been, and to determine what therefore
is the case, without any critical examination
of the facts.

In recent philosophical estimates these mediæval
lords of thought have been, after centuries of
contempt, restored to their thrones. This fresh
appreciation of their merits is due not only to
a recognition of the vast bulk of their achievement, and of their enormous influence on European thought in their period, but also to the
perception of the vast addition which they made

---

[1] His theory was condemned at the Council of Valence as
merely so much "Scots porridge."

to the power of the human mind to construct
a precise and complicated train of argument,
to estimate exactly what it implies and what
it does not, what it excludes and what it does
not. Their vast enrichment of the furniture of
the human intellect passed to the sons of the
Renaissance who were most inclined to scoff at
them. For the reaction against their method
was violent. Dr. A. N. Whitehead describes
the later scholasticism as " an unbridled rationalism," " an orgy of rationalism." Surely it is
true that the scholastic thinking and reasoning
whether from received dogmas or *a priori*
principles was almost entirely " unbridled "
either by any criticism of their sources or by
any considerable experimental knowledge of
what the ascertainable facts of the universe
actually are.

Thus, the first dawn of historical criticism
and scientific exploration brought the scholastic
fabric into discredit and contempt. All the stress
comes to be laid on criticism and experiment.
Knowledge is specialized into departments. The
unity of knowledge disappears in the process of infinite subdivision. In some quarters the very suggestion of a universal theory of things brings a man
into contempt. A very acute Cambridge man of
the last generation—Henry Sidgwick—used to say
that if a man is to obtain ungrudging recognition
in a modern university he had better know nothing outside his own subject. It could hardly be
denied that the real advances in knowledge since
the Renaissance have been due to the inexorable
determination on the part of our scientific men

and our historians to repudiate *a priori* judgments and to study with minutest analysis the actual facts. Nevertheless, the *a priori* dogmatic spirit has not been killed and cannot be killed. Hegel has been an enormous influence in the modern world, and Hegel's vision of history as the manifestation of spirit in the threefold moments of thesis, antithesis and synthesis, was an intellectual construction which, while no doubt it represents something in actual experience, also largely forced the facts, in violation of their natural meaning, into conformity with an *a priori* assumption.

In the world of to-day the *a priori* spirit is certainly not dead. In many brilliant histories written by Nationalists or Catholics or Modernists we cannot fail to recognize an *a priori* conception of what " must have been," prevailing over any candid examination of the facts. Meanwhile the men of science have been giving violent shocks to those who hoped that they had been imbibing the " assured results " of physical investigation. Mathematical physicists have been proclaiming that there is to be found at the very basis of nature a region of indeterminism. The ultimate elements of what we used to believe to be atoms appear to be acting not according to invariable laws, but with something like arbitrary choice. We may only speak of their average behaviour. The intelligent public cannot understand the argument of the mathematicians, but the outcome of their bewildering conclusions has given a shock to the state of mind which used to think itself scientific.

" Anything may happen in a world which is fundamentally indeterminate."

Once more there is apparent among us a rather widespread revolt from the intellectual traditions of Europe—a revolt which is set to maintain the superiority of Indian subjectivism over European belief in objective reality. This sort of subjectivism is deeply fostered by the dubious suggestions of contemporary psychology. And this widespread subjectivism in our present intellectual society leaves a great many " intelligent " men and women the prey to any *a priori* theorist who attracts their fancy.[1]

This somewhat chaotic condition of the contemporary mind is, no doubt, largely due to the deep disturbance, and disillusionment as to established standards and ideas, wrought by the experience of the war in the mind of Europe. The intellectual disturbance may be only temporary. The chaos may yield to a renewed cosmos. Meanwhile one who still believes that the Western tradition of civilization, science, morality and religion rests on secure foundations and is capable of renewal may hope to get a

---

[1] This " modern " state of mind is described vividly, if with some exaggeration, thus : " Humanity has in fact revolted against the tidy, cast-iron, orderly, rational idea of the universe presented to it by the older science. Such an idea it has found insufferably dull, prosaic and uninspiring. Men and women have reacted against it by asserting their freedom, and by giving vent to their hunger for irrationality, for adventure, and for disorder. Humanity has indulged in the bizarre in art, in free-verse in poetry, in revolutionism in politics. People are more interested in primitive instincts than in rationality." This quotation is made from a paper by H. N. Baker contributed to an Australian journal.

hearing, like anyone else. To me, then, it seems that the philosophy which is capable of ministering to this renewal is that which keeps closest to experience—the prolonged experience of our race whether nature-ward, man-ward or god-ward. No doubt this experience, as vulgarly interpreted, has proved to be full of illusions, and progress has frequently passed into deterioration and collapse. It is the function of the philosopher to rectify the interpretation of experience, and of the statesman and prophet to point the way of secure advance. But an experience which has so richly justified the instinctive belief in human progressiveness, and has so fully vindicated the potential glory of human life, in spite of widespread vice, in spite of actual retrogressions, cannot fundamentally be based on illusion. And the spirit of indiscriminate revolt can hardly fail to lose out of the tradition elements which are of incalculable value for the making or the redemption of mankind. I proceed, then, to my review of the historical conceptions of the good life. They at least deserve our respectful consideration.

It must of course be admitted that if a student to-day reads in succession the works of a number of contemporary or almost contemporary philosophers—surrendering himself to each in turn before he seeks to estimate the ultimate value of his speculations—he will be impelled towards a final scepticism, because he will find the conclusions, confidently presented to him for acceptance, so different and irreconcilable. But to acquiesce in the sceptical attitude which is content to find all views interesting, while abandoning the attempt to reach a conclusion or conviction of one's own, is to abandon the very aim of reason, which is the conviction of truth; and my contention is that the supreme test of truth among theories is the capacity which each theory in turn exhibits, or fails to exhibit, upon mature consideration to interpret the experience of mankind, as well its moral and religious experience as also every other kind of abiding experience.[1]

" Philosophy," says Dr. F. R. Tennant, " is unavoidably a matter of individual predilection, as its whole history reveals, save on the one condition that it sets out from and abides by fact or objective datum, and not from ready-made abstractions in which individual predilection is already involved." [2]

APPENDED NOTE TO CHAPTER I

THE TRINITY OF VALUES—GOODNESS, BEAUTY, TRUTH

Frequent mention is made in these lectures of the idea of a trinity of values—which plays a great part in recent literature. The contention is that these are ideals of which the human mind is specially susceptible, but which it does not create. They are in some sense objective. The human soul appreciates them as real elements in the world which it comes to know—as real as other experienced things. It is further contended that such values presuppose an intelligent mind revealed in nature—a personal spirit of goodness, beauty and truth. They are different aspects of the mind or character of God. Thus, as existing in God,

---

[1] I have attempted, in an appended note, p. 313, to distinguish the appeal to religious experience which I believe to be justified from one which makes itself heard to-day but which cannot be justified.

[2] *Miracle and its Philosophical Presuppositions*, p. 88.

or as appreciated by the human mind, they are not separate entities. All the same it is contended that, as appreciated in the human soul, we are bound to distinguish them, not as if there existed distinguishable faculties in our souls corresponding to those different ideas, but because different souls are specially susceptible of one or the other—as men are specially saints or artists or philosophers, or have such dispositions as that they tend to rate most highly virtue or beauty or truth. But we are not to imagine that they can be sharply divided, or that we shall not find that they inevitably overlap. No man wishes to be good without feeling also that vice is ugly and is out of harmony with the truth. You may find an artist, like Benvenuto Cellini, who appears to describe himself as altogether destitute of moral sensitiveness, but this is probably an exaggeration, due to an eccentric sort of vanity.

I have been asked what I mean by truth as a " value " of which we are sensitive, and of which we feel the obligation. I mean that to be fully human we must recognize the duty of knowing things as they really are—of subjecting our desires and fancies to reality, as experience reveals it to us. Curiosity—the pure desire to know—is an essential quality of the human spirit as it develops ; and this is accompanied by the recognition that to refuse knowledge, even in the supposed interest of edification, is a kind of rebellion against God. Saints have sometimes disparaged the pure love of truth for its own sake—like St. Bernard—but to do so is to repudiate one of the most distinctive excellencies of the rational nature.

CHAPTER II

SPITAMA ZARATHUSTRA [1]

§ 1

MORE and more real knowledge of prehistoric " civilizations " is being accumulated, but these discoveries necessarily tell us little about the accompanying moral ideas. For a more or less concrete idea of the good life for man we must come down to a more recent but still very ancient date. Thus in the sacred books of the Persians, the Zend Avesta or Commentary Lore—which according to the late Persian tradition were scattered and destroyed at the time of Alexander the Great's conquest, but finally re-collected and re-compiled under the first Sassanian king in the third century of our era—there are embodied in the liturgy of sacrifice (the Yasnas) seventeen [2] very ancient metrical hymns (Gâthâs),

[1] Having no knowledge of the language in which the Zend Avesta is written, I am simply dependent on authorities, especially on the translation of the texts by L. H. Mills, in *Sacred Books of the East*, vol. xxxi, and by James Hope Moulton, in *Early Zoroastrianism* (Hibbert Lectures, 1913). For interpretation I have relied chiefly on the latter book, on Ed. Meyer, *Ursprung und Anfänge des Christentums*, vol. ii, pt. ii, pp. 58 ff. (1921), on the *Encyclop. of Religions and Ethics*, " Zoroastrianism " (Prof. Carnoy), and Dr. Sydney Cave's *Introd. to Study of Living Religions of the East* (Duckworth, 1921). There is no important difference between these authorities.

[2] Seventeen, as cut into portions for recitation ; but Mills reckons them as originally five. A peculiar efficacy was ascribed to those ancient hymns as chanted in the sacrificial liturgy—

which there is every reason to believe are the genuine utterances of Zarathustra or written under his immediate influence. The language and style in which they are written is greatly different from that of the formulas which surround them. They are closely akin to the Vedic Sanskrit, and must proceed from an Iranian people belonging to the Aryan stock, akin to that which had invaded India. The gulf which separates the religious thought and social outlook of these hymns from the rest of the Avesta, or from the Persian religion as we hear of it in the sixth century B.C. and later, must represent a great interval of time. One of our authorities, Dr. J. H. Moulton, is content to postulate a date not later than the eighth century B.C. But Ed. Meyer and others—with reason, as it seems to me—require us to go back to some date not earlier than 1000 B.C. Let us be content to leave the date in uncertainty.[1]

What is of much more importance is that we should be satisfied that these are very ancient documents which give us authentic information about a hero prophet of Eastern Iran, who had become in later Persian legends a miraculous

" correctly uttered words," " intoned with sanctity." Hence, no doubt, their accurate preservation. " Constant repetition with traditional music " kept the Gâthâs from corruption (Moulton, p. 15). Hence " In the Gâthâs Z. speaks in his own person, wholly or nearly so " (p. 17). So Meyer, p. 58.

[1] The later Parsi priesthood, perhaps influenced by the desire to bring the now mythical and divinized Zarathustra nearer to their own time, put him in the seventh century B.C. But the Greeks, relying on earlier tradition, assigned to him a very remote antiquity—6000 years before Alexander or 5000 years before the Trojan war (Plutarch).

3

and divine being, but who is presented to us in
these Gâthâs; in unmistakably historical fashion,
as a purely human being on a remote but intelligible background, living, striving, failing, suc-
ceeding, desponding, rejoicing, but all through
his experiences proclaiming himself as the inspired herald of a gospel of the kingdom of God
which is profoundly ethical, enforcing an ideal
of " the good life " for man, which in its main
outlines is as clear as it is deeply impressive.
Darmesteter, at the end of the last century,
endeavoured to maintain the idea that Zarathustra was not an historical character at all, but
the product of mythical imagination, and that
the Gâthâs were artificial productions of the
second century B.C.   The scholars have, however,
refused this suggestion almost with unanimity.
For my own part, having read the Gâthâs again
and again, I cannot understand how their
antiquity and authenticity can be doubted.

Zarathustra appears as belonging to a pastoral
and agricultural community which is subject to
constant assaults and outrages from nomad free-
booters, of Turanian, that is non-Aryan, stocks,
who made their life a burden to them, and who
appear to be largely in possession of the country.
In Zarathustra's mind all that is good is identified
with the quiet pastoral life, to which no doubt
he belonged by tradition.[1]   " The soul of the
kine " in these Gâthâs represents this quiet life,

[1] His own name and that of his father-in-law Frasa-ustra
are compounded of *ustra* (camel) : his father Pourusaspa and
his son-in-law Jamaspa had their name from *aspa* (horse). His
mother's name Dughdhova means " who has milked cows," and
the clan-name of his wife, Hvogva, " having fine oxen."

and its "wail," as it is harried by the free-
booters, goes up to heaven. This struggle of the
pastoral peace-lovers against the violent and
aggressive nomads becomes in Zarathustra's
imagination the world-wide struggle of good
against evil—what seems the almost desperate
struggle of the feeble good in the world against
overwhelming evil. The picture of the divine
commission entrusted to Zarathustra to be the
champion of the good cause [1] is very vivid.
The wail of the kine goes up to the divine being
or beings. "For whom did ye fashion me?
who created me? Violence and rapine hath
oppressed me and outrage and might. I have
no other herdsman (shepherd) than you: prepare
for me, then, the blessings of pasture." The
divine beings thus appealed to confer among
themselves and the plea of the kine is accepted
by the supreme being, Ahura Mazdah. "Destruction is not intended for the right-living, nor
for the tender of cattle, at the hands of the
Liars" (that is the characteristic name in these
hymns for the adversaries of truth and right).

Again, the plea of the soul of the kine comes
before one of the divine beings. "Whom hast
thou among men who may care for us?" Then
Zarathustra is named by one of the divine
ministers as the one righteous man who will
faithfully declare the divine purpose, but who
needs for this high function to be endowed with
the gift of acceptable speech. But the Soul of
the Kine protests against so lowly a guardian.
"Alas! that I must be content with the in-

[1] Yasna 29.

effectual word of an impotent man for my
protector, when I wish for one who commands
mightily. When shall there be one who shall give
us effectual help ? " The " Most High " takes
no notice of this objection. Only the voice of
Zarathustra is heard pleading for divine assistance,
and also pleading with men to acknowledge him
as the instructor of the faithful community. And
the cattle, representing the pastoral people, do
accept him. " Now help is ours : we will be
ready to serve those that are with you."

Throughout the hymns, which give us but a
dim picture of the external fortunes of the good
cause, Zarathustra evidently relies upon the
divine appointment and upon divine inspiration.
Sometimes the cause seems to be in the gravest
peril. But Zarathustra appears as having won
the protection of the chieftain or king, Vishtaspa,
a relative of his own, and of two of his chief sup-
porters, Frasa-ustra, whose daughter Zarathustra married, and his own brother Jamaspa ; and
under the urgent insistence of Zoroaster they
are ready to defend the cause by force of arms.
Throughout the prophet is convinced that the
good will prevail ultimately and the evil be
utterly vanquished. That is the divine will
and purpose, and the prophet is its minister.
But he also with a pathetic earnestness desires
some token for good here and now.[1] His petitions for such present recognition are urgent,
and they concern particular things—" ten mares,
a stallion and a camel " which Ahura Mazdah,
the good God, had promised him, as well as the

---

[1] Yasna 34. 6.

future gifts of welfare and immortality [1] : also " two cows in calf " promised to a faithful follower as a pledge to-day of the Life Beyond.[2]

We must seek to gain as clear and detailed a conception as we can of the religious and ethical system which Zarathustra promulgated and sought to propagate. But, before this, we must ask what religious and ethical ideas he inherited and found around him. And we shall also want to know what measure of success his mission won. We will deal *first*, very briefly with the traditional background ; *secondly*, more at length with the teaching of Zarathustra himself ; *thirdly*, again very briefly, with its consequences in the Persian religion of later days.

§ 2

To the first question the answer of the experts is largely conjectural. The Iranian tribe to which Zoroaster belonged must, we should suppose, have inherited the Aryan tradition of religion—its great nature gods and minor departmental gods, its spirits good and bad, its sacrificial system and the priesthood to administer it. We know this religion in its Indian development in the earliest Vedas, and some of its features we find recognized by Zarathustra. Others are quite absent from the Gâthâs, but reappear in later Zoroastrianism, which in all probability represents in this respect a reversion to type. Thus Ahura Mazdah,[3] Zarathustra's

[1] Yasna 44. 18.   [2] Yasna 46. 13.
[3] " The Lord Wisdom," according to Carnoy ; " The Wise Lord," according to Meyer. He is, of course, the Osmuzd of later tradition.

supreme god, was an ancient Aryan god, parallel
to the sublime Varuna of the earliest Indian
tradition. But by his side were others, notably
Mithra, who holds so great a place in later
Persian religion, but was rejected by Zarathustra
probably as associated with the cultus of the
intoxicating drink (saoma).   " When," he cries
to Ahura Mazdah, " when will the nobles understand the message ?   When wilt thou smite the
filthiness of this intoxicant ? " [1]   Minor departmental gods of the tradition, also originally
nature gods, we shall see surviving in Zarathustra's religious system as divine attributes, to
reappear in the later Zoroastrianism as the Am-
shaspands, " The Holy Immortals," the seven
" Archangels."   The Dævas in Zarathustra's
system are the evil spirits, the servants of the
Lie (Trug), the constant and inveterate enemies
of the Truth. These were the minor gods
" devas " of the Vedic tradition ; but they were
the chief objects of worship among the enemies
of Zarathustra's tribe, and appear therefore as
devils in his teaching.

It was from tradition that he received the
idea of the world as a mixed result of the activity
of good and bad spirits, and the scene of their
perpetual conflict. But there does not appear
to have been any precise dualism in the tradition
as he received it, though there was undoubtedly
polytheism ; nor does he himself seem to recognize any good spirits, other than the supreme
Ahura and his attributes or " holy spirit." The
traditional veneration of the sacred fire he

[1] Yasna 48. 10.

received, no doubt, and found a place for it, but, the sacrificial system he ignored, and, though once he calls himself a priest,[1] he took no account of priestly ministrations. Of the Fravashis also, the geniuses of individual souls and the spirits of the dead, he took no account, but their cultus reappears later in full force.

On the whole we can draw a fairly distinct conclusion. The religion of his tribal tradition—a religion of many gods, primary and secondary, and of spirits good and bad, with its sacrifices and charms and priesthood—Zoroaster does not appear directly to have combated,[2] except where it was associated with vice, as in the cultus of the Saoma, and probably of Mithra ; but, concentrating his attention on certain elements in it, he converted it in his own mind and teaching into what was practically an ethical monotheism, claiming the co-operation of all loyal men in the purpose of the good God ; and so went out on a purely prophetic mission, to inaugurate a reformation which was fundamental indeed, but which he strove to make effectual rather by affirming and deepening the better elements in the tradition which the inner light showed him to be alone the truth, than by starting afresh, like Ikhnaten in Egypt, or Muhammad in Arabia, in direct hostility to the accepted religion. He would, we may suppose, have left the unworthy elements in the traditional religion to die of them-

[1] Yasna 33. 6 : " I who, as a priest [Zaota, the old Aryan title, not the word used in the Avesta otherwise], would learn the straight way."

[2] There is some difference between the authorities on this and other details.

selves. Alas! Judged by the outcome, this method, as we shall see, cannot be said to have been successful. But of his profound originality there can be no question. Meyer calls him "a completely independent thinker," "one of the very few real founders of religions," "one of the most important figures in religious history."

§ 3

The religion of Zarathustra was deeply ethical, but it was based upon his dominant conception of God; and we must turn our attention first to this. He was neither a mystic nor a metaphysician, and his theological ideas lack precision; but for all practical purposes he was a monotheist and a monotheist by profound conviction. The one God of his devotion was the Aryan deity, Ahura Mazdah—the Lord Wisdom—associated in tradition with Mithra, whom Zarathustra seems to have rejected as morally inadequate, isolating Mazdah into a sole supremacy, as "God of Gods," "the first and the last," "the creator of all things by the holy spirit," the fount of all goodness, the supreme and omniscient judge, the only ultimate power.[1] The tradition ascribed the world to a mixed creative activity of good and bad spirits, and Zarathustra retains this convenient belief, so apparently congruous to experience; but his supposed dualism has been misconceived. Let us examine the only proof-texts.

" Now will I proclaim to those who will hear

[1] Yasnas 31. 8 ; 44. 7, etc. (see Moulton, p. 140).

the things which the understanding man should remember. . . . Hear with your ears the best things; look upon them with clear-seeing thought, for decision between the two beliefs. . . . The two primal spirits, who revealed themselves in vision as twins, are the Bad and the Good in thought and word and action. And between the two the wise ones chose aright, the foolish not so. And when these twain spirits came together in the beginning, they established Life and Not-Life. Of these twain spirits, he that followed the Lie chose doing the worst things; the holiest spirit chose right, he that clothes himself with the many heavens as a garment; so likewise they that are fain to please Ahurah Mazdah by dutiful actions. Between these twain the Dævas [the minor nature Gods of Aryan tradition] also chose not aright, for infatuation came upon them as they took counsel together, so that they chose the worst thoughts. Then they rushed together to violence, that they might enfeeble the world of man." [1]

Again,[2] " I will speak of the spirits twain at the first beginning of life, of whom the holier thus spake to the Enemy. [Here only does the name Ahrim(an) appear in the Gâthâs.] ' Neither thoughts nor teachings nor wills nor beliefs nor words nor deeds nor selves nor souls of us twain agree together.' "

Here we get a clear idea of two primeval Spirits good and bad. The evil spirit is Druj, the Lie, the Enemy—later known as Ahriman. Whether the primal good Spirit is to be identified

---

[1] Yasna 30. 1–6.　　　　[2] Yasna 45. 2.

with Ahura Mazdah is not clear. But three points must be noticed.

(1) The power of the evil one is to destroy or spoil, not to create. Evil is, in this sense, negative, not positive. His product is "not-life."

(2) The conflict of good and evil is due to an original (and ever-repeated) choice of wills. The primeval spirits *choose* good or evil. They must have existed therefore before they chose; and, like the Dævas, who followed them, they appear therefore as *fallen* spirits, like Satan and his angels in Christian belief. So also we seem to trace a dim allusion to a fall of man, led by a primitive man, under the inspiration of the Dævas, who gave them forbidden food, "portions of beef, to eat."[1] "Ye (the Dævas) defrauded mankind of happy life and of immortality . . . so as to ruin mankind." At any rate, it is fairly clear that evil throughout is attributed to an original bad choice made by beings already in existence endowed with free wills; and what lies behind (the really primal being) is left in obscurity. Practically, however, Zarathustra treats Mazdah as the only Creator and supreme God; thus the ultimate controlling will in the universe is only good.

Further (3), though Mazdah is now in conflict with a kingdom of evil, and needs the help of men "to make the world advance,"[2] his final victory in the whole universe of things at the

---

[1] Yasna 32. 8 (see Moulton, p. 148); cf. 32. 5. But it is not at all clear that the reference is to any original sin.
[2] Yasna 30. 9.

great consummation or " the last turning-point
of creation "[1] is assured. He is ultimately
omnipotent; and the forces of evil, higher and
lower, are destined to utter defeat and woe.
But of this more hereafter. Zoroaster is to all
intents and purposes a monotheist.

There is another problem, which, however,
appears to admit of fairly easy solution. Above
(p. 85), in the scene of Zarathustra's call and
commission, and constantly throughout the
Gâthâs, we are confronted not only with the
Most High, Ahura Mazdah, but with what are
apparently other divine " holy ones," who share
his supremacy. These are, in the front rank,
Asha (truth or right), and Vohumanah (best
thought); then Khshathra (kingdom or sovereignty, sometimes *desired kingdom*, as being
future); Aramaiti (piety); Haurvatat (welfare); Ameritat (immortality). There is also
Sraosa (obedience); Spenta Mainyu (holy
spirit). The first six of these appear in the later
Persian religion as the six, or seven, Amshas-
pands, commonly translated " archangels."

But, though Zoroaster appeals to some of them
and speaks of them as persons, it is fairly plain
that the first two or three are not really separable
from Ahura Mazdah himself, but are simply his
effective attributes, like the Divine Wisdom in the
Old Testament.[2] Moreover, the two first are communicated to men to possess and guide them;

[1] Yasna 43. 5.

[2] The supreme triad of Ahuras (Holy Ones) consists of Mazdah,
Asha, Vohu Manah (see Yasna 30. 9; 33. 6, etc.). The six are
named together in Yasna 45. 10.

mankind is to think God's "best thought" after
Him and to embody His truth or right; and
the others are rather divine gifts for man than
attributes of Mazdah, though they belong to his
being. Nor does the "holy spirit" appear to
be anything else than a summary expression
for the divine activity.

Mazdah is thus an utterly transcendent being
—Zoroaster is as far as possible from pantheism—
but he is also immanent in obedient mankind,
in the obedient community to which Zoroaster
would convert all living men,[1] and his Haurvatat
and Ameritat (welfare and immortality) are
to become the very substance of the blessed
future state. On the whole, then, we need not
hesitate to think of these holy beings as in the
religion of Zarathustra no more than personified
attributes of Mazdah and of his activities among
men.[2] It is to be observed, however, that the
names were not new, and that many of them—
Aramaiti, Haurvatat, Ameritat—were originally
minor nature gods, representing earth, water
and plants. But the use of them by Zarathustra
would appear to be thoroughly original; Moulton
calls them "the most distinctive features of
Zarathustra's own thought."[3]

On this basis of theology stood Zarathustra's
conception of mankind. Man is a being endowed
with reason and freedom of will. His vocation is
to correspond by a deliberate act of choice with

[1] Yasna 31. 3.

[2] This matter is discussed at length in Moulton and the
other authorities cited above, with substantial agreement
in conclusions reached.

[3] P. 87.

the beneficent purpose of the good God, finding
his happiness in dedicating all his faculties to his
service ; and in describing this service the phrase
constantly recurs " in thought and word and
deed." This is a message for " all living men," [1]
and not for any class or race of men; and it is
for women as for men. All possible stress is
laid on individual responsibility—" each man
for himself "—and the choice is to be made in
view of the divine assurance of everlasting bliss
for those who choose the right, and everlasting
misery for those who choose otherwise. Thus
man has the making of his own heaven or his
own hell.[2] By co-operating with God—" making
the world to advance "—he accumulates merits,
and by the opposite conduct, demerits; and
according to the ultimate balance of one over
the other will he be dealt with when he reaches
the final " bridge of the separation " which
connects this life with the hereafter at " the last
turning-point of creation." [3] We hear rather
dimly of a middle place in the Beyond for those
whose merits and demerits balance.[4] But this
perhaps only concerns an " intermediate state "
before the final consummation. As to this there
is no certain information.[5]

But the picture of the human vocation and
destiny is startlingly clear and delivered with
the assurance of inspiration. The appeal to
individual responsibility is a ringing appeal,

[1] Yasna 31. 3.   [2] Yasna 46. 10, 11.
[3] Yasna 43. 5.   [4] Yasna 33. 1 ; 48. 4.
[5] Meyer is inclined to read back into Zoroaster a more precise
eschatology than the evidence of the Gâthâs justifies.

and it is much more than an appeal to avoid offences. Every man is to be active and militant in the divine cause. Even the followers of the Lie may be converted and saved.[1] For the divine piety strives with the sinner. " Passing from one to another, she pleads with the spirit in which there is wavering." [2] But the conversion of the Liars is not seemingly much expected. And so long as they remain unconverted they are to be hated with a holy hatred, as the enemies of God. " He is himself a liar, who is good to a liar " [3]; nor does Zarathustra shrink from identifying with the enemies of God those who have done him a particular injury. He has a vivid memory of an occasion when a certain follower of the Lie refused hospitality to him and his two shivering horses on some occasion of great peril.[4] And he thirsts for vengeance at the hand of God. All this hatred of the hateful, this active hostility to the enemies of the true religion, is a necessary part of a service of God. All the desire of " the friends of Ahura Mazdah " is indeed for peace. His kingdom is a kingdom of peace. But to the violators of the righteous law there is to be no peace. They are the Dragvans—the lovers of the Lie—and the prophet thunders curses upon them.[5]

In Zarathustra's disclosures of his own inner life we are given a wonderfully vivid impression

[1] Yasna 46. 12 ; 28. 5 ; 33. 2.   [2] Yasna 31. 12.
[3] Yasna 46. 6 ; 47. 4, 6.
[4] Yasna 51. 12.   But the translation appears to be very doubtful.
[5] Yasna 53. 8.

of a life of constant and importunate prayer to
Ahura Mazdah—for particular physical blessings,
but much more for speedy vindication of the divine
law. It is only by prayer, we gather, for oneself
and for others, that the soul of man can keep in
correspondence with God.[1] And the ethical
content of human life is determined by the
thought that God's own attributes as explained
above (or God's own spirit) possess the soul of the
righteous man, who is his fellow-worker and
" friend." [2]

In all this Zarathustra is speaking of himself
just as a man. But he is a man with a special
vocation—to be the proclaimer of the Message,
the good tidings of the kingdom, speaking with
authority. Man, he conceives, needs a prophet
much more than a priest—a spiritual guide to
show him the way. As such, then, Zarathustra
knows himself divinely appointed. Even in the
worst times he seems to expect God's immediate
coming in judgment, and he himself in that
dread hour is to be the saviour (Saoshyant) and
judge.[3] But he does not isolate himself in this
respect or make any exclusive claim for himself.
He speaks of other saviour judges,[4] many whom
Mazdah will appoint to prepare his way. The
idea of the one saviour in a far future does not
appear in the Gâthâs.[5]

---

[1] Yasna 43 (the whole) ; 44. 1, etc.   [2] Yasna 44. 4.
[3] Yasna 44. 16 ; 45. 11 ; 48. 9 ; 49. 9 ; 53. 2.
[4] Yasna 46. 3 ; 49. 9.
[5] I have not thought it necessary to refer to the later legends
about the preservation of Zarathustra's *semen* by 99,999
Fravishis in a lake, whence the final Saviour is to be born. (See
Moulton, p. 310, and note.)

It must be noticed that " the bridge of separation " connecting this world with the world to
come was apparently a traditional conception.
Those who could walk over what was in later
Zoroastrianism defined as its sharp razor-edge,
would be only the righteous helped by the
Saviour, while the friends of the Lie, the wor-
shippers of the Dævas, would fall off into hell.
Zarathustra is very sparing in his use of metaphor
or symbols.   But he introduces into the picture
of the day of judgment at " the bridge of separation " the symbol of the Holy Fire, " for the
faithful visible delight, but for the enemy visible
torment, according to the pointings of the hand " [1]
—this last expression, which recurs several times,
refers to the gesture of the Supreme Judge
separating the saved from the lost.   There is also
the flood of " molten metal " which presumably
both purges the good and consumes the evil ;
once more there is " the weighing of actions by
the good Spirit." [2]   These images are used
without explanation or elaboration, and Zarathustra is never carried away by such imagery
from a strictly rational and spiritual conception
of heaven and hell as the region of " the best
thought " and " the worst thought," " the best
[and the worst] state," the " better than good "
and the " worse than evil " : [3] and he speaks of
both as everlasting. [4]   Whether Meyer is right in
thinking that he carries into eternity the accom-

[1] Yasna 34. 4 ; cf. 43. 4 ; 50. 5.
[2] Yasna 48. 8.   The weighing may result in an even balance
of good and bad.
[3] Yasna 43. 3 ; 51. 6.
[4] Yasna 45 ; cf. 33. 13, where the lost cry in vain for mercy.

paniments of pastoral life—cows and abundant pasture, etc.—seems to be doubtful.[1] But heaven is certainly to be full fellowship with Ahura Mazdah and with his faithful servants.

The blessed in Paradise are not to be disembodied souls. There is to be apparently for the virtuous dead a resurrection of the body.[2] For Zoroaster the body, or matter, is not evil. There is no trace in him of the sort of asceticism which is based on such a conception; thus he has a high ideal of marriage. He rejoices before God in the prospect of his own marriage. "The fair form of one who is dear has Frashaostra Hvogva promised to me. May sovran Mazdah Ahura grant that she attain possession of the right for her good self."[3] And on the occasion of his youngest daughter's marriage,[4] the bridegroom, Jamaspa, makes profession: "Earnestly will I lead her to the faith, that she may serve her father and her husband, the peasant and the nobles, as a righteous woman serving the righteous. The glorious heritage of good thought shall Mazdah Ahura give to her good self for all time." And the ruler of the feast, or Zarathustra himself, addresses all married couples. "I address teachings to maidens marrying, to you bridegrooms also giving counsels. Lay them to heart, and learn to get them within your own selves in

---

[1] The wicked, however, in hell are said to be given " foul food " by the souls who have died earlier. Yasna 49. 11.

[2] Yasna 53. 9. Whether this extends to the unrighteous is doubtful. They are said " to forfeit their own body." But the translations of this Yasna vary considerably.

[3] Yasna 31. 11 ; 43. 3 ; cf. Moulton, pp. 147–148.

[4] Yasna 51. 17.

4

earnest attention to the life of good thought.
Let each of you strive to excel the other in the
Right, for it will be a prize for that one. So it is
in fact ye men and women . . . if only faithful
zeal be in the wedded pair." [1]

We do not find in the Gâthâs much ethical
detail. The virtuous life is the life of the good,
peace-loving peasant or noble—peace-loving
save that there is to be truceless hatred and
war to the death against the servants of the Lie.
And the agricultural life centres in the home.
There is no occupation for the good man contemplated except the agricultural. " The love
of the kine " is essential.[2] Further than this, the
attributes of right and truth, in thought and
word and deed, and piety and obedience, and
conformity to the good thought, and constant
watchfulness against the machinations of the
spirit of the Lie and his servants, give us his
general character ; but there are no detailed
enactments for the direction of the community
or the individual, such as we get in the Code of
Hammurabi or the Jewish Code.

Throughout this description I have been con-
fining myself to the Gâthâs. As will appear, we
have no right to rely upon the later developments
of Zoroastrianism as reflecting the spirit or
teaching of Zarathustra. Moulton may be justified in speaking of his religion as " aristocratic "
in the sense that, while his teaching is undoubtedly intended for man as such and not for
any particular class, and while he has a horror

[1] Yasna 53.
[2] Yasna 48. 6–7 ; 51. 14 ; 28. 5.

of any oppression of the poor—indeed, in one place he calls his religion a religion of the poor—yet he takes for granted the authority of the ruling family, and he certainly makes no attempt to be popular. It is a dry, austere, abstract teaching that we find in the Gâthâs. There is little of the fascinating metaphor and splendid rhetoric which we find in the Hebrew prophets, no story telling, no ritual, to attract and attach the people. Doubtless this was one of the causes of the seeming failure of his reformation. This dryness will appear if I copy out, with a few alterations in phraseology, the summary of Zarathustra's religion as given by Dr. Carnoy in the article already referred to.

" By his right choice the man who obeys Law (Asha-van) helps in the final victory of the good spirit, the spirit of the Lord Wisdom (Ahura Mazda), over the Spirit of Deceit and Treachery (Druj, Avigra-Mainya). Inspired by Right Mind, he takes his stand against the whole world of the Druj, its satellites (the Dæva), its priests, its sorcerers, its fairies and its cult, sacrifices of living creatures and of the intoxicating haoma. He repudiates with special emphasis nomadic life with its brigandage and strife, the life of the Infidels. He lives with Wisdom of Purpose an Orderly Existence, according to Law, in obedience to the Good Spirit, represented by a moral adviser (or judge). In this way he will realize in this world and hereafter the Wished-for Kingdom, the Kingdom of Blessings, the Kingdom of the Best, the Good Reward, with perfect Happiness and Immortality, that will follow the Last Ordeal and the Restoration of the World."

Clearly it is not possible to suggest that this lofty religion—however closely resembling the Jewish faith—could have been borrowed from the Jews; its date renders that impossible. (The question whether and how far it influenced the Old Testament must be kept till we are considering the religion and morality of Israel.) Nor is there any other alien source to which it can be attributed. It remains in its lofty severity a momentous creation, if it be not wiser to call it, as Zoroaster himself would have called it, a signal inspiration by the divine Spirit of an individual prophet. It exhibits at a very early stage in the history of mankind a clear conception of the Good Life for Man. It is puritanical—that is, it has no flavouring of art and gives but few signs of accommodation to ordinary human desires for relaxation and enjoyment; but it is in the highest degree lofty and inspiring, and, full as it is of the sense of pity for the oppressed and miserable, it can rightly call itself a gospel; further, it is conspicuous for the simplicity and decision with which (on the basis of a highly ambiguous tradition) it exhibits in the boldest outline the theology by which this good life is controlled and justified, and the eschatology by which it is supported. The longer one thinks about Zarathustra's religion and allows it to absorb one's mind, the more central, the more illuminating, the more divine, it appears. But in fact, if it was truly a light shining in a dark place, it shone in its purity but for a very little while and in a very restricted area.

§ 4

All the scholars are agreed that the light shed
by Zoroaster was swallowed up in darkness.
There must have been a counter-reformation
following on what Zoroaster speaks of as his
" reformation." The deeply ethical tone of
his religion was gradually lost in a welter of
superstition and magic. Anyone who tries to
read the Avesta at length will certainly be convinced of this deterioration, and will find it
highly significant that what survives of the
Gâthâs (which is probably only a portion of
the whole) has survived because the hymns
were regarded as effective charms to be scru-
pulously preserved and recited. There seem to
be stages in the process of deterioration. First,
we have a prose appendix to the Gâthâs called
the Gâthâ Heptangaiti,[1] in seven chapters, still
more or less in the dialect of the older Gâthâs,
and therefore presumably not so very much
later in date, but exhibiting a very different
spirit. It is noticeable that the name of Zarathustra does not occur either here [2] or in the
famous inscriptions of Darius at Behistan
c. 518 B.C. The personified attributes have
become distinct divine persons, and sacrifice is
offered to them, while the deep ethical meaning
of their names is no more apparent : the Fravishi
and their cult have become again prominent :
fire and earth and grass are also worshipped.
What we seem to be witnesses of is a rapid

---

[1] Yasnas 35–41 or 42.

[2] If (as is probable) Yasna 42, is of later date.

recovery in the generations after Zarathustra of
the older tradition of religion.

On the other hand, the Heptangaiti Gâthâ
is widely different from the later Yasnas; and,
whatever may have been the case for a while,
the name and fame of Zarathustra could not
be permanently suppressed. Thus in the later
religion of the Persians, such as we know it
under the Achæmenid Kings following Darius,
he is worshipped as a divine and miraculous
being; but though his teaching still gave to
the Persian religion an ethical tinge, which it
was never to lose [1]—the emphasis on truth remains constant—yet the elements which were
really Zoroastrian were greatly obscured or
submerged in superstition. " The religion of
the Persian court was practically the old Iranian
polytheism, with the reformer's name retained
to atone for the absence of his spirit. What new
elements there were came not from him but from
Semitic sources, or through the powerful influence
of the Magian priesthood already at work." [2]
Still later, when this priesthood had won a
complete triumph, their religion was still further
removed from Zarathustra's own. For the
purpose of this book, however, we need not
concern ourselves with the later eclipse of the
real Reformer. For present-day Parseeism (i.e.
the Zoroastrianism which survives almost only in

[1] This is apparent in the accounts of it given by Herodotus.
But later Greek accounts give a less favourable impression.

[2] Moulton, pp. 78 f. On many points in this paragraph there
is difference among the authorities, e.g. between Moulton and
Ed. Meyer; but the differences only concern points with which
we are not concerned.

Bombay, whither its followers fled from Muhammadan persecutions) an outside observer would
say that nothing is more to be desired than a
movement " Back to Zoroaster."

The teaching of Zarathustra as presented in
the Gâthâs, when it is considered as a whole,
and its early date taken into account, is of even
startling significance. According to it the life
of man, in spite of all the evils which imperil
and beset it, in spite of the enormous abuses
of life which prevail, is a good thing, of eternal
and immeasurable worth. The responsibility
of saving one's soul or realizing one's being is
the supreme responsibility of men and women,
as free and rational beings. The adventure and
the opportunity is for man as man, not for any
class or any race or either sex in particular.
For there is a good purpose running through
creation, though there are many adversaries.
The supreme Lord Wisdom, the creator, the
final judge, omniscient and (ultimately) omnipotent, is the only God to be worshipped, and
is one day to come into His own in His whole
creation, awarding just judgment of eternal
bliss or eternal woe on all men according to their
deeds. The function of man is therefore to co-
operate with this good God, who through all the
present age has to win His way by struggle
against evil spirits and evil men—the Truth
against the Lie. Man's vocation is to put his
whole self, body and soul, thought and word and
deed, at the service of the Holy Wisdom, by prayer
and by work, by living the peaceful, beneficent
life and loving the lovers of truth and peace,

but also by fighting hard against the followers
of the Lie, and hating them with a holy hatred,
even while seeking their conversion. There is
no way of fellowship with God by charms or
sacrifices, but only by the way of likeness to
God. And what He is we know. Transcendent
and supreme, He is yet, by His attributes and
holy spirit, immanent in the world and in men of
good will. We know His character of truth and
justice, purity, goodness and pity, and can live
according to His spirit which works in us in
devout obedience. We can live in the certainty
of the final day of infallible judgment with its
eternal issues.

Here is indeed a theory, as intelligible as it is
magnificent, of the good life for man in fellowship
with God. And the prophet who, relying upon
divine inspiration and divine appointment, spent
his life in proclaiming it, is morally worthy of
his high vocation. Through the mist of ages
we can discern him, afar but distinct. We note
the close resemblance of the ideal which he
proclaims to that of the Jewish prophets (of
whom, however, he is completely independent)
even in their limitations, though in one respect
the difference is marked. For, if Christianity
be taken as the fulfilment of Judaism, Judaism
is a strictly national religion which at last expanded to become universal, but Zoroastrianism
is at starting a universal religion for man as
man which ultimately narrowed into an intensely
national form in the Persian religion and Parseeism. But both are alike in making the essence
of the good life for man to be correspondence

with the purpose and character of God, and in finding the knowledge of his character and purpose to depend not on the labours of the human intellect but on his own self-revelation.

We shall have to return upon Zoroaster's religion and its principles. But first we must continue our long search for ideals of the good life for man among the nations of the earth.

CHAPTER III

INDIA AND BUDDHISM

§ 1

WE are engaged in a survey of the distinctive
conceptions of the good life for man which are
found in possession among the different races of
mankind in different ages, such, that is, as have
been left on record in a more or less consistent
and intelligible form, and have been based upon
or have become the basis of an intelligible
theory or philosophy of life. We have seen how
out of the primitive Aryan polytheism there
emerged in Eastern Irania the exceedingly definite
moral construction of Zarathustra, and we have
noted that the language in which it is expressed
is closely akin to the language of the Aryan
invaders of India in which the Vedas were com-
posed. And it is obvious, when the Rigveda
is studied (? 1500 to 1000 B.C.), that from the
primitive customs of life and worship, based
upon a primitive polytheism, disclosed in these
hymns, there might have developed as definite
a moral system based on as definite a theory of
the universe as Zarathustra gave to Iran. The
majestic Varuna might have taken the place
of Ahura Mazdah; and, as he is the guardian
and source of Right,[1] the sovereignty of the
moral law would have been secured in his person.

[1] The Vedic *Rita*, which equals the Persian *Arta* or *Asha* in
the Zend Gâthâs.

But Dr. Cave [1] is probably right in telling us that the old polytheistic nature worship appears in the Rigveda as already "unstable and in decay"; and the thinkers and teachers of India did not in fact give themselves to ethical studies, but to the more abstract study of the nature of reality, and their metaphysical thinking was not such as to provide a basis for a consistent doctrine of the good life. It was, we may almost say, essentially unpractical. Everywhere, no doubt, mankind has experienced more or less deeply the sense both of the vanity and of the misery of life; but in India this sense appears to have become so strong as to overwhelm the sense of joy and hope in life, which found expression in the Vedas, and to have occupied the soul and thought of India with a permanent and profound pessimism of outlook over the world of present experience, as being both unreal and evil, such an outlook as, on the one hand, left them without any zest for the systematic study of experience, and, on the other, drove them to seek—not a redemption of life from its attendant evils but rather a redemption from life itself.

The causes which have hindered the development in India of the conception of the good life for man, other than physical and political causes, appear to have been specially three.

(1) The first is the doctrine of Karma, which is commonly translated "transmigration." This appears for the first time in the earliest Upanishads as new knowledge—" which never before

[1] P. 22 (see above, p. 32, n. 1).

now dwelt with any Brahman " [1] ; but it is definitely pre-Buddhist—certainly not later therefore than *c.* 600 B.C.

The word " transmigration " suggests the real existence of a persistent individual soul passing through different incarnations and carrying with it the consequences of its behaviour in its previous states. And such is the meaning assigned to the doctrine of Karma as it appears in the Upanishads and elsewhere—even in the Buddha's popular teaching. But all the time the philosophers were expressing their disbelief in the reality of individual souls and of the world of common experience. Nothing is real but the one Self, unchangeable, inexpressible—the Self (Atman) which is identical with Being (Brahman). Thus original Buddhism, which is largely built upon the doctrine of Karma, refuses, as we shall see, to hold or to teach that there is any such thing as a permanent soul which could migrate from one body to another. What is popularly called a soul is a combination of elements which are dissolved at death. But there is a fatal force of *desire*, acting like a law of attraction among atoms, which tends to produce a new combination—a new individual life, human or divine or animal or vegetable, according to the summary result of past action. This is Karma. Strictly, then, it is the consequence of past actions, not the individual soul, which is permanent.[2]

This philosophical conception makes " trans-

[1] Cave, p. 32.
[2] See Copleston's *Buddhism*, pp. 71 ff. ; Cave, p. 121.

migration " a seriously misleading rendering
of Karma, which meant originally only " work "
or " action." However, whether in its popular
or its philosophical form, the doctrine of Karma,
which has seized and possessed the soul of
India, is deeply hostile to the formation of any
firm idea of the good life for man, which involves
an acute sense of both personal and social
responsibility. The doctrine of Karma under-
mines or weakens disastrously the sense of
personal responsibility in the present individual,
for it makes him think of his life as the bearing
of the penance laid upon him by an irresistible
fate for things done in some other existence of
which at least he has no memory and for which
he can feel no present responsibility. Thus it
destroys, or if it cannot quite destroy it dimin-
ishes, the sense of moral freedom and obligation.
But, much more, it must beget a fatal individualism, and the sense of social responsibility cannot
grow under its shadow. The high-caste man
contemplates the out-castes as individuals suffering—not the consequences of the selfishness and
cruelty of society which a newly awakened
conscience of man's duty to his brethren can
and ought to reverse, but as suffering by a law,
which no efforts of ours can counteract, the
inevitable consequences of unknown crimes committed by unknown persons in previous states of
existence. From such a point of view it is a
blind and irreversible law which makes men
what they are ; and it is not rightly described
as a law of justice ; for justice is a personal
quality ; and, if a divine justice exists, it must

constantly be found appealing to the justice of man to rectify what only selfishness and injustice have brought into being. Thus it is that the doctrine of Karma, however understood, seems only calculated to lead to passivity under evil, and has in fact led to it.[1]

(2) The second tendency which seems to have affected deeply the whole development of life in India is that the mind of its best men and ablest thinkers has been dominated by an intellectualism of a highly abstract kind—a passion for the One, the Absolute, which has not applied itself to the interpretation of present-day experience or the scientific study of nature, but has tended to regard it all as illusion—as a baneful veil which hides the face of Reality and on which the wise man in his search for truth had better turn his back. This sort of intellectualism has brought it about that the best men have been for ever searching for some escape from life, and not for its improvement—the escape being by way of highly abstract thought or of mystical devotion based on ascetic practice.

(3) The third force has been the constant pressure of a priesthood powerful enough to maintain a religion, or an amalgamation of religions, which on the whole has been divorced from morality and indifferent to morality.

To these considerations, thus briefly indicated, we shall have to revert. But we must first apply ourselves to study what is, I suppose, the greatest product of India—the system of thought

[1] It gained, as we shall see, a certain hold in Greece, but never to the same extent as in India.

and life which we owe to Siddartha Gotama, the Buddha ; for here at least we have a profound attempt to contemplate human life steadily, to analyse its meaning and interpret its secret, and, as a fruit of this concentrated intellectual effort to deal practically with human life, to show men the Way and to proclaim the Law. Here then, it may be said to me, you have precisely what you have been complaining of India for not producing. We shall see whether this is so. Certainly it is true that the Buddha turned his back decisively and deliberately on some of the most dominant forces and tendencies of Indian life—on its metaphysic, on its asceticism and on its priesthood.[1]

In considering Buddhism as a system we shall have to do what we did in considering Zoroastrianism—we shall have to distinguish between the system of the Founder and the ultimate and general outcome of his work. The broad consideration of the history of religion and morality among men leads to an interesting conclusion, that at each stage where conspicuous advance is made the best comes first. Religion and morality would no doubt have been the subject of some sort of development like all parts of human life, apart from the great creative founders. But in fact the main actual force, in promoting higher spirituality or morality among men, has been the apparition of prophetic souls whose teaching cannot be accounted for by what went before them, and who appear by their commanding

[1] See the Tevigga Sutta, *S.B.E.* (*Sacred Books of the East*), vol. xi, p. 168, and *The Foundation*, pp. 146 ff.

influence to drive men by a new impulse in a new direction. This new impulse is, perhaps, never afterwards wholly exhausted or lost. But it becomes merged in the general channel with other currents, and though it adds something to the whole, it tends to become less and less distinctive. Thus the prophet Zarathustra's teaching was something much nobler and much more distinctive than historical Zoroastrianism or Parseeism. And, as we shall find, the system of the Buddha was something far more distinctive and nobler of its kind than the Buddhist religion as it has appeared in the life of the nations reckoned as Buddhist. Thus it is Buddhism at its source that we must seek to appreciate first of all.[1]

§ 2

Siddartha Gotama[2] was a son of the chieftain of the Sakyan tribe, whose home was within

[1] I should advise a student who desires as real acquaintance as possible with the original Buddhism to study some modern books first, especially Rhys Davids' *Buddhism* (S.P.C.K.), R. S. Copleston's *Buddhism* (Longmans, 1908), and Dr. Cave's *Living Religions of the East*, pt. iii. He will also find illumination in Tolstoy's estimate of Buddhism in his *Confession* (Aylmer-Maude's trans., Oxford Press), pp. 42–4, and Lowes Dickinson's in *The Magic Flute*, pp. 100–109. The modern books—and they are many—which, based on the principle that there is really only one religion under many forms, assimilate Buddhism to Christianity are uncritical and untrustworthy. And the student who studies modern books, whether the more or the less trustworthy, must at least revise his impressions by a careful reading of the Buddhist Suttas in the eleventh volume of the *Sacred Books of the East* (referred to in what follows as *S.B.E.*), which are among our earliest authorities for the teaching of the Buddha.

[2] The names by which the founder of Buddhism is called are many. *Gotama* was the family surname. His personal name (which he is said to have renounced on leaving his home) was *Siddartha*. He was known later as *the Buddha*, " the enlightened

(what is now called) Nepal, about 100 miles north of Benares. He was probably born about 540 B.C. The story runs that his father brought him up surrounded by every kind of luxury and sensual indulgence, and endeavoured to screen him from all the evidences of " this life's undelight." But he found himself satiated with this protected life. In spite of the protective barriers he saw the evidences of human misery— a decrepit old man, a diseased man and a dead man. His soul came to be possessed with disgust of existence. Like many another in India, in his time and in subsequent ages, at his twenty-ninth year he renounced the world, and, kissing his wife and child, left them and his home for ever. " The air of India " at that time was already " full of intellectual effort and of the earnest search for deliverance from the ills of life." [1] He sought two of the wisest philosophers of his time and became their pupil, but in vain. They had nothing to teach him which really got at the root of human misery. But he appears to have become well acquainted with the current philosophy of an age marked by intense and widespread interest in the most highly speculative problems.[2]

one," i.e. one of a class of illuminated beings. He speaks of himself as the *Tathagata*—" the one who has arrived," while his disciples speak of him as *Bhagavat*, the blessed one. The names by which he is commonly known in China and Japan are derived from *Sakyamouni*, that is, " the Sage of the Sakyan race."

[1] Copleston, p. 8.

[2] The first dialogue of the Sutta Pitaka, or *Sermon Basket*, one chief authority for the teaching of the Buddha, enumerates sixty-two " heresies," that is, metaphysical doctrines contrary to Buddhism, many of a very subtle kind, but this may represent a later age than the lifetime of the historical Gotama.

5

Gotama, however, found no satisfaction in these speculations. Then he tried the most strenuous asceticism, all the possibilities of which he is said to have exhausted, under the guidance of five famous masters. But that way too seemed to him as fruitless as metaphysical enquiry, and the ascetics, who said that he had " given up his exertions and returned to an abundant life," left him in disgust. He does not appear, however, to have returned to any mode of life which we should call " abundant," but to have given himself, unassisted, to the profoundest efforts of thought, and at last, as he sat beneath a bo-tree, illumination came to him. He saw the secret of human misery and found therewith the way of deliverance. Under that tree and other trees he is said to have passed four weeks in fasting and meditation. During this period of complete abstraction from the world he reviewed the series of causes which lead to suffering till all doubts and obscurities were dispelled and the true nature of things became clear to his mind. Thus " he enjoyed the bliss of emancipation."

Then the tradition represents him as subject to a great temptation. His secret—the ultimate truth about life and the way of emancipation from its misery—was " profound, difficult to perceive and understand, unattainable by reasoning, abstruse, intelligible only to the wise." He reflected, " If I proclaim the doctrine, and other men are not able to understand my preaching, there would result but weariness and annoyance to me. . . . When the Blessed One pondered over the matter, his mind became inclined to

remain in quiet and not to preach the doctrine."
But the great Lord of all the gods, Brahma,
fearing for the world if it lost its one chance of
hearing the truth, came and did homage to the
Buddha on one knee, and thrice implored him
not to withhold his doctrine from such as have
ears to hear it; and at last the Buddha, "looking
compassionately towards sentient beings over
the world," consented to his entreaty. Then
Mara the Tempter—the ruler of the sixth and
highest heaven of sensual pleasure—came and
made a terrific attempt to divert him from his
purpose, urging that " now was the time for the
Blessed One to pass away." But the Buddha
answered him. " I shall not die until this pure
religion of mine shall have become successful,
prosperous, widespread and popular in all its
full extent." [1] These stories, though in their
present form they cannot be dated within two
centuries of the actual events, and though they
are fairly full of miraculous adornments which
seem childish and absurd, may very well embody
the historical truth.

Then it is represented that the Buddha
" breathed forth the solemn utterance which
has never been omitted by any of the Buddhas " [2] :

Through birth and rebirth's endless round,
Seeking in vain, I hastened on
To find who framed this edifice.

[1] *S.B.E.*, p. 43.

[2] The new Buddha, we must observe, frequently insisted on
the *novelty* of his message. See *S.B.E.*, pp. 147 and 150. " It
was not among the doctrines handed down." It was " discovered
by the Tathagata." And it is exclusive of all rival systems.
" Void are the systems of other teachers " (p. 107).

What misery !—birth incessantly !
O builder, I've discovered thee !
This fabric thou shalt ne'er rebuild !
Thy rafters all are broken now,
Thy pointed roof demolished lies !
This mind hath demolition reached,
And seen the last of all desire.[1]

His first thought was to impart his message to the two philosophers who had taught him in vain. But it was supernaturally communicated to him that they were dead; and his next thought was for the five ascetics who had witnessed his asceticism and mourned his relapse. After much reluctance they agreed to listen and were converted, and became the first five disciples—the first members of a definitely monastic and mendicant Order, with a precise doctrine and precisely defined methods of obtaining its end, and with the Buddha for its infallible teacher and head; and they were the first-fruits of a great harvest. Their ideal may be gathered from a reported saying of the Master : " So long as the brethren shall not engage in, or be fond of, or be connected with business . . . or be partakers in idle talk . . . or indulge in slothfulness or in society . . . nor fall under the influence of idle desires, nor become friends, companions or intimates of sinners, so long as the brethren shall not come to a stop on their way to [Nirvana], because they have attained to any lesser thing—so long may the brethren be expected not to decline but to prosper." [2]

It should be observed that in one sense the

[1] The translations of Pali texts in the above narrative are taken from *S.B.E.* or Cave or Copleston. There does not seem to be much disagreement as to the matters of importance.

[2] See *S.B.E.*, pp. 26, 223 f.

mission of the Buddha was to all men, and that he recognized no distinctions. Thus he refused to recognize the authority of the Brahman priesthood—not yet grown to its height—and the distinctions of caste, in this matter acting probably like other contemporary ascetics [1] ; but in fact his real message made no popular appeal, and it was in no sense aimed at relieving the miseries of the poor and oppressed by re-forming the conditions of the common life. His appeal was in the highest degree intellectual, and such as the uneducated or those who were unversed in abstract speculation could not have understood. " The Buddhist texts tell us with some complacency that his converts were wealthy and of noble birth." Very few low-caste people are represented as entering the order under his preaching ; and he showed also the greatest reluctance in admitting women. He was in truth very suspicious of woman-kind. Ananda, his closest follower, asked him, " How are we to conduct ourselves with regard to woman-kind ? " The reply was, " Don't see them, Ananda." " But if we should see them, what are we to do ? " " Don't speak to them, Ananda." " But if they should speak to us, Lord, what are we to do ? " " Keep wide-awake, Ananda." [2] However, he yielded to pres-sure. But when he yielded and made rules for his nuns he prophesied that, if this had not been done, the pure religion would have stood fast for a thousand years, but now it would stand fast for only half that period.

[1] Cave, p. 110.   [2] *S.B.E.*, vol. xi, p. 91.

Nevertheless, though the fundamental appeal was not what could be called popular, and seems to have been greatly hindered by acute divisions within the order, yet the converts were very many. The monks wore the yellow robes of the ascetic, had their heads tonsured, and lived the mendicant life in chastity, free from all earthly ties and without any recognition of distinctions of caste. Though their Master often went alone and was constantly passing from place to place, the brethren were stationary and went out always in pairs.[1] Outside the Order were pious laymen who did not share the aspiration of the monks to win Nirvana, but did aspire to improve their lot in a future rebirth by obeying certain moral precepts, by works of charity, and especially by gifts to the Order.

It is plain that the success of the Buddha was due in great measure to the beauty and attractiveness of his character—to his patience, his courtesy—even to the courtesan[2]—and his gentleness. As one reads the dry formalism of his teaching as the tradition gives it us, one cannot but suspect that the aroma of sweetness must have been allowed to evaporate in the process of reducing it to a technical form, adapted to be a " memoria technica " ; for there was no writing in the early centuries of Buddhism.

The mission of the Buddha—chiefly in the regions of which Benares was the centre—lasted for some fifty years, till he was eighty years

[1] The form of their dismissal is given, " Go forth, mendicants, on your rounds."
[2] *S.B.E.*, p. 30.

old. In the " Sutta of the Great Decease " we have a moving account of his last days and death.[1] Knowing himself to be very ill, he restrained his sickness by a deliberate act of his will (" I will bend this sickness down again, and keep my hold on life ") that he might take leave of the Order before he died. He refused the urgent request of Ananda that he would give some instruction for the Order in their future career. He reminded him that he had never made a mystery of his doctrine. He had explained it fully, making no distinction of esoteric and exoteric truth. He had never kept " a closed fist." He had nothing else to leave them but the truth. " The Tathagata thinks not that it is he who should lead the brotherhood, or that the Order is dependent upon him. Why should he leave instructions on any matter concerning the Order ? Therefore, O Ananda, be ye lamps unto yourselves. Be ye a refuge to yourselves. Betake yourselves to no external refuge. And whosoever, Ananda, either now or after I am dead, shall be a lamp unto themselves, and a refuge unto themselves, shall betake themselves to no external refuge, but holding fast to the truth as their lamp, shall not look for refuge to anyone beside themselves . . . it is they, Ananda, who shall reach the very topmost height." [2]

He would not refuse a meal of boar's flesh

---

[1] *S.B.E.*, pp. 1 ff. The narrative is interspersed with miraculous incidents which have no interest and are easily detachable.

[2] This is not easy to reconcile with the formula of admission to the Order—" I betake myself to the Blessed One as my refuge, to the Truth, and to the Order."

which Chunda, the worker in metal, provided
for him, though he recognized that it was un-
healthy, and such as none but the Tathagata
could digest; it caused, however, a painful
dysentery, of which he very soon died. But in
the interval before his death he showed a touching solicitude that Chunda should not experience
any remorse. Before he died he questioned his
monks as to whether they had any lingering
doubts about his doctrine, but they were silent,
and he bore witness that " even the most backward of these five hundred brethren has been
converted, and is no longer liable to be born
in a state of suffering and is assured of final
salvation." Then he addressed them : " Behold now, brethren, I exhort you, saying :
Decay is inherent in all component things !
Work out your own salvation with diligence ! "
This was the Tathagata's last word. So he passed
away. His body was cremated with the greatest
reverence and his ashes divided among his
kinsfolk and various nobles. The portion received by his kinsfolk was buried under a monu-
ment in an urn, which was discovered in 1898,
claiming in an inscription to contain "the remains
of the exalted Buddha of the Sakyan clan."

§ 3

The centre of the Buddha's doctrine—the
secret which he had discovered in his intense
meditation, after he had turned his back both
on current metaphysical enquiries and on ascetic
practices, as guides to the light of truth—was
that what causes rebirth is the existence of desire.

It is assumed that misery is inseparable from life, or in other words that life is an evil to be got rid of, if possible.[1] Now at death the components of the individual life are dissolved. What brings them together again to form another individual life is the persistence of desire. Thus if once desire—not what we call lust merely, or misdirected desire in some form, but desire as such, every form of clinging to anything, divine, human or sub-human—is utterly eradicated, then there is nothing left which can bring about any re-collection of the components of life which have been separated by death. The individual person or being will have altogether ceased to exist.

The central heresy in the Buddha's eyes was " the heresy of individuality " or " the doctrine of soul or self "—the notion " I am," " This I exists," " I shall, or I shall not, be," or " have such and such qualities." This is one of the three fatal delusions—the other two being belief in the efficacy of rites and ceremonies, and doubt as to the truth of the Buddha's message—which must be abandoned at the very first stage of the path to perfection.[2]   Alike the early Buddhists and their Brahman opponents recognize in this doctrine something essential to Buddhism. The Buddhist must utterly purge himself from " the struggle to maintain his individuality " ; and " the desire for a future life " is as pernicious as what we should call *wrong* desires.[3] It is

[1] Not, however, by suicide. That, presumably, was regarded as contrary to the state of passivity proper to the perfect.
[2] See Rhys Davids' *Buddhism*, pp. 95 f.   [3] *S.B.E.*, p. 148.

because a Tathagata is utterly free from desire
as such that at death he passes entirely away
" with that utter passing away in which nothing
whatever is left behind." [1]

It would appear that Nirvana is strictly
speaking the name, not for the utter nothingness
into which the life of the perfect passes away, but
for the state of mind—the absolute tranquillity,
or emancipation of heart and mind from all
desire, which constitutes Aratship, and *merits*
the final transition.[2] It should be noted that
the gods—even Brahma, reckoned the supreme
deity by contemporary Brahmans—were, in
Gotama's view, like all other beings, "evanescent,
bound by desire to the chain of existence, the
result of ignorance, and could only find salvation
by walking along the noble Eightfold Path." [3]
He who attains Nirvana is thus superior to all
the world of gods. And any disciple who
retains a desire to belong to one or other of the
divine or angelic hosts and who directs his
conduct accordingly, is to be regarded as still
bound in mental bondage.[4]

All the opinions of the philosophers, so eagerly
discussed in his day,[5] Gotama ranked as *dilthi*
(" views " or " heresies "), of which sixty-two
are enumerated in one of the Suttas. To the
question, " What became of the enlightened man
after death ? " he answered " Where does the fire
go, when it goes out ? " To all possible questions

[1] P. 48.
[2] Rhys Davids' *Buddhism*, pp. 111 f. ; see *S.B.E.*, p. 218.
[3] See *S.B.E.*, pp. 162 f.   [4] *Ibid.*, p. 227.
[5] See *Ibid.*, pp. 167 ff.

about the eternity of the world or about the soul—" Do you hold " this, that or the other opinion ? he answered merely " No." All these " views " belong to " the jungle of mere opinion, the writhing of opinion, the bonds of heresy." They involve pain, vexation, etc. They do not tend to dissatisfaction and the putting away of desire, and the real knowledge, and the absolute insight, and Nirvana.[1] He equally repudiated all the science of his time—all astronomy, geography, astrology and occult investigations.[2] The " knowledge " of his disciples was to include nothing that we should call culture—nothing that did not aim directly at the extinction of individuality by the extinction of desire.

He was equally in antagonism to religion— that is, to all that is associated with priesthoods and worship and prayer and sacrifice—what he called " the belief in the efficacy of outward acts." [3] Such practices are as vain and useless as metaphysical and scientific occupations. As to theology, no doubt Gotama accepted as a fact the existence of gods and spirits ; but they all, like human " selves," belonged to the world of the compounded and evanescent, and he was bound to regard speculation about them as a waste of time, to be deprecated.

All such enquiries, then, are met by a deliberate agnosticism. The dogma which is to be believed

[1] Copleston, p. 68.   [2] S.B.E., pp. 196 ff., 299.
[3] Ibid., pp. 10, 27, 169 ff.   There was no prayer or praise in early Buddhism.   See on prayer, Copleston, p. 269.   There is an interesting comparison between the " learned men " whom the Buddha confronted and the " Scribes and Pharisees " of the Gospels made by Rhys Davids in S.B.E., p. 160.

is strictly confined to the one central point—
that what lies at the root of misery (which is
inseparable from life) is desire, and that the total
eradication of desire brings life or soul and all
its attendant misery to an absolute end with
death. All other dogmas of the metaphysicians
Buddha insisted should be—not denied or discussed but ignored. He was the first thorough-
going agnostic. On the basis of this fundamental " discovery," he formulated " the Noble
Eightfold Path " for all those who have the
courage to walk in it, which formed " the Law "
for his Order, and the Four Noble Truths.[1]

The system of the Noble Path is divided into
eight sections : the first is *Correct* [2] *views*, i.e. the
steadfast holding of the fundamental Buddhist
dogma, free from all superstition or delusion.
The second is *Correct aims*, i.e. constant direction
of the intention away from all vain things
towards the one great end. The third is *Correct
speech*, which means not only inflexible veracity,
but also kindly speech which is unwilling to hurt
or injure anyone. The fourth is *Correct conduct*,
peaceful, honest and kind. The fifth is *Correct*

[1] In *The Foundation of the Kingdom of Righteousness*, the
central discourse attributed to the Buddha (*S.B.E.*, vol. xi,
pp. 146–155), his doctrine appears as the Middle Way between
licence and asceticism. Avoiding these, we follow the Noble
Eightfold Path, based upon the Four Noble Truths. This
teaching is addressed to the Five Ascetics, and produced their
conversion.

[2] I have preferred the word " correct " to the more common
translation " right," because it suggests the highly doctrinaire or
dogmatic style of the Buddhist teaching and its sharp-cut edges.
It would seem as if that quality must have belonged to the
teaching of its founder.

occupation or livelihood. The sixth is *Correct efforts* in obtaining complete self-control. The seventh is *Correct memory*, or the constant having in mind of the fundamental doctrine. The eighth is *Correct contemplation*, that is constant meditation on the fundamentals. The aim of " the Path " is shown by the insistence under this last head upon regular and protracted meditation on all that sustains *disgust* with life, on all the degrading and foul aspects of physical life, on its diseases, its decay and its corruption. This permanent disgust with life is essential to keep alive in a man's mind the *Correct aim*, viz. redemption from something so altogether and irremediably loathsome. " A man should do his best, when a good point of meditation has occurred to him, to keep it before his mind, such as the idea of a skeleton, a corpse eaten by worms, a corpse turning blue, etc." [1] He is also to meditate constantly on the dreary prospect of innumerable lives—the impression of their number being conveyed by every kind of incredible metaphor, such as that the tears which each individual has shed over his fathers in the succession of lives amount to more water than is in all oceans—until the sense of weariness generated by such an interminable succession arouses disgust and the resolution to have no more of it.[2]

It is plain that both the third and the fourth requirements of the Noble Path would produce a character in the Buddhist monk, who should follow it faithfully after his master's example, in a high degree amiable and kindly, and in a true

---

[1] Copleston, p. 82. [2] *Ibid.*, p. 90.

sense beneficent, even if no permanent or real remedies could be applied to the evils of human life. And truthfulness, honesty and kindliness were to be conspicuous features, outside the circle of the monks, in the laymen or attached disciples who did not aim at perfection, but only at a rebirth under good conditions.

The Four Noble Truths, which are the basis of the Noble Path, follow the lines of the medical science of the time which " dealt with disease under the categories of its symptom, its cause, its cure, and the way to obtain the cure." [1] Buddha, as the physician of souls, adopted these categories. The symptom of disease in humanity is the noble truth of suffering, which is the thing to be remedied ; the noble truth of the cause of suffering is desire ; the noble truth of the cessation of suffering is the thorough extinction of desire ; the noble truth of the path which leads to the cessation of suffering is the Holy Eightfold Path already described.

We find in the Suttas a vast number of other numbered lists of requirements or hindrances or methods for the monastic life—there are the *Eight Positions of Mastery*, the *Ten Fetters*, the *Thirteen Links in the Chain of Causation*, etc., etc.,[2] but it is the discourse delivered at Benares, later called *The Foundation of the Kingdom of Righteousness*, containing the eight divisions of the Noble Path and the Four Noble Truths, which we have the best right to ascribe to the Buddha

[1] Cave, p. 105.
[2] See *S.B.E.*, pp. 181, 213 f., 222 ; also Copleston, pp. 76 f., on the unintelligibility of the last of these enumerations.

himself and not to later tradition. Fundamentally it is by this discourse he must be judged.

§ 4

We must seek to form some estimate of the Buddha's formulation of the best life for man, given, as it seems to have been, in a singularly dry and precise form—the life which in its perfection is possible only for the mendicant monk.[1] He must get rid of all the vices—" lust, hatred, stupidity, fear," or " greed, malice, sloth, pride and doubt."[2] Each vice is to be got rid of at the root, that is, in the thoughts as well as in the words and actions. The instructions on the overcoming of anger and pride are especially touching and edifying. More or less the same ground is gone over in the treatment of the virtues to be cultivated, but the virtue of loving-kindness is specially emphasized. The true monk " lets his mind pervade each quarter of the world with thoughts of love. And thus the whole wide world—above, below, around and everywhere— does he continue to pervade with heart of love, far-reaching, grown great and beyond measure,"[3] and this love is interpreted as pity, sympathy and equanimity, which means a " quietude of

[1] Copleston, chaps. viii–xvii. The form of the teaching, which I have described as singularly dry and precise, may have been exaggerated in the tradition before it was written down. But we cannot doubt that the form was impressed upon it by the founder originally.

[2] Cf. *S.B.E.*, vol. x, p. 41: "Anger, intoxication, obstinacy, bigotry, deceit, envy, grandiloquence, pride, conceit, intimacy with the unjust—that is uncleanness, but the eating of flesh is not."

[3] *S.B.E.*, pp. 201, 211, 273.

heart which springs from within " and is bred of " the ecstasy of solitary contemplation, looking through things." Much attention is paid to love of the brethren, or the spirit of unity among the monks dwelling or journeying together, and the temper of meekness necessary for such companionship is much dwelt upon. Moreover, the love insisted upon is extended to animals as well as men, and consideration for them is to reach far beyond the scrupulous refusal to take animal life. Thus the credit of having first founded hospitals—and even for animals—undoubtedly belongs to Buddhism.

Extensive lessons on vices and virtues are given in the process of elaborating the Five Precepts—against destroying life, against taking what is not given, against sexual offences (which are horribly detailed), against lying, and against drinking intoxicating liquors. (As regards the first of these precepts it must be remembered that the offence of personally taking the life of an animal did not extend to eating the flesh of an animal killed by someone else. Gotama himself habitually did so.[1]) Where the monk has offended against any of the precepts, he is required to make confession in Chapter, and is liable to excommunication. There is very little said about the life of the nuns, and it would appear that they were never an element of importance in the community.

In admiring this strenuous and exacting ideal it is necessary to entertain certain considerations.

(1) The life contemplated is that of one who

[1] *Buddhism*, p. 76.

has absolutely separated himself from the world.
The separation [1] is to be not only from vices,
not only from noxious practices, such as magic,
not only from luxuries, but from amusements,
games and athletic exercises of all kinds, from
all kinds of business, buying and selling, etc.,
from all holding of property, except the necessary
clothing and implements like the beggar's bowl,
from all adornment of the person, and from almost
all subjects of conversation, as well as from
" mean talk." In the long lists of things from
which the monk must abstain, the real vices are
curiously mixed up with actions we should
call innocent. It should be noticed that the
Buddha is said to have prophesied that Rahatship
(that is the higher practice for the attainment
of which he founded his Order) would not exist
for more than a century. And, as far as Southern
Buddhism—the most primitive sort of Buddhism
—is concerned, it does not ever appear in the
tradition to have been believed to be possible
among contemporaries. It appears only as a
remote ideal.[2]

(2) The only motive assigned for the pursuit
of virtue and eradication of vice is the selfish
motive, the escape from the chain of lives.
This is quite explicit. It is so with those who
are seeking Nirvana, and with those who minister
to them—not themselves aiming so high but
only aiming at rebirth in a better condition.
The thing to be sought by either class is simply

---

[1] See especially the " paragraphs on conduct," *S.B.E.*, pp.
189–200.

[2] Copleston, p. 267 ; cf. *S.B.E.*, p. 245, referring to Northern
Buddhism.

6

merit. Thus the laity are said to be injured when good monks leave a place, because " the opportunities of almsgiving are spoilt." When a bodhisat (i.e. one on the way to become a Buddha) is represented as making monstrous sacrifices, such as leaping into the fire, as a hare, to be cooked for a Brahman's dinner, he is made to say, " If I do not make this surrender, I shall not attain Buddhahood." But this leads us on to notice what seems to be a blessed inconsistency in Gotama's life and teaching. As we have seen, he is said to have deliberately abstained from " passing away " when he had obtained complete emancipation, in order that he might propagate his gospel in fifty years of laborious life for the love of men. And the description given of the universal love which every perfect man is to acquire and exercise treats it as a positive quality which goes far beyond the mere absence of the disturbing feeling of hate. We cannot but ask ourselves whether this noble charity can be interpreted with any reality on the basis of the utterly pessimistic estimate of life which Gotama preached. Must it not mean that positive love is a quality of human life, which subsists and deepens and broadens as selfishness and vice is conquered ? And must not this mean, further, that there is something worth living for—some noble purpose that life can subserve—which must have its root in the innermost nature of things ?

(3) We have said that the infinite love for man and for the whole universe which Gotama preached was a positive thing and not a mere absence of

hatred or anger. That is true. But it must also
be observed that in the story of the Blessed One
and his companions very little is said of works
of mercy done to others.[1] Their love is a disposition of mind which does not generally appear
to prompt any kind of redemptive action. The
blessedness of " giving " appears almost always
to mean " giving to monks." For the monks
themselves the idea seems to be that " it is
more blessed to receive than to give." They
stand before men regularly as the perpetual
opportunity for the acquisition of merit by giving
them good food.

When we pass from the monks to the laity
and the " householders," we find among the Suttas
a very attractive outline picture attributed to
the Buddha of the duties of parents and children,
teachers and pupils, husbands and wives, friends
and companions, masters and servants, laymen
and religious.[2] It is permeated by a thorough
spirit of kindness and friendliness. In particular
the tone of the Buddhist books towards women
in the lay life is excellent. But the whole life
of the married man is put on a decidedly lower
level than that of the religious. Its aim is
different. For example (in spite of the Five
Precepts) it is assumed that by the necessity of
killing animals for food, or by drinking intoxi-

[1] Copleston, pp. 99, 107. He notes one exception.
[2] Rhys Davids, cap. v. The five fundamental precepts
which monks and laymen alike must vow to observe are these :
not to take life, not to steal, to abstain from impurity, not to
lie, to abstain from intoxicating drinks. For the monk " impurity " meant all sexual intercourse. For the layman it
meant " unlawful sexual intercourse."

cating liquor, he will be constantly storing up
demerit with its necessary consequences in a
future life. He may, if he is good, even go to
heaven ; but he cannot " reach the end of
sorrow." [1] The religious aim of the layman is,
then, the acquisition of merit, available to procure
him a better condition in the next life ; and
we cannot but notice how prominent a place in this
process of acquisition is occupied by " giving "
to the monks.[2]

Thus, whether we are considering the life
of the Order or the life of the layman we are
never allowed to forget, however carefully defined are the duties of life, and however thoroughly analysed are the vicious tendencies of
mankind, that the sole motive for self-improve-
ment is the selfish motive of obtaining a better
future for oneself ; and that the only really
satisfying motive is the motive of getting utterly
rid of individual life by the utter extinction of
desire. All generations all the world over can
join in veneration for Gotama, but his secret,
his principle of enlightenment, must surely
remain abhorrent.[3]

[1] However, he is much better off than even the ascetic, who
is not a Buddhist.

[2] Copleston (pp. 136 f.) gives a very good account of the gradua-
tion of the Buddha's teaching—how he first taught men to be
good laymen, and when their hearts were opened, taught them
the much higher blessings of the mendicant state. It is to be
noticed (pp. 141 f.) that Gotama, though in principle he refused
to put non-caste people under any taboo, and sternly rebuked
Brahman pride, yet accepted the caste system as he found it
and commended the observance of caste rules.

[3] I have referred above (p. 64, n. 1) to the estimate of
Buddhism by Tolstoy and Lowes Dickinson.

§ 5

I shall not attempt to trace the history of Buddhism. Between the time that Gotama died and the middle of the third century B.C.—some two centuries—his system received form and elaboration, and the " canonical literature " was for the most part compiled. This takes us to the epoch of the King Asoka, the great patron of Buddhism, which is the epoch of its glory. " In him Buddhism inspired perhaps the greatest effort, in scale at any rate, on behalf of good, than was ever made by man, outside of Christianity." " He was not merely the Constantine of Buddhism, he was an Alexander with Buddhism for his Hellas."[1] He found in Buddhism—that is, the Buddhism of the third century which had already abandoned the pursuit of Rahatship and the stringent discipline which Gotama had established for his monks—both an ideal of personal life, especially in its emphasis on kindness and the refusal to take life, and also an instrument of justice for his kingdom. We know so little about the period subsequent to his death that we cannot tell what permanence his ideals had.

We owe to his son, Makinda, the conversion of Ceylon, and to Ceylonese Buddhism the preservation, so far as it has been preserved, of original Buddhism ; Buddhaghosha (about A.D. 420) in that island has merited the name of " the second founder of the Buddhism of Ceylon " ; and it was from Ceylon that Burma and Siam were converted. For the history of Southern Buddhism and for the present state and influence

[1] Copleston, p. 165.

of Buddhism in Ceylon I can refer to no more candid and just estimate than Copleston's.[1]

The Northern Buddhism diverged from the principles of the Founder more widely than the Southern, which in consequence condemned it and held it in abhorrence. It was the Buddhism of the Northern tradition [2] which penetrated into China and Thibet, and thence to Korea, to Japan and elsewhere, in the early centuries of our era. In India it had a constant struggle with Brahmanism, and before the twelfth century it had been extirpated; but it still holds its ground in the other countries named, though in a form very far removed from the intentions of its founder. It has abandoned the extreme discipline which embodied his secret; it has become a religion of elaborate ceremonial in the worship of Buddhas and Bodhisattvas, of gods and goddesses; it has associated itself with all sorts of magic. It appears to have retained very widely the beauty of tranquillity or passivity of character and the virtue of kindness. But the fundamental principle of its founder, from which it never can cut itself loose—that personal life is an evil, not a good—vitiates Buddhism at the core. We must content ourselves with having examined the fundamental Buddhism.

[1] Cap. xxvi–xxviii. Copleston's great book contains some passages, written from the point of view of the Christian missionary, which one may wish away. But this point of view never seems to me to hinder the justness and generosity of his estimate either of original or of later Buddhism. It is the most illuminating account of Buddhism we have.

[2] Called the Mahayana, or Great Vehicle (of Salvation); by contrast to the Hinayana, or Lesser Vehicle, which is the Southern Buddhism.

CHAPTER IV

FURTHER SURVEY OF THE EAST

§ 1

WE have been occupied in considering two concrete and intelligible conceptions of the aim
which men should set before them in living their
life and of the means of attaining it—two definitely ethical systems based on specific theories
of the universe—the Zoroastrian and the Buddhist. In both cases we have studied the theory
and ethical system at their best—that is at their
fountain-head—for in their subsequent propaga-
tion both alike were so fully accommodated to
their surroundings that their essential character
was almost lost.[1] Thus in India we see Buddhism
first transformed (in Northern Buddhism) and
then expelled by the victorious power of Brahmanism[2]; and, outside Buddhism, anything
like a definite theory of the good life for man
in general we shall not find in India, on account
of the indiscriminate toleration which is the

[1] See *The Interpretation of Religion*, by John Baillie (T. and T.
Clark, 1929), pp. 386 ff.

[2] It would appear probable that many Buddhists remained
in India by professing the Jain religion. Jainism at its origin
was a movement akin to that of the Buddha. It was not strictly
a religion. The cry was, "Man, thou art thy own friend! Why
wishest thou for a friend beyond thyself?" (see Baillie, as
above, p. 389). But, like Buddhism, it was accommodated to
the surrounding polytheism, retaining as its most distinctive
feature the scrupulous refusal to take life.

principle (or absence of principle) in Hinduism. On this subject there appears to be general agreement. I will quote at length from a correspondence between a sympathetic English-man and his Indian friend.[1]   The Indian writes :

" You asked me to give a definition of Hindu-ism. I am afraid I must disappoint you. Hinduism is not one religion, not one creed, not one faith. It is a jumble of all the religions, all the creeds, and all the faiths that have swept the land through the course of ages. Further, Hinduism covers all the stages through which religious instinct has passed and philo-sophic thought has travelled, developed and advanced. Nor is this all. Hinduism is not confined only to religion in the ordinary accept-ance of the term.   It also brings under its shelter-ing wings all the religions, semi-religions, and social practices and observances of the Hindu race (or races). Do not imagine for a moment that I have exaggerated matters. Polytheism, monotheism, pantheism and atheism have all flourished under the auspices and in the name of Hinduism, not necessarily at different times, and still form an integral part of recognized Hinduism. Demon worship, hero worship, ancestor worship, worship of animate and inanimate objects, wor-ship of natural forces and worship of God have all been woven into its web. It caters for every taste, every grade of life, every stage of develop-ment. This at once constitutes the bane and beauty of Hinduism, its weakness and strength. From the purest to the vilest form of worship, from the sublimest heights of philosophic thought

[1] *Sidelights on the Crisis in India*, by H. Harcourt (Longmans, 1924), pp. 28–29, slightly abbreviated.   A valuable book, with a preface by Dr. Norwood, the Head Master of Harrow.

to the meanest and crudest phrases of intellectual and religious developments, all the stages are provided for."

In *The Hindu View of Life* the eloquent Prof. S. Radhakrishnan,[1] the panegyrist of Hinduism, gives us (notwithstanding his exaggerated and uncritical estimate of the merits of Hinduism) the same impression, if we read a little between the lines. I am not attempting any independent estimate of Hinduism. I am only urging that this atmosphere of indiscriminate intellectual, religious and moral toleration is not likely to generate a definite conception of the good life for all men based on any definite principle. I will justify this opinion by pointing to the great Epic, the *Bhagavadgita*[2] (the Lord's Song). "It would be difficult," says Dr. Cave, "to exaggerate the importance of the Bhagavad-gita in India to-day. By men educated on Western lines the Vedas are praised, but often left unread; but the *Gita* is known and loved, and to many such the Krishna of the *Gita* seems a worthy rival of the Christ of the Gospels. No Hindu book so merits study by those who would understand the vital forces of modern Hinduism."

It starts by stating a moral problem with pathetic power. Arjuna, the warrior chieftain

[1] King George V Professor of Philosophy in Calcutta University (George Allen & Unwin, 1927), see pp. 37, 41, 46, 48.

[2] Dr. Barnett's translation (Dent & Son) in the Temple Classics. The introduction to the translation and Dr. Cave's analysis, pp. 42 ff., should be consulted. The poem dates probably from the first century A.D.

of the Pandavas in their struggle against the
Kurus, to whom they are united by kinship,
is paralysed by an overwhelming scruple at the
thought of the slaughter of his kinsmen, which
he and his are about to undertake from no other
motive than ambition. " Ah me ! a heavy sin
have we resolved to do, that we strive to slay
our kin from lust after the sweets of kingship."
" Verily it were more blest to eat even the food
of beggary in this world, without slaughter of
noble masters." [1]   But the divine Lord Krishna,
who is acting as his charioteer, seeks to remove
his scruple first by philosophical doctrine.   The
self (or essential reality) of each man is indestructible, and therefore unaffected by any physical
experience in the cycle of births.   It passes
from body to body unchangeable in essence.
" This slays not, neither is it slain.   This never
is born and never dies."   Therefore it is wrong
to deplore the sufferings or deaths of men.
" Thou dost not well to sorrow for any born
beings."   Moreover, the individual selves have
no reality : they are but phases of the un-
changing universal soul.   The real is one, and
the differences of selves are illusory.

Then he passes from metaphysics to the
practice of the *Yoga*—the ascetic discipline.
Thereby Arjuna must seek to realize indifferency.
He must fulfil his caste duties—and he belongs
to the Warriors whose duty it is to kill—but he
must rise to do these things without any thought
of gaining benefit for himself thereby. He
should pass to the highest state, which is a

[1] Pp. 86–87.

profound apathy of body and mind, the prelude to emancipation and union with the divine.

The poem, it must be confessed, is full of vital contradictions. Thus in spite of this supreme unselfishness which Arjuna is to cultivate, Krishna does not hesitate to represent to him the dishonour which will be his, if he fails to fight, and the honour which will accrue to the victor. " They that seek thy hurt will say many words of ill speech, crying out upon thee for thy faintness ; now what is more grievous than this ? If thou be slain, thou wilt win heaven ; if thou conquer thou wilt have the joys of the earth ; therefore rise up resolute for the fray."

So far Arjuna is not satisfied. " If thou deemest understanding more excellent than works . . . then wherefore dost thou engage me in a grim work, O Long-Haired One ? Thou confoundest my understanding with seemingly tangled utterance." Krishna proceeds to explain to him how " worklessness " is, by mental abstraction, compatible with the works of his calling, for such work becomes no-work. The man may do them while he himself is utterly selfless— wholly detached from what he does with his body. " He who on every side is without attachments, whatever may happen, whether fair or foul, who neither likes nor dislikes, of such a one the understanding is well poised." But as the " lessons " proceed the conception of the one supreme being changes.

He is now presented as one who seeks divers incarnations. He is incarnate, especially in Krishna-Vasudera, and he can most effectively be sought and found of men by Bhakti " devotion "—that is, faith and love and joyous self-surrender to the personal God incarnate. In this idea of the God of Love and the love of God the poem reaches its highest level. But the devotion is still free from positive ethical obligation. " I am indifferent," says Krishna, " to all born beings ; there is none whom I hate, none whom I love. He who regardeth indifferently friends and foes, also the righteous and unrighteous, he excelleth. But they that worship me with devotion dwell in me and I in them. Even if he that worships me with undivided worship should be a doer of exceeding evil, he shall be deemed good ; for he is of right purpose. Speedily he becomes righteous of soul, and comes to lasting peace. O sons of Kunti, be assured that none who is devoted to me is lost." [1]

The universality of Krishna, as the All in All incarnate, is then illustrated in a torrent of expressions ; and afterwards he reveals himself in his body—the universe—to Arjuna, who is overwhelmed with the awful spectacle. " I behold in thy body all the gods and hosts of the orders of born beings . . . all the saints and heavenly serpents. I behold thee of many arms, bellies, faces and eyes, on all sides endless. . . . Looking upon thy mighty form the worlds and I quake. For as I behold thee touching the heavens, glittering, many hued, with yawning mouths . . . my inward soul trembles. The sons of Dhritarashtra [his adversaries in the war]

[1] Pp. 129–130.

and likewise the chief of our warriors hasting enter into thy mouths, grim with fangs and terrible ; some caught between thy teeth appear with crushed heads." As rivers into the sea, as moths into the fire, so all worlds pass into thy mouths to perish. " Grim grow thy splendours, O Vishnu." This awful demonstration is to render Arjuna indifferent to slaughter—" Therefore rise up and get thee glory; by conquest of thy foes enjoy ample empire. By me have they already been given to death; be thou the mere occasion thereto, O left-handed archer." [1]

Having thus smitten Arjuna's soul with terror, " Vasudeva [Krishna] once more displayed his own form ; and . . . again assuming a pleasant shape, comforted him in his terror." The ideal of devotion to the Lord, while doing the works of his calling in absolute detachment, is again set before him. " He who rejoices not, hates not, grieves not, desires not, who renounces alike fair and foul, and has devotion [bhakti], is dear to me—one indifferent to foe and to friend, free of attachment, possessed of devotion, is a man dear to me." The noble virtues of such a man are contrasted with the vices of the sceptic.

Then the different works of the castes— brahmans, knights, traffickers and serfs—are described. " Restraint of spirit and sense, mortification, purity, patience, uprightness, knowledge, discernment and belief are the natural Brahma-works. Valour, heroic temper,

[1] This is one of the examples of the "numinous" in poetry given by Otto, *The Idea of the Holy*, App. ii, p. 193.

constancy, skill, steadfastness in strife, largesse and princeliness are the natural knightly works. Tilling the ground, herding kine, and trading are the natural works of traffickers ; and the natural work of the serfs is service. According as each man devotes himself to his own proper work does he attain to consummation." But finally, the way of consummation which " wins to Brahma " is explained to be the way of absolute detachment from all earthly things, free from all thought of *I* or *mine*, the way of one who does his works of caste and religion in a spirit of total " worklessness " absorbed in devotion to the Lord. So, finally, Arjuna is rid of his doubts and scruples about the slaughter of his kinsmen. " My bewilderment has passed away. . . . I stand free from doubt ; I will do thy word."

I have thought it worth while to give this sketch of the argument of the Bhagavadgita because, while even in an English translation we can feel something of the splendour of the poem, it leads us to see that we cannot expect from Hinduism any firmly conceived ideal of the good life. Original Buddhism can supply one, because, however wrong we think its fundamental dogma, it does, in the form in which its founder inaugurated it, demand acceptance of that fundamental principle to the exclusion of all others, and a mode of life according to it. But Hinduism is infinitely tolerant. The way of real salvation is the way of intellectual abstraction, casting off all belief in real selves or the distinctions which belong to human experience. The real self is unaffected by deeds which belong only to the material—unreal—world. This leaves it possible for a man to fulfil the works of his calling, the laws of his caste, but in a spirit of indifference which is inevitably contemptuous. What we call ethics remains a matter of caste requirement or of religious observance according to the sect each man belongs to. How unlikely either caste or religion in India is to provide any worthy ethical standard for man as man we can easily ascertain. We have to accept the fact that, almost all the world over, the "natural religions" are ceremonial and non-ethical. They are divorced from morality, and often positively immoral. So it was and is in India.

There are noble examples set before India both in its myths and in its history, like the noble example of wifely purity and devotion in the heroic Sita in the *Ramayana*. But there are so many other examples. The Krishna of the Bhagavadgita is also the Krishna of the licentious stories of the Vishnavite *Puranas*. "Imagination can be foul as well as pure, and, in the popular mind, the ideal Krishna of the *Gita* is inevitably confused with the Krishna of the *Puranas*, who is the product of an imagination both lewd and foolish."

There are so many writers to-day who are claiming for India that even we Western people should seek a new spiritual home in her thought and tradition that it is necessary to ask for serious consideration to be given to the fact that neither in the religion nor in the philosophy of India is any stable foundation to be found for ethics.

§ 2

The world is a large place. History sets before us for our consideration many nations, and within nations many races, and each has its own traditions of belief, practice and worship. But there seems to be everywhere something in human nature which responds to an ideal of conduct, transcending alike traditional customs and utilitarian necessities. To the Chinese sage, Mencius, the follower of Confucius, who gave Confucianism its final expression,[1] and is called " the Second Inspired One,"—an optimist who always emphasizes the natural goodness of human nature— is attributed a saying with which the unsophisticated among us would agree. " From the feelings proper to it [mankind] is constituted for the practice of what is good. Benevolence, righteousness, propriety and knowledge are not infused into us by external influences. We are certainly furnished with them " [i.e. from within].

Thus the traditional wisdom of China finds at the basis of all things a divine principle or law—Tao [the way]—closely akin to what the Stoics described as Nature, to which all things in heaven and earth must conform, and to which human nature is akin ; so that for man the highest knowledge is to know the Tao and the highest wisdom is to live by it. In the Chinese Classics [2] the Rites, religious and social, of the

---

[1] Confucius died in 479, Mencius in 289 B.C.
[2] *S.B.E.*, vol. iii.

Chinese tradition are regarded as the will of "Heaven," which is the name for the Supreme Power ruling the affairs of men as an omnipotent and omniscient righteousness.[1] "These rules [the Rites] are rooted in Heaven, have their correspondences on earth, and are applicable to spiritual beings."[2] The principle of Tao was already the governing idea of the system of Lao-tse, the older contemporary and traditional rival of Confucius, though his system, known as Taoism, became a pantheistic mysticism, indifferent, like the Indian metaphysic, to all considerations of difference between one thing and another, and having a pure impassiveness for its ideal of character. Later, it degenerated into a profuse polytheism and the practice of exorcism as a defence against demons,[3] in this respect sharing the fate of Buddhism, with which it had joined hands.

But the principle received a different development at the hands of Confucius. His treasured sayings [4] are sometimes enigmatical; but they are full of a ripe and shrewd wisdom, and on the whole one gets a clear picture of the mind of a great and good man. To quote a Chinese historian of the second century B.C.: "Countless are the princes and prophets that the world has seen in its time, glorious in life, forgotten in death. But Confucius, though only a humble member of the cotton-clothed masses, remains

---

[1] See *S.B.E.*, vol. iii, Dr. James Legge's preface, p. xxiv.
[2] This is a response of Confucius to a question as to the value of the Rites.
[3] See Cave, pp. 159–161.
[4] See L. A. Lyall's *Sayings of Confucius* (Longmans).

among us after many generations. . . . He may indeed be pronounced the divinest of men." Certainly he was one who loved and lived by the eternal virtues—justice, truth, self-control, kindness, faithfulness, and courage—holding, however, in especial veneration man's duty to parents and to the King. " The duty of children to their parents is the fountain whence all other virtues proceed."

His idea of authority was not, however, absolute authority. He found the moral principle of life in reciprocity. The duty of the governed was reciprocal to that of the governor. The duty of obedience presupposes just government. He expressed the principle of reciprocity in the words, " What you do not want done to yourself, do not do to others." Lao-tse had said, " Recompense injury with kindness." " No," said Confucius. " Recompense kindness with kindness, and injury with justice." That is reciprocity.

He was a grand conservative. His ideals lay in the past as tradition glorified it. He laboured hard, so long as he was allowed, to restore the ancient standards of discipline and obedience. Except for a few of his disciples, his " little children," his " two or three lads," he had the poorest opinion of his contemporaries, high and low. Perhaps you cannot find in his sayings much attempt to base the good life upon principles valid for mankind in general. " He threw no light," says Dr. Legge, " on any of the questions which have a world-wide interest." But this is not wholly true. No doubt it was of his own country and its tradition that he

chiefly thought.   No doubt also it is the case
that, living in a world of disorder in which there
was only too much religion of a kind which
could give him no assistance, his aim was only
to restore morality and peace on the basis of
the Chinese tradition of duty.   But though he
rarely spoke of religion, he certainly claimed a
divine sanction for his utilitarian morality—
its roots were to be found not in human necessity
but in the divine order.[1]

His later disciple Mencius, developing his
thoughts, is the author of a system of conduct
and a political economy which have a remarkably
modern ring, and he appears to be even more
purely secularist than his master ; but while
affirming the natural goodness of man, he finds
this in kinship to some vaguely conceived divine
principle.

Apart from the influence and authority of the
three philosophers we have noticed, there appears
to be found in China an amorphous mass of
traditional beliefs and practices, not capable
of being reduced to any system.[2]   China at
present is confronted with a formidable task
of political, moral and spiritual reconstruction.
The source of her traditional morality, Confucianism, is so bound up with a vanished regime that
it does not seem likely to be of much avail for
the establishment of a new order.   But those
who study China deeply seem always to discern
in her a moral capacity which has deep roots in

---

[1] Cave, p. 156 ; see also Christopher Dawson's *Progress and
Religion*, pp. 119 ff.

[2] Cf. L. Hodous, *Folkways in China* (Probsthain).

her traditional doctrine of a divine order to which man must conform or he will perish.

§ 3

We find in Japan an extraordinary confusion of religious and ethical theories. The traditional Shinto mythology appears to be quite meaningless, but it is identified with patriotism and loyalty to the Emperor.[1] It has no other meaning. " It was too unreflective to be ethical." But Japan has shown an extraordinary power of assimilating foreign cults and ideas. In the sixth century A.D. Buddhism—of a kind far off from the teaching of Gotama—was introduced from Korea, and became gradually the established religion. Later Christianity became a dangerous rival to Buddhism, but it was almost extirpated in the sixteenth century. Shinto was again established ; but the real rival to Buddhism, which still prevailed in its various sects, was Confucianism, introduced from China, modified, however, from its Chinese form,[2] and made to minister to the military ideal of unconditional and absolute loyalty to the Emperor, be he good or bad. At present it would appear that Buddhist quietism, Confucian morality and Christian ideals in a vague form, coming as part of Western civilization, are contending for the mastery in Japan ; but except in the great tradition of patriotism, no definite ethical standard or theory is to be found there which can claim our consideration.

[1] Cave, pp. 173 ff.
[2] In which stress was laid on " reciprocity," see above, p. 98.

§ 4

Nothing like an ethical system or clear ethical theory has come down to us among Egyptian or Babylonian records ; but it is interesting to notice that the Hebrew Book of Proverbs has recently been shown to depend in part upon the Teaching of Amen-em-ope, contained in a papyrus which may date from the period of the twenty-fifth dynasty, to which Tirhakah belonged, who helped King Hezekiah of Judæa against Senna-cherib. Hezekiah's scribes, who " copied out " proverbs, or their later followers, may have used those of the Egyptian wise man, contained in thirty chapters, which are now available for our study.

Amen-em-ope is said to represent a higher tone of religious and moral reflection than appears in any other specimen of Egyptian wisdom. His proverbs—which seem to have been used as a school-book—illustrate the appreciation, which is general among men, of the virtues of justice, truth, mercy and self-control (" tranquillity "), not only for their utilitarian value but also for their conformity with the divine will.   Amen-ophis, who is a " superintendent of land and of corn " for the king and " for all the gods "—i.e. all the temples—is giving advice to his son, who appears to be a young priest; and the gods he appeals to are various, but supreme among them appears to be the Sun-God (Ra) in his visible disk (Aten), whose approval all good people desire to win.   Unlike the Hebrew compilers of proverbs, his vision of the advantage of virtuous living extends beyond this world to that which lies beyond.[1] The following are specimens of this Egyptian wisdom :

The beginning of teaching how to live, guidance for welfare . . . to direct a man in the path of life and make him prosper upon earth.

Beware of robbing a poor man, of being valorous against the man who has a broken arm.

Give way unto him that attacketh ; sleep a night before speaking ; leave the passionate man to his own devices. God will know how to reply to him.

The truly tranquil man . . . is like a tree grown in a plot (?) : it grows green, it doubles its yield, its fruit is sweet, its shade is pleasant.

Remove not the landmark on the boundaries of the sown fields, nor shift the position of the measuring-rod . . . mark well him who hath done this on earth, for he is an oppressor of the weak. [But] his goods are taken out of the hand of his children and his property is given to another. . . . A man propitiates God by the power of the Lord [Aten], when he defines the boundaries. Desire then to make thine own self prosperous ; beware of the Universal Lord. Better is a bushel that God giveth thee, than

[1] For the above see the translation of the Egyptian document in F. H. Griffith's article in the *Journal of Egyptian Archæology*, vol. xii, October 1926, and Prof. A. E. Morris, in *A New Commentary* (S.P.C.K.), pp. 382 ff., and Oesterley's *Proverbs* (Westminster Commentaries). The portion of the Book of Proverbs which especially shows dependence upon the Egyptian document is capp. xxii. 17 to xxiv. 2. It is not, however, certain that we are justified in speaking of this specimen of " wisdom " as of Egyptian *origin*. Sir E. Wallis Budge would find its home in Asia : and Oesterley (pp. xxxiv. ff.) would have us recognize a wisdom of the proverbial sort as characteristic of the whole Middle East and only receiving a special development in Israel.

is still the formidable rival to Christianity in Africa and elsewhere.

But I do not propose to examine Islam (the great " submission " to the call of God) or the Quran (the Lesson or Recitation) at any length. Confessedly Muhammad was deeply influenced in the beginning of his mission by what he had learned of Judaism and Christianity. At first he taught his disciples to turn to Jerusalem, not to Mecca, in prayer, and to observe not the Fast of Ramadan, but the Jewish Day of Atonement. His system is, like that of the Bible, an ethical monotheism. Comparing, then, the theology and morality of Islam at its best with Judaism at its best, I suppose that hardly anyone can hesitate to give the preference to the latter or to exalt the Old Testament above the Quran.[1] Still less, if Islam is compared to Christianity and the Quran to the New Testament, will any of us hesitate to give the preference to the latter. Thus, if there be such a thing as one specific religion and morality for the world, it must be sought in Christianity at its best rather than in Islam at its best. I propose accordingly only to make three remarks on Islam.

First, it has often been observed that the Muslims on the average are better specimens of their religion than Christians are of theirs. This has been true on a large scale, though with great reservations ; and if we are to justify our-

[1] On Muhammad's defective conception of God (" In Allah the numinous is absolutely preponderant " over the rational, " This will account for the fanatical character of this religion "), see Otto's *Idea of the Holy*, p. 94.

selves hereafter in taking the religion of the Bible as our supreme type of " ethical monotheism," we should take this fact—granted that it is a fact—of the greater success of Muhammadanism in impressing itself on the mass of its converts into account.   The truth seems to be that the success of Muhammadanism is due to its limitation—that very limitation which makes it unprogressive and renders it impossible to consider it as a religion for humanity.

Muhammad must have had a very shrewd perception of what the Arabs, with whom he was primarily concerned, would be content to do, or refuse to do, in order to procure the rewards of Paradise and avoid the horrors of hell.   Thus—they would accept a creed on absolute authority ; they would transact religious forms such as the Five Duties—the recital of the confession of faith, the recital of the set prayers, the fast of Ramadan, almsgiving, and the pilgrimage to Mecca, specific duties which, considerable as they are, would involve no deep transformation of character ; they would fight courageously for the victorious faith, and die for it, like brave soldiers the world all over ; they would avoid certain sins and submit to certain limitations on conduct, such as the avoidance of alcoholic drink, or the flesh of the pig, and perform certain penances or make required compensations for a neglect of specific prohibitions.

This obedience to specific commands was what Islam involved ; and the prospect of obtaining heaven and avoiding hell was put in a form which the natural man would find fully attractive. But Islam made no searching claim for a radical reformation of character. Christianity, however, wherever it has been at all true to its New Testament, has made so deep a claim that men must "die to live," as to make them feel that mere conformity, mere "works," are not worth while. Christianity, where it has been content to become a religion of moderate conformity to an external rule, has been as successful as Muhammadanism in dealing with uncultured people; and indeed at some periods and in some countries in retaining the allegiance of highly cultivated people. But at least in countries where the New Testament is well known, even where people have not broken away from Christianity but have maintained a certain measure of conformity, they have not done so with any strictness, because they have fully recognized in their hearts that what Christ required of them was something very much deeper than this. Thus, for us the Muhammadan idea of God and of religious authority, and the Muhammadan satisfaction with conformity as the passport to heaven, has become wholly impossible. We could not be persuaded to believe that such "works" would carry us to heaven, for heaven is fellowship with God, and such fellowship is impossible without a very radical conversion. Thus the relative success of Muhammadanism as compared with Christianity over the mass of its adherents, so far as that is a fact, appears to be due to the essential defectiveness of its moral claim.

Secondly, the success of Muhammadanism,

where it still appears as the rival to Christianity, as among African tribes, is largely due to something highly meritorious—something which Christianity, according to its principles, ought to have exhibited in an even higher degree, but to its shame has not—that is, that it incorporates weak races into a great world-wide fellowship, of which they at once feel the sustaining force. The principle of brotherhood they see among the Muhammadans really exemplified. They feel its support. Whereas Christianity, as Africans (or Asiatics) have seen it exemplified in the European, nominally Christian, community, so far from welcoming them into brotherhood, has been scandalously exclusive and even hostile. But this is a mere negation of fundamental Christianity, to which it is to be feared the British nation has been peculiarly liable. Racial narrowness and pride have been besetting sins which our Christianity has never at all effectively undermined. But no one can deny that the principle of a catholic fellowship was inherent in Christianity from the start, and is of its essence, and that in a higher form than in Muhammadanism, which maintains slavery and the depreciation of women.

Lastly, something must be said about the mysticism which has been a conspicuous growth upon the Muhammadan, as upon the Indian, the Hellenistic and the Christian soil. That it is not a natural outcome of Islam is not disputable. It has lain always in Muhammadanism under suspicion of heresy. Nevertheless it has flourished at certain periods and in certain regions, and has exhibited beautiful fruits, such as that wonderful Mallorean saint, Ramon Lull—of the thirteenth century—frankly recognized.

Mysticism—Indian, Hellenistic, Muhammadan and Christian—presents a remarkable similarity. " We cannot honestly say," writes Evelyn Underhill, " that there is any wide difference between the Brahman, the Sufi (Muhammadan), or the Christian mystics at their best." [1] The mystics start from different traditions, theological and moral, and a mystic, like St. Theresa, or El-Ghazali among the Muslims, may remain a devoutly orthodox adherent of the tradition ; but the substance of the mystics' quest is union with God, and God being above all that human speech can utter and human thought conceive, there has been a tendency among them to depreciate the specific doctrines of positive religion. Not only so, but mysticism, being " the flight of the alone to the alone," has been deeply individualistic, and has taken wing to the skies above the common life of men. On the contrary, the religion of Muhammad and the religion of Jesus Christ have from first to last concerned themselves primarily with the common and social life of man ; and, though there is an element of mysticism in all true religion, yet in the quest which we are now pursuing—the quest of the good life for men in general—we have not much concern, at least directly, with the mystics in any religion.

[1] See *Essentials of Mysticism* (Dent), p. 4.

CHAPTER V

WE turn now to Greece, and in Greece especially to Athens, which became its intellectual centre.

The influence of Greece on the civilization of the world it is impossible to ignore and difficult to exaggerate, and in no department of civilization, except perhaps in that of art, has its influence been greater than in ethics, or the science of the conduct of life. The cities of Greece had of course their own traditional ethical standards, which varied considerably, and were all seriously weakened by demoralizing mythologies. At Athens the enumeration of what came much later to be called " the cardinal virtues "—justice, self-control, courage and wisdom—was, it seems,[1] traditional in Socrates' time. These were civic virtues, which could be justified on merely utilitarian principles, but, in spite of the bad example set by the gods of the mythology, there was probably a general recognition that morality had ultimately a divine sanction. The great dramatists seem to take this for granted. Thus Æschylus, in the *Prometheus Bound*, recognizes the glory of the hero's rebellion in the interests of humanity against the tyranny of Zeus, and implies the assurance that there was something,

[1] See A. E. Taylor's *Plato, The Man and his Work*, p. 222.

even beyond the irresistible power of Zeus, which would vindicate him at last[1]; while in the *Agamemnon* he gives to Zeus ("whoever he be") something of the moral dignity which belongs to the Hebrew Jehovah.[2] Sophocles, in the *Antigone*, presents to us his heroine as appealing beyond the ruler of the city to the eternal moral laws which are there identified with the sovereignty of Zeus.   Euripides, like Æschylus, makes Hecuba appeal to a Something, called by many names, which lay beyond the unjust or careless gods of Heaven and Hades—Something "which, moving in its silent path, guides mortal destinies according to justice."   "Unrighteousness is not to be found with the gods."[3]   These great poets probably represent the common conscience of their people in elevating Right to the dignity of a divine law, beyond the authority of states and mythologies.   But at Athens especially, in the fifth century, the principle of morality was seriously threatened.[4]

Democracy, of which Athens was the stronghold, was the political system which gave equal opportunity—not to all the inhabitants of the city, for the citizen body was sustained by slave labour, and there was no movement to enfranchize

[1] We cannot, however, answer the question of what was contained in the lost drama of the *Prometheus Freed*. "There is perhaps no piece of lost literature that has been more ardently longed for " (Gilbert Murray).

[2] *Ag.*, pp. 155, 353 ff.

[3] *Fragment*, p. 609. For the above see Gilbert Murray's *Literature of Ancient Greece*, pp. 225, 265 f.

[4] *Thuc.*, iii, 82, gives an account of a universal degeneracy throughout the Greek cities as a result of wars without and party spirit within.

the slaves—but to the whole body of the citizens.
For them all, under democracy, there was an
open career. The writing or reading of books
was not yet in fashion. The opportunity and
the power lay with the public speaker. Unlimited success was to be won by the power of
persuasion in law courts and assemblies. Under
these circumstances a host of professional teachers
(sophists) had appeared who offered to show
men how to succeed. Though some of them
were great and good men, their method was
" Machiavellian "—they owned no principle but
success ; so at least Socrates and Plato thought.
But it would have been in vain for those who
dreaded their influence to appeal merely as con-
servatives to tradition. For mere tradition had
been discredited, and to appeal to religious tradition in particular would have been useless. It was
under such circumstances that Socrates, and
Plato after him, laboured to re-establish morality,
social and individual, on a firm foundation of
eternal principles.[1]

§ 1

Socrates (c. 470–399 B.C.) is said by Cicero[2]
to have " called philosophy down from the
heavens to earth (or ' away from the secrets

[1] For what follows I am depending upon Ueberweg's *Hist.
of Phil.*, vol. i, pp. 83 ff. ; John Burnet's *Greek Philosophy*, pt. i,
also his *Platonism* and *Essays and Addresses* ; A. E. Taylor's
Plato (Methuen) and *Platonism* (Harrap) ; R. C. Lodge's *Plato's
Theory of Ethics* (Kegan Paul) ; William Temple's *Plato and
Christianity* (Macmillan), and W. D. De Burgh's *Legacy of the
Ancient World* (Macdonald and Evans), cap. v.

[2] *Acad. Post.*, i, 4, 15 ; *Tusc.*, v, 4, 10.

and obscurities of nature' with which it had
previously been occupied[1]), and introduced it
into the cities and houses of men, compelling
men to enquire concerning life and morals and
things good and evil"; and the truth of this
description of his activity is acknowledged by
everyone. It appears that he himself took for
granted the obligation of morality and the
divine authority of conscience and the moral
law. "For," he said to his judges,[2] "whereas
I know but little of the world below [Hades],
I do not suppose that I know; but I do know
that injustice and disobedience to a better,
whether God or man, is evil and dishonourable,
and I will never fear a possible good [death]
rather than a certain evil [to do wrong]. Men
of Athens, I honour and love you, but I shall
obey God rather than you." This is the rock
on which Socrates stood. He was a martyr for
righteousness and truth, and Phædo, in the last
words of the dialogue called by his name, calls
him "the best man of whom I have ever had
experience and the wisest and justest."

How was it, then, he came to be condemned
to death?[3] The plea was "that he did not
worship the gods whom the city worships, and
corrupted the young men." The latter part of
the charge no doubt expressed the resentment

[1] In the *Phædo* (96) Socrates himself is represented as having
taken a deep interest in these matters, but abandoned it in
despair of obtaining satisfaction.

[2] See above, p. 9; cf. *Phædo*, 118.

[3] The answer to this question in part is that Socrates would
have nothing short of acquittal. Probably if he had acquiesced
in banishment it would have contented his judges.

of the newly restored democracy of Athens at
Socrates' friendship with the hated traitor
Alcibiades and the fallen oligarch Critias.   But,
at the bottom, the cause of his condemnation
was their alarmed aversion from his whole
principle and method, and their sense of his
formidable power.   For he hated rhetoric, and
the worship of success, and the clamour of the
popular voice, and he believed himself to have
a divine vocation to " examine men " and to
plant the morality of the city life on a foundation deeper than political expediency.

His " ironical " method was to address some
grown citizen or distinguished sophist, or brilliant
young man, whom he heard speaking about
piety or justice or temperance or courage, as
if he were himself quite ignorant and were seeking
enlightenment—" What is this virtue you speak
of ? "   Then with his incomparable power of
dialectic he would show the inadequacy or
absurdity of their attempts to define, one after
another—contenting himself often with nothing
more than the negative result of having exploded
the false assumption of knowledge in others.
That was, no doubt, an " unsettling " method of
instruction, calculated to inspire nothing more
than a distrust of popular rhetoric.   But Socrates'
aim went beyond that.   He described himself
as practising the art of his mother the midwife.
He was the midwife of the intellect to bring to
the birth something latent but innate in the
intelligence of ordinary men.   His aim, as Aristotle describes it, was through induction, that is,
the examination of particular instances, to arrive

at an adequate general definition of each ethical notion. That definition would represent reality —something true and abiding which could be relied upon. He did this in the region of ethics exclusively. He held that the virtues were rational—that rationality and virtue were inseparable, and that vice was mere ignorance.[1]

Thus by means of the definition of particular virtues he sought to aim at such a trustworthy science of good living as that henceforth virtue might be taught, and good parents and teachers would be able to hand on the science to their children and pupils, as securely as any other kind of solid knowledge. And he did all this in the assurance of a divine commission, confirmed by the Delphic oracle, with the safeguard of a divine restraint—a mysterious inward voice which warned him when he was going wrong— and in the conviction that the good life was the will of God for men.

Undoubtedly the most lifelike, as well as brilliant and fascinating, picture of Socrates that we possess is that given us by Plato in the dialogues in which Socrates is the dominant speaker. The question is at the present moment much in dispute—" How far down in the course of Plato's Socratic dialogues, as they advance from criticism of the loose popular definitions of the virtues to the positive doctrine of the eternal " forms " [2]

---

[1] Cf. Aristotle, *Eth. Nic.*, 1145 (vi. 13).

[2] The word commonly used by Plato is εἶδος or ἰδέα. So we talk of the Platonic " doctrine of *ideas*." But the English word means only a conception in the mind, and that is precisely not the meaning of the Greek word. One may translate it " form," using inverted commas to indicate that it is not what

(or principles), centring in the form or principle of the Good, is it really the historical Socrates which is represented ?[1] But we can leave that question aside. For however much or little of " Platonism " is to be ascribed to Socrates as its real originator, at any rate it is as Platonism in its full development, and not as Socratism, that this philosophy influenced Greece and the world. Socrates remained in the memory of man not as the author of a philosophical system, but rather as the very type and model of philosopher, saint and martyr, who had taught men to care for their souls,[2] and had believed in the capacity of the average man to think accurately and to come to the knowledge of the truth.

It is indeed much to be remembered that ethical idealism in Greece depended not on any sense of gradual progress in the ethical standard of society, but on the reverence in which outstanding historical individuals were held. The standard of the good in Aristotle is " as the Wise

we mean by form. But *principle* or sometimes " *value* " (in the modern philosophical sense) better conveys to us the real meaning of the word.

[1] Dr. A. E. Taylor, following Burnet, is the advocate of the position that so long as Socrates is the dominant speaker in the dialogues, the teaching is that of the real Socrates in substance ; but he admits that in the *Parmenides* Plato " frees himself from the responsibility for the strict accuracy of his narrative " (*Plato*, p. 352). It is very difficult not to feel, as one reads, for example, the *Republic* or *Phœdrus* or *Symposium*, or *Theœtetus*, that a much wider admission is needed, in spite of the dramatic devices by which the connection of the dialogue with the real Socrates is maintained.

[2] " ' To care for their souls ' was what Socrates urged on his fellow-citizens " (Burnet, *Essays*, etc., pp. 138 ff.). He discovered " the soul " in the sense of the spiritual personality.

Man would determine ": Socrates remained in
memory as this ideal Wise Man—just as later
Plotinus did among the Neo-Platonists.

§ 2

We may well imagine that Plato (427–347 B.C.)
would have said that he owed his soul to Socrates.
But he had other teachers. From Cratylus,
Aristotle tells us, he derived the tradition of
Heracleitus—the idea of the everlasting flux
and instability of all sensible things—of the
whole phenomenal world : and from the Pytha-
goreans he derived his veneration for the mathematical elements, numbers and figures, which,
though they are suggested to us by our senses,
are yet something which sensible experience
never realizes in perfection, while at the same
time they are supremely real and the very basis
of exact science.   These were the main influences
which met in Plato. Socrates convinced him
that " the moral values " (as we call them),
goodness and the separate virtues, and truth
and beauty, are realities eternal and divine behind all the varieties and fluctuations of opinion,
and that it is the salvation of the soul to live
according to these eternal principles, and real
knowledge to apprehend them. From Heracleitus he learned to appreciate the changing
character of sensation and opinion, and contrasted
it with the other realm of stable reality—the
realm of forms or principles—the realm of science.
Finally, and more and more as his thought
developed, he found in mathematics, side by side
with ethics, the type and the standard of science.

Throughout, then, Plato presents to us the conviction that it is only on the background of the world of eternal principles that this world of changing experience can be given any intelligible meaning, or that any real satisfaction can be found in living our present life. But we do well to observe at once that Plato is never a mystic in the sense that in the vision of the eternal and unchangeable world he is prepared to turn his back on this world.[1] No; as it is from the passing experiences of the senses and the needs of the earth-bound soul that we get the suggestion of the world of stable being, so one who by strenuous thought has won his citizenship in that higher region must return to earth to practise what he has learnt there. Here it is, in the actual city life of his day, that he has to save his soul, and do his duty, and win his spurs. Moreover, though the knowledge of the forms is contrasted, as being real knowledge, with the mere opinion of those who are content with sense-experience, yet Plato does not exaggerate the knowledge which can be gained of the Beyond. When he has need to speak of the Hereafter—of heaven or hell or purgatory—he passes at once into glorious " myths " which he declares to be only profitable lies.

---

[1] Burnet insists that Socrates was much more of a mystic than Plato. " There can be no doubt that Plato means us to believe that Socrates had actually attained to this beatific vision [of] the eternal forms. It is not for nothing that he is represented as having one of his trances just before the conversation recorded in the *Symposium* " (see *Greek Philosophy*, p. 140 ; cf. pp. 131, 168, 244).

Thus though the " heavenly things " are more real than the earthly, our only profitable knowledge of heavenly things is what we derive from earthly experience by analysing its implications and suggestions. For the earthly things, however transitory, " partake of " or " imitate " the eternal, and only from them can we get the starting-point of real knowledge. Moreover, Plato has no idea of solitary virtue or of a solitary conscience or of solitary salvation. A man realizes himself only in the close human relationships of the city. In all this Platonism is to be distinguished from the Neo-Platonism which has often usurped its name.

Plato's conception of the Forms, as we find it in the Dialogues, varies very noticeably. If they are to be equivalent to Socrates' definitions or general notions, then there must be forms of material objects, such as beds and tables, as much as of virtues, such as courage and self-control. Along this line of thought we reach the idea of an eternal world of forms, in which the prototypes of all the things of this world exist in perfection, so that earthly things are " the copies " of, or " partake in," the heavenly. And this eternal, or real, world is presented to us as an ordered world, where supreme among the forms is the Form of Good, in which is found also the ultimate motive of the universe. Things are what they are because it is good that they should so be. Thus the Form of Good tends to appear as a force, bringing things into being, and not only as a static intellectual principle. But in a later dialogue (the *Parmenides*, 130 C)

Socrates confesses to a sense of absurdity, at any rate in suggesting a " form " of mud or of anything disgusting, and the difficulty of discrimination is not faced.   Then there are dialogues where we hear nothing of the forms, or where, as in the Sophist,[1] " the friends of the forms " are shrewdly criticized by the Eleatic Stranger in the presence of " Socrates," who is silent. In one (the *Theætetus*, 191 C) we are led by " Socrates " himself on the way to the doctrine that our knowledge of real objects is not derived from sensations passively received, but is due to the intelligence which holds together the data of sensation.   We seem to be moving towards a doctrine of mental categories like that of Kant. But the suggestion is found to involve difficulties, and is not pursued.

In the *Timæus*—which we must remember was the only dialogue of Plato known (in great part) to the Middle Ages—and in the *Laws*, Plato's latest work, we are presented with a definite cosmogony or philosophical theism.   We must not of course assume that Timæus, who gives the cosmological lecture in the dialogue named after him, and who represents a type of Pythagoreanism, expresses exactly Plato's own conclusions, or that the unnamed Athenian of the *Laws* is to be identified with Plato, but undoubtedly both these dialogues give us our best insight into the final tendency of Plato's mind and the principles upon which his Academy was founded to work.   In these dialogues, then, we are presented with a definite doctrine of the Creator

[1] 248 A.

God, the supreme soul or person, whose existence we are bound to postulate to explain our world, which shows such unmistakable marks of order and design. He, out of the formless chaos which lies beyond time,[1] creates the orderly world out of his pure goodness : " He was good, and no goodness can ever entertain jealousy of anything. Being free from jealousy, then, he desires that all things should be as like himself as possible. This is the true beginning of creation and the world, which we should do well in receiving on the testimony of wise men : God designed that all things should be good and nothing bad, as far as this could be accomplished." [2] And the idea of the eternal forms reappears here in the sense that God is represented as creating the world, like any other creative artist, on the model of an eternal self-existent and complete ideal world, present to His mind. (Of the relation of this eternal "living being " to the Creator God nothing is said, nor of the relation of God to formless matter.) The content of this Divine Ideal is found to consist of the mathematical and moral principles on which science and life are based.[3]

In view of this changing conception of the Forms which the dialogues present to us, we must remember that Plato had no love of written systems of philosophy. He would not write out, or sanction the writing out of, his own

---

[1] Plato asserts that Time and Creation are correlative and begin together.

[2] *Laws*, 29–30.

[3] On the *Timæus*, A. E. Taylor is our leading authority. See his *Plato*, cap. xvii, and his edition of the *Timæus*.

system. What he set most store by was the Academy which he founded, where students living long years in close association in the " great business " of thought should catch the light of truth, which once kindled in the soul " feeds upon itself." His dialogues, intended for general reading, he would have us regard as " belonging to Socrates, turned young and handsome "— that is (we may perhaps paraphrase), as embodying the spirit of his master, without regard to any explicit system.[1] Platonism has gone through many phases—during Plato's own life and the life of his Academy and in Neo-Platonism and in the later world of philosophy. But the principle has been constant through all those phases that the temporary can only be understood on the background of the eternal ; that experience itself suggests, even forces upon our notice, eternal realities ; that if any real knowledge is possible it must be knowledge of those things ; and if any worthy life is to be lived, it must be in the conviction of divine laws of right and wrong.

We must certainly attribute to Plato a final theism, but not any complete or consistent doctrine about God. In his highest flights and moments of vision he uses language which only the conception of personality can satisfy. Thus in the *Sophist*,[2] he puts into the mouth of the Eleatic visitor this question about God (Zeus) :

[1] These last sentences depend upon the *Letters* of Plato (vii, 341 C, and ii, 314 C), now recognized again as authentic (see A. E. Taylor's *Plato*, p. 23). The translation of the last phrase I have borrowed from Burnet.

[2] *Soph.*, 248–249.

" Can we ever be made to believe that motion and life and soul and thought are not present with perfect being, or that it exists as holy, awful, mindless, motionless fixture ? " In more than one place he tells us that the good life is the imitation of God, and that no being on earth is so like God as the just man. In the *Timæus*,[1] as we have just seen, he tells us that God made the world because He was free of all jealousy, and would have creatures to share in His perfection ; but he holds it for certain in the *Laws* that there must be one or more evil souls at the root of things to account for the evil in the world, and he leaves the position of the " formless matter," into which God in creation introduced form and order, quite undetermined. He has no hesitation, moreover, in speaking of " Gods " as well as of " God." [2]

---

[1] *Tim.*, 29 E.

[2] There are other matters, beside the nature of God, as to which we cannot speak certainly of any definite doctrine as " Platonic." Thus, (1) while the doctrine on which he always insists is that the good life—the life in correspondence with the Form of Good or with God—is, wherever lived, essentially eternal and godlike, and while he certainly believed in the persistence of the soul beyond death, and in something real adumbrated in the myths of hell and purgatory and heaven, we cannot feel sure that he does more than play with the doctrine of the pre-existence and reincarnations of souls or with the idea of *anamnesis*—that the way in which the embodied soul awakes to recognize eternal principles is by " being reminded " of what it had known in a previous state of existence. The *Meno* (86 B) suggests as much as this (see also Taylor's *Plato*, cap. viii, and Lodge, cap. xvi). (2) We cannot speak definitely as to Plato's doctrine of matter or of evil. Certainly he does not hold that matter is evil or the source of evil as such. But he sometimes talks of the body as the degrading prison-house of the soul, only by emancipation from which it can attain its true liberty

But what most concerns us is to gain as exact an idea as we can of Plato's conception of the good life, individual and social. It is quite untrue to describe Plato as lacking in the sense of the value of individual personality. The whole purpose of the state is to educate good souls. No work is to be compared to that of " saving the soul," or, as we say, making the best of the latent capacities of the individual. And he is deeply conscious of the dominion of sin in the world—of what a precarious adventure life is in such a world as ours. He gives us vivid pictures of temptation. He compares the real self to a charioteer who has to control two winged horses, the nobler fiery steed, which we may call ambition or pride or the spirit of adventure, and the baser, which is lust or appetite. Out of the warring elements within it, the soul has to fashion a co-operative unity, and that he can only hope to do with the help of God—that is, by having some real vision of eternal principles. This constitutes the supreme importance of education.

Developed virtue must be rational. It must be able to receive and give rational account of itself. But it is not barely or only intellectual ; thus the most important period in the education of the soul is the pre-rational, the education of

and life, in the Orphic or Pythagorean manner. Certainly he propounds the idea of the absolute creation by God of all things in nature through the lips of the Eleatic Stranger (*Soph.*, 265 C). But (as mentioned above) in the *Timæus*, in speaking of creation, he seems to presuppose chaotic matter, and, in the *Laws* approves a belief in evil souls and their influence in creation, without explaining whether these evil souls are so originally or by a fall from goodness.

children to love and hate the right things.   The
rational habit can only grow out of the right pre-
disposition, which is the right direction of the
emotions.   The training of children—the stories
they are taught, the songs they sing, the dances
they practise—is to train the soul to love order
and beauty and to *feel* aright, so that later, when
the period of conscious reason comes, they can,
by a sound prejudice, distinguish truth from
error and right from wrong.   Among the most
justly famous passages in Plato are the passages
in the *Republic* and the *Laws* about the emotional
training of children which is the only adequate
preparation for the later life of rational principle.
Also beyond the period of childhood Plato shows
an admirable appreciation of the adaptation of
various human occupations to the stages of individual life.

In most of his dialogues Plato is markedly
not ascetic or puritan.   The evil is not that men
love pleasure and pursue it—he is even prepared
to argue for the virtuous life on the ground that
in the long run it is the most pleasant—but
that they mistake the nature of the soul and its
true satisfaction, and pursuing pleasure, as it is
depicted by unregulated fancy, they altogether
miss the real happiness.   All the common aims
and activities of life are good, as the body and
its natural impulses are not in themselves evil
but good.   Money and power are goods if
rightly used.[1]   The one thing needed is the

[1] But there is a recurrent note of *contempt* for business as
commonly understood (see *Rep.*, iii, 416 ; iv, 425 ; and *Theœtetus*,
173–175.

control of the whole of life by the consecration
of it to the true aim—which is the good life
lived in accordance with eternal principles or
the following of God.

Nor is the emotional nature to be regarded
as only valuable in childhood. Among the
most memorable of Plato's dialogues are those—
the *Phædrus* and *Symposium*—which treat of
love—not the Agape of the New Testament,
which is a settled disposition of the will, but the
Eros of Greek poetry, the irresistible passion.
Here, in expressing his sympathy with the passionate affection of young men for one another,
Socrates (or Plato) is, we feel, on very dangerous
ground.[1] But he sees in such passionate love
something capable of sublimation. Behind the
beautiful body is the beautiful soul, and behind
the beautiful soul is the pattern of all loveliness,
the ideal beauty. For the supreme good is
beauty as well as truth, and it is the object of
passion as well as of intellectual research. Thus,
beside the philosophers as guides to truth stand
the inspired men who have seen the vision of
the Eternal Beauty, or in a divine madness have
received the afflatus, the inspiration of God.
Or perhaps it may be more truly said that the
philosopher, to be worthy of the name, must
be the lover also. We should judge that Plato,
as truly as Pascal, felt that " the heart has its
reasons " as well as the speculative and logical
intellect, and that what claims to be the truth

---

[1] Finally, in the *Laws*, Plato does pronounce a severe judgment
on all " unnatural vices " as being really unnatural, and banishes
the practice of them from his state (see *Laws*, 836–842).

must satisfy the whole soul of man, which loves and wills as well as thinks.[1]

Plato, I say, was not an ascetic or a puritan —unless indeed by asceticism we mean merely self-control. (Socrates, his ideal, is, we notice, in spite of his sympathetic attitude towards very dangerous fashions of the day, represented to us as himself in absolute control of sensual passion.) He recognizes how all that belongs to normal humanity—all that makes human life happy and wholesome—can be consecrated and used in loyal subjection to the Right.   This at least is true throughout the greater part of the dialogues, and when he is speaking of the ordering of his own life by the individual.   On the other hand, he would never allow us to imagine that anything but the life of the city can educate and develop the individual.   It is the city—which is both State and Church, as we should say— which is to impress upon each of the citizens the true principles of the good life, and every citizen is bound to remember that no man lives to himself but to the community.   But he is convinced that the actual city-states of Greece have very poorly fulfilled the function of developing character on the eternal pattern.

Moreover, though he has a deep and true conception of progress in the life of the individual, he is almost wholly without the conception of human society as advancing by gradual improve-

[1] A great part of the unparallel fascination of Plato's dialogues depends on his wide humanism ; but it cannot be denied that in his latest dialogues, just as his literary style has lost so much of its glory and charm, so his spirit has become doctrinaire and dogmatic.

ments, or as moving towards any final consummation.[1] If he does not believe in a golden age in
the past, he certainly does not believe that
humanity or the city-state, as he knows it,
is advancing towards any state of perfection in
the future. His sense of all-pervading sin and of
progressive deterioration, is so strong that his
hope for mankind seems to lie in nothing else
than in securing a completely fresh start. He
builds his Utopias therefore. The construction
of the ideal city, whether in the *Republic* or
in the *Laws*, assumes the necessity for starting completely afresh and in isolation in the
Building of the City.

It is true that he did not think that the con-
structions which he imagined could be realized in
their entirety, but he probably did really think
that the only way in which a city-life, such as the
wise man could approve, could become an actual
fact on earth would be through the emergence of
the philosopher king, or group of philosophic men,
who would be able to command the allegiance of a
whole body of citizens, and would be entrusted
with power absolute enough to make a really
fresh start in organizing a common life dedicated
to the true ideals. But it is when we consider
his ideal cities (perhaps especially in the more

---

[1] Prof. Lodge, in his *Plato's Theory of Ethics*—a very valuable
book—is fond of speaking of " the process of social evolution "
or "the long upward struggle of humanity" as if these ideas
were to be ascribed to Plato. He does indeed show in the *Laws* a
real sense of the initial stages through which civilized life
evolved ; but when he is considering the phases of civilized life
he shows no sense of a progressive purpose to be gradually
realized. Prof. Lodge himself acknowledges this, p. 162.

prosaic presentation of the *Laws*) that we become
perplexed and astonished at the amount of
drastic regimentation to which he seems seriously
to suppose that the citizen body must be subjected if the real city-church is to exist.
We have grown so used to Plato's wonderful
sympathy with various types of man and his
astonishing versatility and abounding sense of
humour, that his ideal of government amazes
and irritates us. It seems to involve such a
complete ignorance of human nature, not less
of Greek human nature than of the human nature
we ourselves know.

That he should think it worth while to suggest
that human governors, however philosophic,
would be able to distribute human beings into
classes, not according to their birth in this or
that caste, nor by giving free opportunity to
everyone to make his own position, but by a
quasi-infallible insight into the latent capacity
of each, leading to an autocratic distribution of
functions, seems incredible ; that in one picture
of the ideal city he should establish a communism in wives and children utterly abolishing
the family, and in the second picture, when
family life is recognized and maintained, that
he could demand a eugenic despotism which
would leave no " private life " to the individuals
and no real control over the education of their
children ; that he should demand the expulsion
of the poets in general, and a censorship of
literature of the most exacting kind—excites the
same feeling of amazement. It is perhaps
deepened when we find Plato to be the first

9

clear formulator of the principle of religious persecution as necessary for his city-church.

That God (or gods) really exist; that God is good and only good; that God is incorruptible, and that bribes and sacrifices cannot deflect him from the path of perfect justice, are indeed noble dogmas. But for their maintenance Plato established a Nocturnal Court of Inquisition bound to visit recalcitrant heretics with lifelong confinement or death. Plato, who, following Socrates, had seemed the very apostle of peaceful persuasion and free-thinking, reappears as an autocrat indeed, and that so rigid and doctrinaire that his hope for the maintenance of his city is based on the fact that it has been found possible in Egypt—the very type of immobility, the very antithesis of Greece—to preserve for countless ages the rules of art and practices of religion.[1] "If the fable about Cadmus has been found credible, who can set limits to what a beneficial lie may not establish as an immutable law?" "But Plato is only playing with us," you may say. That is true in a measure in the *Republic*. But in the *Laws* it is hardly to be imagined. And at any rate, if he is only "idealizing," at least we shiver at the severity of the regimenta-

---

[1] *Laws*, 798–800. Incidentally we should notice that it is misleading to speak of Plato's political theory as Socialism or Communism. It is socialistic in the sense that the individual can only realize himself in the state and that the state is supreme over the individual. It is communistic (in the Republic) as applied to the governing classes. But the economic life, the life of productive industry, on which the whole fabric depends, is left outside any communistic legislation. It is assumed that the wealth-producing or money-making classes will be permanently content to submit to the governing classes.

tion to which he dreams humanity must be
subjected if the good life is to be realized at all
on earth. The regimentation is so complete that
it even excludes from the life of the city the
very possibility of real self-sacrifice. It is
indeed a splendid idea that the adepts in philosophy should be called to come down from their
lofty seats of intellectual contemplation to become
rulers and politicians. But it is not allowed to
be a matter of free choice. It is all to be done
under compulsion.[1]

Perhaps the strangest feature in the whole of
Plato's thought is that it does not appear that
he—he whose conception of the power of love
is so entrancing—ever realized at all what the
love of man and woman can be, or the glory of
the home, or the power of the mother's love as
the very root and inspiration of the good life.
Any worthy conception of distinctive woman-
hood, such as we find in the Greek dramatists, is
quite lacking.

The name of Plato is perhaps the grandest
name in the history of philosophy and in particular of moral philosophy, and Platonism has
been so permanent and ennobling an influence
on the life and thought of mankind that criticism
of him seems almost irreverent. In fact, however, his immediate influence on the ethical life
of Greece does not seem to have been considerable.
His ethical ideal still centred wholly upon the
city-life. According to the latest tendencies of
his thought, his Academy, the foundation of

[1] A German commentator, quoted by Lodge, speaks of Plato's
ideal state as a " Zwang-Anstalt."

which he regarded as his permanent work, gave itself not only to mathematical studies which had become the basis of his philosophy, but to constitution-making for cities.[1]

But the days of the city-state were passing. Plato's death was shortly followed by the establishment of the Macedonian supremacy in Greece, and the Macedonian Empire was the prelude to that of the Romans. Until that was firmly established, which was still centuries ahead, the Greek world was in a state of disintegration, confusion and uncertainty. What was in question was no longer how the city-state could be best ordered in the ethical interest of the citizens—which was the question for Plato and Aristotle—but how the individual in a world of disorder and fear could save his own soul. Thus it was through Zeno, the founder of Stoicism, and the later fusion of Platonism with Stoicism, that the power of Plato's idealism made itself widely felt as a master influence in fashioning the individual life, and indeed, through the profound influence of Hellenistic thought on Roman law, in fashioning the society which was to be ; but it was thus as a generalized influence that it prevailed—the influence of the general idea that human life, if it is to be noble and worthy, must be lived on the basis of eternal principles frankly recognized, and that such principles the reason of man has the power to apprehend and embody.

[1] Taylor, *Plato*, pp. 5 ff. and 464.

§ 3

Zeno [1] (*c.* 350–260 B.C.) appears to have been a Phœnician by race, whose home was in Cyprus, but who, under the influence of the story of Socrates, was converted from trade to philosophy and, after trying in vain to find satisfaction in the various philosophic schools at Athens, established himself about 310 B.C. in the Painted Colonnade (*Stoa*, whence the name of his philosophy) as a prophet and teacher of the good life, the life which is victorious over fear and desire and doubt. His physics and psychology were quite different from Plato's. He may be described as a materialistic pantheist—the God of whom he spoke as immanent in the universe, and as the principle of order, being Heracleitus' element of Fire, conceived of as a refined material force or "spirit"; but this fire or spirit was also Heracleitus' "reason," [2] and the reason in each man was a fragment of this divine reason, whereby the man can, if he will, live in accordance with "nature," that is the all-pervading and all-prevailing divine purpose or providence ; and where this is deliberately and consistently done, a man can attain to perfect tranquillity of mind, accepting indifferently all accidents, as being the will of God, and rising superior to all doubt or fear or preference of pleasure to pain. As for the wicked who follow their lusts and appetites, in neglect of the will of God, they

[1] The most illuminating account of Zeno is to be found in Edwyn Bevan's *Stoics and Sceptics.*

[2] In fact Fire, Spirit (Breath), Ether, Nature, Reason, Providence, Destiny and Zeus seem to be identified in Stoicism.

would suffer as all must who set themselves against omnipotent Nature.

Zeno, however, in spite of the " self-sufficiency " which he proclaimed for the individual man, was not wholly individualist. He asserted the essential equality and independence of all men of all races and all classes in virtue of the share of each in God. But he would have all men regarded as forming one city—one " city " of God, which indeed included the whole universe ; and he insisted on the duty of mutual service to the whole by each of its members [1]— distinguishing, however, active service from any inward emotion of compassion for human suffering. The *feeling* of compassion he regarded as an emotion destructive of tranquillity, and therefore is a vice rather than a virtue. The good man's humanitarianism was to be simply an attitude of will—not a feeling but simply a motive to action. (It is obvious how closely Zeno's conception of the highest state for man— absolute detachment—resembles that of Indian sages and of Lao-tse in China.[2] But it was not in this sense that Stoicism coalesced with Platonism and later with Christianity.)

It should be added that the Stoics believed that the soul survived death, but that there could be no *immortality* for the individual.

---

[1] " You are part of a social system," wrote the Stoic Emperor, Marcus Aurelius ; " a factor necessary to complete the sum ; therefore your every action should help to complete the social life. An action of yours which does not tend, directly or remotely, to this social end, dislocates life and infringes its unity. It is an act of sedition " (*Meditations*, ix, 23 (Rendall's trans.)).

[2] See especially Bevan, *op. cit.*, pp. 77 ff.

The destiny of all individual souls, " fragments "
of the one divine fire, would be reabsorption into
their source.   And much as Zeno insisted on the
reality of providence and upon a divine purpose
in events, he had no conception of any final
consummation   or   ultimate   purpose   for   the
universe—any kingdom of God to come.   He
conceived of a cycle of universes.[1]   The divine
fire brought the universe into being, and it
gradually   " ran   down "   through   stages   of
deterioration till it reached its end in a universal
conflagration, after which another   identical
universe would succeed in its place, and again
run down to another conflagration and so
ad infinitum. There was nothing final, and
nothing individual could survive these cosmic
conflagrations.   The satisfaction of the individual
must be looked for here and now.

It ought to be said that the evidence does not
admit of distinguishing precisely between the
teaching of Zeno himself and that of his school.
For instance, it was the teaching of the Stoic
School that it lay in the legitimate judgment of
the individual to terminate his life by suicide
when it should seem good to him.   It is not
certain, however, whether this was the teaching
of Zeno himself.

Zeno, we have seen, embraced certain psychological and physical theories, derived from the
Heracleitean tradition, perhaps somewhat mis-
understood ; but his method was not that of
the traditional Greek philosopher, but rather
that of the Semitic prophet.   Psychologically

[1] See App. Note 2, at end of chapter.

he derived all knowledge from "impressions" made upon the soul, and he distinguished impressions according to their intensity. Some impressions, he said, have such intensity as to be irresistible—they, as it were, "take hold of one by the hairs of one's head and drag one to assent." They become convictions which can be proclaimed without argument. Zeno's teaching appears to have consisted mainly of such affirmations. He trusted not to intellectual arguments, which breed scepticism, but to dogmatic statements which, because of their self-evidence, produce faith in the souls of those who have ears to hear. Accordingly he preached, and his successors preached, effectively to select souls, the way of emancipation from fear and doubt and the tyranny of desire. And the emphasis of Stoicism on its being man's vocation to reduce his whole nature into subordination to his will, and his will into harmony with the will of God or the eternal law of nature, admitted of easy accommodation to the ethical principle of Platonism. So in fact, in the two last centuries before Christ, a fusion of Stoicism and Platonism was effected by teachers such as Panætius and Posidonius. How complete such a practical fusion could be will appear if we have under our eyes two celebrated Stoic utterances —the hymn of the Stoic Cleanthes [1] and a grand Stoical presentment of the Law of Nature from Cicero's *De Republica.*

[1] I have borrowed James Adam's translation from *The Vitality of Platonism*, pp. 104 ff. If it is not very good poetry, neither is the original.

THE HYMN OF CLEANTHES

O God most glorious, called by many a name,
Nature's great King, through endless years the same ;
Omnipotence who by thy just decree
Controllest all, hail Zeus ! for unto thee
Behoves thy creatures in all lands to call.
We are thy children, we alone, of all
On earth's broad ways that wander to and fro,
Bearing thine image wheresoe'er we go.
Wherefore with songs of praise thy power I will forth show.
Lo ! yonder heaven that round the earth is wheeled,
Follows thy guidance, still to thee doth yield
Glad homage ; thine unconquerable hand
Such flaming minister, the levin-brand
Wieldeth, a sword two-edged, whose deathless might
Pulsates through all that nature brings to light ;
Vehicle of the universal Word,[1] that flows
Through all, and in the light celestial glows
Of stars both great and small.   O King of Kings
Through ceaseless ages, God ! whose purpose brings
To birth, whate'er on land or in the sea
Is wrought, or in high heaven's immensity ;
Save what the sinner works infatuate.
Nay, but thou knowest to make crooked straight ;
Chaos to thee is order ; in thine eyes
The unloved is lovely, who didst harmonize
Things evil with things good, that there should be
One Word through all things everlastingly.
One Word—whose voice, alas ! the wicked spurn.
Insatiate for the good their spirits yearn,
Yet seeing see not, neither hearing hear
God's universal law, which those revere
By reason guided, happiness who win.
The rest, unreasoning, diverse shapes of sin
Self-prompted follow ; for an idle name
Vainly they wrestle in the lists of fame ;
Others inordinately riches woo,
Or dissolute, the joys of flesh pursue ;
Now here, now there, they wander, fruitless still
For ever seeking good and finding ill.
Zeus the all-bountiful, whom darkness shrouds,

[1] The Greek should rather be translated " Reason."

Whose lightning lightens in the thunder-clouds,
Thy children save from error's deadly sway ;
Turn thou the darkness from their souls alway ;
Vouchsafe them unto knowledge to attain ;
For thou by knowledge art made strong to reign
O'er all, and all things rulest righteously ;
So, by thee honoured, we will honour thee,
Praising thy works continually with songs,
As mortals should ; nor higher meed belongs
E'en to the gods, than justly to adore
The universal law for evermore.

THE LAW OF NATURE

" There is a true law which is right reason,
agreeable to nature, diffused among all men,
constant, eternal, which calls us to duty by its
injunctions, and by its prohibitions deters us
from wrong : which upon the good lays neither
injunction nor prohibition in vain ; while for
the bad, neither its injunctions nor its prohibitions
avail at all. This law admits neither of alteration
nor subtraction nor abrogation. The vote of
neither senate nor people can discharge us
from our obligation to it. We are not to look
for some other person to expound or interpret
it ; nor will there be one law for Rome and
another for Athens, nor one at this date and
another later on ; but one law shall embrace
all races over all time, eternal and immortal ;
and there shall be hereby one common master
and commander of all—God, who originated
this law, and proposed it and arbitrates concerning it ; and if anyone obeys it not, he shall play
false to himself, and shall do despite to the nature
of man, and by this very fact shall pay the greatest
penalties, even if he should escape all else that
is reckoned punishment."

There will be something more to be said
about the ethical conceptions which the Christian-

ity of the early centuries found current in the Græco-Roman world, and which it in part readily assimilated and in part criticized and repudiated. But there can be no question of the enormous influence which this Platonic and Stoic conception of the eternal law of right and wrong, for the individual and for the society, was to have in the evolution of modern Europe.[1]

APPENDED NOTES

A. ON ARISTOTLE AND EPICURUS

I have passed over Aristotle's treatment of ethics and politics not from any lack of respect, but because it is substantially a critical republication of Platonism, only robbed of some of its brilliant and appealing qualities— " a little coarsened and with a certain diminution of moral fervour," Taylor's *Platonism*, p. 56. " For the most part," says W. D. Ross (*Aristotle*, p. 190), " he accepts the opinions of the Academy as his own." See for details Taylor's *Plato*, pp. 61, 64, 176, 235, 269, 324 n., 406, 410, 413 n., 415.

I have also passed over the famous Epicurus, Zeno's contemporary. He was a man, it seems, of great attractiveness and even severity in his own habits of life. He saw mankind degraded by fear—fear of death and fear of the gods, and from both these kinds of fear he sought to deliver

---

[1] The definition of S. Thomas Aquinas runs thus : " Participatio legis æternæ in rationali creatura lex naturalis dicitur." " That is, that the immanent and all-present reason, which penetrates the universe, rises in man to a height or climax in which it becomes the conscious law of liberty and truth. Here Platonist, Stoical and Christian ideas meet in a splendid unity." " On the first view crudely expressed the Law of Nature is a code which is discovered and rules are based upon it. On the second it is the inner law of an unfolding organism which is observed, the reason and value of which are to be found, not in its obscure beginnings, but in the richness of the end to which it moves " (C. E. Osborne, *Christian Ideas in Political History* (John Murray), pp. 62–64 ; cf. p. 14).

men by pure Naturalism. It was a highly sublimated
sensuality that he taught. His ethical doctrine was that
happiness was identical with pleasure, which accordingly
was the only aim that a man could set before himself ; but
that wisdom consisted in the weighing of pleasures, in
respect of intensity and permanence, as a result of which it
would appear that a virtuous life was the pleasantest.
There were, no doubt, many noble Epicureans, like Lucretius
or such men as Pater has described with wonderful subtlety
in *Marius the Epicurean*. There have in later times been
Hedonists who put a fresh aspect on Hedonism by taking
account of the will of a righteous God and life beyond the
grave, but any such considerations Epicurus rigidly ex-
cluded. Death was final, and the gods were not concerned
with human life. The outlook being thus limited, it did not
seem to Greek thinkers in general that those who cared for
the good life could find support in his principles, and they
fell into disrepute. It would seem that just as Stoicism
was gradually refined into such an appealing form as
appears in Marcus Aurelius's meditations, so Epicurus'
doctrine became coarsened and vulgarized.

B. ON THE THEORY OF CYCLES (see above, p. 135).

The theory that the history of the universe would be
found to consist of an infinite succession of cycles, each
exhibiting progressive deterioration and reaching final
dissolution, is to be found in the thought of the *Vedanta*
in India. It was apparently (whether borrowed from India
or no, directly or indirectly) an Orphic idea. The law of
deterioration is clearly in Plato's mind as regards human
societies, though the idea of cycles does not appear : but the
doctrine of cycles, each identical with the last preceding
even in detail, was a recognized doctrine of the Stoics (see
Bevan, *Stoicism and Scepticism*, pp. 50 f.). The idea of a
progressive development in the universe or of any ideal
climax to universal history does not seem to occur in
classical literature. De Burgh (*op. cit.*) instances Lucretius
as an exception (B. v, ll. 771 onward, esp. 1454-7). But
Lucretius is also responsible for the saying " Eadem sunt
omnia semper " (iii, 945), and the melancholy conclusion

of B. ii. He perhaps conceived of *development through each cycle* to end in destruction and a fresh beginning, without any final purpose or culmination.

C. THE PLATONIC AND ARISTOTELIAN CONCEPTIONS OF GOD

Plato finally certainly conceived of God as personal—self-moved and the author of all *orderly* movement in the universe —as purely good, and as creating the world that His creatures might share His goodness. This comes very near to the Christian conception that God is love, though the limits to such an identification have been noticed (above, p. 123). Aristotle's conception of God, as expressed in a famous passage of the Metaphysics, as the Supreme Thought—thought thinking upon itself in supreme satisfaction—is also a personal conception ; but the idea of God conveyed in this passage is very different from Plato's. God is not self-moving but unmoved. He is neither creator nor sustainer of the universe, of which he is unconscious, and to which he is wholly indifferent. He is the author of all movement in the universe, only because in his supreme perfection he kindles love in all that is, so that all things move towards him as an object of desire. But this strangely mystical notion of a universal movement in the world towards a self-conscious but otherwise unconscious and indifferent God (see Ross's *Aristotle*, pp. 183 f.) is not the only one to be found in the Metaphysics. There is another passage, much less often quoted (1075*a*), which discusses the relation of the world to God under the figure of an army. " The question must now be raised in which of two ways the nature of the universe possesses the Good and the Highest Good— whether as something existing separately and of itself, or as the order of the whole ? Perhaps we should say in both ways, as in the case of an army. For the Good in the case of an army is both its order and its general, but the latter especially, for the general does not depend on the order, but the order does depend on him.'' If the Supreme Good is identified by Aristotle (as it surely is) with God, here he suggests that it is not enough to conceive of the Good, i.e. God, as an immanent and unconscious principle of organiza-tion in the universe. It or He must be also independent of the world and its director, like the general of an army (see Baillie, *Interpretation of Religion*, pp. 292–293). It certainly looks as if in this passage Aristotle was suggesting a conception of God very different from what he suggests elsewhere. We must recognize that neither in Aristotle nor in Plato nor in the Stoics is there a consistent theology.

CHAPTER VI

ISRAEL

§ 1

THE idea of the good life in the religious tradition
of the Jews is a much more familiar matter to
us than that which is to be found in the nations
of the remoter East, or even among the Greeks.
For the last fifty years books based upon a
critical study of the Old Testament documents
have been pouring from the press ; and for the
most part their drift is identical, and their sense
of the world's debt to the ethical monotheism of
Israel is expressed in similar terms.   No one who
has any belief in a superintendent Providence
in the world's history would be inclined to doubt
that a special providence was at work to preserve
Jewish nationality from extinction, in spite of
the overwhelming risks which it ran in its rough
history of being absorbed into more powerful
empires ; nor could anyone who believes in a
divine providence doubt that the purpose of this
protection of Israel was that its faith, which it
had at last learned to guard so jealously, might
become available for the nations of the earth
when it had been emancipated from a narrow
nationalism.

Moreover, we have learned to see that this
attitude of special reverence towards the Old
Testament is not dependent on any such belief
in its inspiration as would make it equivalent to

143

historical infallibility, or would hinder us from
recognizing in the literature of the Jews the
features which are common to all national
histories. I will confess myself to be a conservative critic. I mean, for instance, that, while
recognizing to the full that in the Pentateuch a
great deal is attributed to Moses, the great
founder of Jewish nationality, which was in
fact elaborated in a gradual historical process,
the stages of which we can trace more or less
clearly in the literature, yet I find it difficult to
doubt that the fundamentally ethical character
of Israel's worship of Jehovah must be traced
back to its Founder, and that the prophets, of
whose ministry authentic records remain to us,
were really, as they believed themselves to be,
in the succession of Moses, while the popular
non-ethical religion which they denounced—
the religion of the Canaanite Baals, adapted to the
worship of Jehovah—really represented a lapse
from what Moses had taught to his people.

Nevertheless, criticism is right in bidding us
start in our investigation of the history and
religion of the Jews from the written prophets,
as from the most solid historical ground, that is,
from Amos and Hosea and Isaiah and Micah,
and Jeremiah and Ezekiel and the second Isaiah ;
and right in bidding us recognize in the message
of these great men a teaching which, through a
long period profoundly unpopular, finally, through
the catastrophe of the Captivity, won a supreme
victory and became the acknowledged glory
of the Jewish people. Gradually and finally it
penetrated all their literature—its folk-lore, its

legends, its history, its cultus, its ethics, its wisdom, its poetry—and gave to the Hebrew Bible a unity and intensity such as belongs to no other national literature.[1]

I do not propose to attempt an answer to the question of how much exactly of the whole final complex of Jewish religion was " borrowed " from other nations with whom they came in contact. The Hebrews appear in the historical scene in the midst of a world penetrated by Babylonian culture, and no one can doubt that its influence, as represented in the legislation of Hammurabi,[2] was very great on the Jewish social law. Again, we cannot doubt that S. Chrysostom was right when he described the material of Jewish religious rites—" the sacrifices, the cleansings, the new-moons, the ark and the temple itself," as derived from their pagan background.[3]

[1] Ewald, whose *History of Israel* dates from 1843, writes, vol. i, p. 4: " This aim [perfect religion] was lofty enough to concentrate the highest efforts of a whole people [Israel]. And as, however the mode of the pursuit might vary, it was this single object which was always pursued, till finally attained only with the political death of the nation, there is hardly any history of equal compass that possesses, in all its phases and variations, so much intrinsic unity, and is so closely bound to a single thought pertinaciously held, but always developing itself to greater purity." But it must be recognized that the " pursuit " was not a continuous advance. It may be said to have reached its climax with the second Isaiah. Certainly the last four centuries before Christ do not represent an advance.

[2] See John's *Oldest Code of Laws in the World* (Edinburgh: Clarks, 1903). This code is based on the idea of the divine authority of social justice. But Dr. Hertz, *Affirmations of Judaism*, p. 138, is justified in noting the absence in this code, as compared with that of the Pentateuch, of the idea of mercy.

[3] *Hom.*, in Matt. vi. 3 (*P.G.* lvii, col. 66).

10

From Egypt, however, they certainly did not derive the spirit either of their religion or of their worship, and what they derived from the Canaanites, with a lamentable freedom, was in great part precisely what the prophets finally succeeded in excluding from the religious tradition of Israel. Prophecy itself had its origin in a sub-rational kind of religious frenzy, common to many nations ; and it would seem that the mass of the prophets in Israel—whom (what we call) the " true prophets " are in the habit of denouncing, and from whom they peremptorily distinguish themselves—remained down to the captivity on the same low level. Amos, Hosea and their successors owed very little to this class or to its traditions. Thus the real religion of the Jews with its accompanying conception of the good life for man—all that formed the basis of the religion of Jesus—was essentially a native growth, and was already in being in all essential points before the Jews came in contact, on their restoration from captivity, with the religion of Persia.

During the Persian period—on which we have little historical light—Judaism seems to have assimilated elements from Persian religion, especially a developed belief in angels, while it studiously refused the element of ultimate dualism which had become so prominent a feature in the Persian creed. Later, in Hellenistic times, the book of the Wisdom of Solomon shows how much of Platonism a loyal Jew could make his own, and the Book of Proverbs borrows from Hellenistic and probably from Egyptian " wisdom." It is a grave mistake to attempt to minimize the borrowings of Judaism, or later of Christianity. Any real belief in one God must be a belief in His universal presence and the universal activity of His Spirit, and a religion of the true God ought to be able to show its affinity with the higher wisdom of all peoples; that is to say, it ought to give evidence of its divine origin by its power of assimilating truth wherever it comes in contact with it. When we come to review the results of our whole historical enquiry, we shall need to lay stress on this consideration. But what it is important to recognize at this stage is that substantially—in spite of their marked resemblance to the religion and the ethics of Zarathustra—the religion and ethics of Israel were indisputably in all their essential qualities a native growth, rightly attributed in their origin to Moses, but fashioned under our eyes in authentic history by the great prophets —who spoke, not as philosophers who had thought and arrived at certain conclusions of their own, but as men who were constrained to speak as they did under the pressure of the Spirit of Jehovah.

I will only add that those of us who hold that nothing can adequately account for the teaching of the prophets of Israel, except a belief that they were really inspired of God, can hardly find any ground for doubting that Zoroaster was equally an inspired man. But there is this marked difference. In succession to Zoroaster we find no signs of a like inspiration. We see his lofty religion being swallowed up in supersti-

tion. What is unique in Jewish history is the
spectacle of a great prophetic tradition from
Amos to Malachi or Joel, extending over centuries
and constantly maintaining and elaborating,
through the mouths of men of very different
personal characteristics, a substantially identical
doctrine about God and human duty, till it
becomes indestructibly embodied in a whole
literature which, as culminating in the New
Testament, becomes the basis of a religion for
the world ; and which in its earliest Christian
form showed its power to assimilate—what in
the world's literature comes nearest to it—the
long tradition of Greek philosophy.

§ 2

There are certain features of the religion of
Israel, and of the ethics based upon their religious
beliefs, which we do well to notice before we
attempt, with something more of detail, to
describe its character.

(1) First that religion, and the good life based
upon the religion, was, as Ewald says, the one
all-absorbing quest in Israel. Of their art—
the art, for example, of Bazalel and Oholiab, who
are described as " full of the spirit of God," to
work in precious metals and precious stones and
woven fabrics for the adornment of the tabernacle,[1] or the art of Huram, of mixed Israelitish
and Tyrian origin, who fashioned the furniture
of Solomon's temple[2]—we know nothing. The
Herodian architecture of later days, so far as
we can judge, owed little to Jewish genius.

---

[1] Exod. xxxi. 1–11.   [2] 2 Chron. ii. 13 f. ; iv. 11 ff.

Again, if an exhaustive science of nature is ascribed to Solomon in the Book of Wisdom,[1] that is due to the imagination of a Hellenized Jew. Israel made no early contribution to science like Babylonians or Egyptians or Greeks. Again, they contributed nothing to political science, and they show no interest in theological or metaphysical speculation. In poetry indeed, and in the art of narration, they reach the highest level, but both their poetry and their prose narratives and their proverbial literature are concerned with the one theme of religion and its ethical fruits. It is a single debt which mankind owes to Israel—not indeed to them only, but to them in an eminent degree. Athanasius's estimate of them is justified—that they were (through the prophets) " the sacred school of the knowledge of God and of the spiritual life for all mankind "—or at least, up to the present, for a very large and important section of mankind.

(2) Their religion was ethical through and through, and not in its main character ritualistic. The earlier prophets, indeed, finding the popular *cultus* non-moral or immoral, like that of the peoples round about them, speak of it with contempt. Their fierce denunciations of idolatry or image-making, and their depreciation of material sacrifices, were doubtless due to their abhorrence of the religions with which they were familiar, which were morally worthless or corrupting. Later, under the guidance especially of the Book of Deuteronomy and the prophesying of Ezekiel, a synthesis was effected between the traditional

[1] Wisd. vi. 17 ff.

sacrificial cultus and the ethical religion of the
prophets ; and the specially priestly portions of
the Old Testament, such as a great part of the
Pentateuch and the Books of Chronicles, show
an enthusiastic veneration for exact ceremonial.
In many of the Psalms, again—those which may
properly be called Psalms of the Sanctuary—
we find the highest spirituality associated with
the worship of the Temple. Such close association of spiritual religion with sacrificial worship
may have maintained itself over periods of Jewish
history of which we know little.

But in the centuries which intervene between
the triumphant success of the Maccabæan revolt
and the time of our Lord, it does not appear as if
the priesthood or the Temple was the real centre
of religion in Israel: that is to be found in the
influence of the Scribes and the Pharisees, who
came to be fiercely opposed to the priest-kings,
and later to the Sadducean family who occupied
the priesthood and had charge of the Temple.
The religion of the Pharisees, while of course
observant of the sacrificial rites, centred in the
Synagogue worship rather than in the Temple.
The strict observances which they accepted and
inculcated were connected rather with details of
personal and domestic life than with sacrificial
worship. The marked alienation of Jesus from
a religion of minute and punctilious observances
is, we shall remark, uncoloured by any depreciation of priesthood or sacrifice. There is, in his
teaching, strangely little attention given to the
latter. In this respect the religion of Israel
is like the religion, not indeed of Zoroastrianism

but of Zoroaster himself : it was predominantly ethical. And this was a very rare feature indeed in ancient religions.

(3) The religion of Israel in the Old Testament is seen in process of development. In the theology of the Fathers of the Christian Church, especially the Greek-speaking Fathers, this point is seized upon and emphasized. I think I am right in saying that the recognition of gradual development, as the characteristic of the method of God, is more distinctly found among them than anywhere else in antiquity.[1] The original creative act of God was, they thought, the creation of something germinal, which would gradually unfold into the differentiated world of life, as we know it. Man, again, was not created perfect, but with such an equipment as would enable him to advance towards perfection. And man's education, as we find it in the Old Testament, proceeded gradually. On this line of thought they explained the moral problems which the Old Testament presents. If they found commandments attributed to God—like the commandment given to Abraham to sacrifice his son or the commandments to sacrifice indiscriminately whole populations—which in days of greater light could not have been given or could not have been attributed to God, that, they held, was because the people were being led by

[1] The Italian philosopher, Croce, gives a preference to the mediæval historians over their Græco-Roman predecessors, in spite of their manifest inferiority in culture and ability, in this respect—that they first viewed history as progress towards a goal (*Teoria e Storia della Storiografia*, p. 188). He does not notice that they owed this vision to the Hebrew prophets.

gradual stages upwards to " the true philosophy." The justification of this divine method
lies in its results—in the very fact that we can
now reprobate in the name of God what was in
earlier days conceded or enjoined. All the laws
concerning animal and vegetable sacrifices are
explained by the same method. God did not
so much enjoin or command as tolerate such
concessions to ignorant customs, and the test of
such a progressive method is to be found in the
attainment of its goal.

All this is very consonant with modern ideas.
We feel that it is very unfortunate that later
theology overlaid these evolutionary conceptions
with more static conceptions of the divine method.
But we have been learning of late years that the
actual development, whether of physical organisms or of individuals or of ideas or of civilizations, is not by any means always on the upward
road. Nature and history are alike full of the
evidences of declension. Catastrophe is as
possible as advance. This was certainly the case
in the development of religious and ethical ideas
among the Jews. You can indeed trace a clear
development from Amos to the second Isaiah.

Thus Amos's conception of Jehovah as the
God of universal nature and the just ruler of
all peoples is a great advance upon the idea of
Jehovah as the God of the land of Israel, with
a limited jurisdiction not seemingly extending
downwards even to Sheol, such as we find in
earlier days. Thus, again, Hosea[1] pronounces
the condemnation by God of the bloody slaughter

[1] Hos. i. 4.

of the whole house of Ahab by Jehu, which
the chronicler of Jehu's reign regarded as the
command of God.   Again, the sense of the equal
value and responsibility of each individual soul
only emerges in Ezekiel, and with this comes the
dawning of the sense of man's immortality and
of the resurrection.   But the advance is not
continuous.   There is here advance and there
retrogression.

Thus in Isaiah (xix. 19–25) we see a magnificent
universalism in his conception of the religion of
Jehovah.   Israel is to be one with Egypt and
with Assyria.   In the second Isaiah the Servant-
People of Jehovah are to be evangelists of all
the world.   The eighty-seventh psalm contemplates all nations as destined to call Jerusalem
their mother.[1]   The Book of Jonah extends the
welcome of Jehovah and His free forgiveness
to the most hostile of peoples, if only they will
listen to His word.   But this high level is not
maintained.   A narrow nationalism revives and
tends to prevail.   What is contemplated is the
bloody triumph of Israel over all other nations
rather than the inclusion of them.   The Pharisaic
Psalms of Solomon, dating about 50 B.C., are
content with such a vision.   Moreover, the
prophetic succession closes under the Persian
dominion.   There is " no prophet more " ; and
the successor of the prophets is not so much the
priest in the Temple as the scribe in charge of
the Sacred Book of the Law, who is occupied in
interpreting, and in the process enlarging, the
prescriptions of the Books of Moses till they form

[1] Ver. 5 is so rendered in the LXX version.

a minute network over the whole surface of
Jewish life, and formalism takes the place of
inspiration. It is certainly not the case that
the religion of Israel in the last centuries of our
era—the religion of Israel as dominated by the
Pharisees—was that religion at its best. It had
long been on the down grade.

§ 3

It has been necessary to entertain these pre-
liminary considerations so that the prophetic
religion of Israel and the conception of the good
life based upon it may be set in the proper
context. The conception in all its grandeur
is exceedingly simple, and is rooted in the
idea of Jehovah. There are no limits to the
divine absoluteness. All local limitations of
Jehovah's jurisdiction are repudiated. He is
the one God of the whole universe of being.
There is no place left for any rival God or
co-existent matter. He is the absolute creator
of all that exists, visible or invisible, material
or spiritual. There is no antagonism between
souls and bodies. No such absoluteness of
statement about God is to be found in Zoroaster
or in Plato.

Moreover, the messages of the prophets are
given not as the conclusion of reasoning but
as the word of God. That word sometimes came
to them through the medium of a vision in a
trance, but that does not appear to be by any
means usual. All we can say is that the intuition
of certain truths, which the prophets experience
and are compelled to utter, they experience not

as derived from any reflection of their own
but from something speaking inwardly in their
hearts which they recognize as God's own
utterance—so sharply distinguished from their
own ideas that they sometimes appear as in
conversation with God, remonstrating with God,
and even as reluctantly submitting to be the
instrument of His will.

This supreme and transcendent God is
absolutely righteous, so much so that there is
nothing He really demands of men but righteousness, and there cannot possibly exist any form
of costly sacrifice or any expedient of magical
knowledge which can for an instant be supposed
capable of inducing him to depart in his judgment
from perfect righteousness. That righteousness
must show itself in judgment on sin, because sin
is rebellion against God ; but God has no pleasure
in condemning or punishing. His righteousness
is love—a love greater than that of a mother to
its child or a husband to a wife, and such as
involves an impartial care of each individual
Israelite, even of each individual human being.

In the earlier stages of prophecy and history
indeed, the thought is merely of the people as
a whole, as consecrated to Jehovah; and there is
little to remind us of the distinct worth and
responsibility of the individual, save of those
individuals who represent the nation, that is,
kings and prophets and priests. The constantly
reiterated lesson is that if the nation, regarded
as a whole, will keep Jehovah and His declared
will for them constantly in mind, and will carefully keep His commandments, then the nation

will be prosperous and happy. But the one God of their worship is a God who will not tolerate a divided allegiance in His people. He is a jealous God, and He treats the nation in its succession of generations as a whole: " He visits the sins of the fathers upon the children unto the third and fourth generation of them that hate him, and shows mercy unto thousands of them that love him and keep his commandments." This double-edged assurance, though it appeals to experience, is plainly not based upon experience. It is based simply upon " the word of God " and the conviction that, God being what He is, so it must be.

It is important that we should still in our day recognize the permanent truth of this assurance. If we seriously set to work to analyse the causes of national miseries and failures, we are, I believe, bound to recognize that among the causes of these catastrophes incomparably the chief is sin—the refusal of men in the mass to set themselves seriously to do right. Is it not a simple truth that if our British nation to-day would in the mass seriously determine to keep the moral law, to be just and truthful, unselfish and kind to all, self-restrained in respect of sensual indulgence, and industrious and thoughtful in its activities, all our social miseries and deformities would speedily vanish, or be reduced at least within very measurable proportions ? But the mysterious fact is that mankind in the mass will not so act even though they faintly recognize that such is the will of God. Meanwhile, the law of judgment on society—the law which the famous agnostic Huxley used to declare as unflinchingly as any ancient prophet—" that fixed order of nature which sends social disorganization upon the track of immorality, as surely as it sends physical disease after physical trespasses," so that it is " the high mission " of science " to be the priestess of a firm and lively faith " in that fixed moral order—that law works with a fearful disregard of individual differences. The righteous suffer with the guilty. They often seem to suffer more than the guilty.

One of the deepest elements of interest in the Old Testament lies in the passionate and profound expression which it gives to the experience of the righteous soul seemingly forgotten and tormented of God. That became the central problem for the religion of Israel. Though the idea of vicarious suffering emerges into recognition, yet the problem of pain is not solved. Individual responsibility and worth is indeed fully recognized by Ezekiel and in the Psalms and Wisdom literature, but till late in the history of Israel, throughout the bulk of the Old Testament, the assumption continues that the justice of God, His dealing with men strictly according to their deserts, must be vindicated *in this life*.

It is a most remarkable fact that whereas in so many religions, such as Zarathustra's, the belief in a future life was part of their substance from the first, the opposite was the case with Israel. Not indeed that they did not retain some dim belief in a world of shadowy souls in Sheol ; but this world below was, it would seem, outside the jurisdiction of Jehovah and altogether dark. All their religious faith was concentrated on this world. This concentration was what gave effectiveness to its intensely ethical character. In the conduct here and now of His chosen people the righteousness of their God had to be manifested and His justice had to vindicate itself.

The strain, however, became intolerable, and the belief in resurrection of the dead and the life beyond emerged in the later stages of Israel's religion on this quite distinctive basis—not as a thing borrowed from Persia or Babylon—but as a growth out of its own soul. The root of the new belief was threefold. It emerged out of the sense of the justice of God—because experience forced the conclusion that God must have some wider area than this world in which to vindicate Himself. " Though after my skin worms destroy this body, yet without my flesh I shall see God." [1] We see this belief established in the age of the Maccabæan martyrs.

It emerged secondly, and we feel it emerging in the Psalms, out of the developed sense of personal religion, the personal relation of the soul to God. " God is not a God of the dead, but of the living; for all live unto him." It cannot be that the souls of men who are taken up into such intimacy of fellowship with God are to be thrust out into nothingness by death. Surely " I shall behold thy face in righteousness : I shall be satisfied, when I awake, with thy likeness." [2]

Thirdly, it emerged as part of the confident

---

[1] Job xix. 26 (the familiar A.V., with the one word " without " from R.V. marg.).

[2] Ps. xvii. 15 (R.V.).

expectation of a kingdom of God to come—that the ideal Israel was, after all disappointments, to be finally realized. Then surely it could not be that those who had laboured and fought and failed and died in the cause of Israel should have no part in that glorious day ? Such is the motive of the cry of Isaiah. " Thy dead shall live ; my dead bodies shall arise. Awake and sing, ye that dwell in the dust." [1]

We need not concern ourselves with the critical question as to the precise moment in Israel's history when the belief in the life beyond and the resurrection from the dead emerged, or in what form precisely. In some respects the belief as it lies behind the Gospels may have owed something to Persian influences. But substantially it was a thoroughly native growth out of the heart of Jewish religion.

The same is true of the belief in the Kingdom of God or the final vindication of Israel. It is a mistake to say that the phrase " the kingdom of God," which seems to appear first in the New Testament, means merely " the sovereignty of God." If we examine the meaning of the idea in the New Testament, or trace it to its root in the Old Testament, our conclusion will be the same. The Kingdom of God means *His sovereignty as at last to be realized in Israel* and through Israel in all the world. The assurance of the prophets is that as surely as God is God He must finally come into His own ; and as Israel is His child and His instrument, Israel—under its king of

[1] Is. xxvi. 18–19.

David's line [1]—must be vindicated over all its enemies ; and this triumphant Israel can be only a morally perfect Israel, an Israel worthy of its God, under a king truly godlike or divine ; and as the whole world is God's, so this perfected Israel, centring in the New Jerusalem and its ideal king, must find a world perfectly adapted to it. This Messianic expectation, in all its elements, we find in very familiar and very glorious passages of the prophets. It is regarded as indisputably bound up with faith in the righteous God.

There are other elements in the expectation which make the enhanced fellowship with God more evident. There is to be a wholly new outpouring of the Spirit of God upon the Anointed King and upon the whole people ; and a new Covenant written in their hearts. Mostly in the prophets the realization of the great hope is anticipated in the more or less immediate future. The glory of Israel is seen as the immediate sequel to the annihilation of some particular enemy of God and His people—be it Assyria or Edom, or Babylon. But this did not happen. Then this anticipated judgment of God upon His enemies tends to be generalized. It is thrown upon the background of a cosmic catastrophe, and more and more, as the hope of a military triumph for Israel becomes a dream, the apocalyptic element becomes intensified. We need not pursue the subject here. The only point with which we are here concerned is that in the

---

[1] The figure of the Davidic king, however, is not always present in the pictures of the Good Time Coming.

religion of Israel the belief in the one Good God
is absolutely identified with the assurance that
in this world—albeit a transformed world—
whatever the cosmic catastrophe through which
it must pass—God is to come into His own,
and Israel purged and made righteous, and finding
its centre in a New Jerusalem, is to be vindicated
as the people of God.

It should be added that, while the conception
of the spirituality of God and His spiritual omni-
presence reaches its climax in such passages as
the 139th Psalm and in the second Isaiah, this
is not felt to be inconsistent with the idea that
God is in some intensified sense present in His
Tabernacle or His Temple.

§ 4

What is the effect of this lofty monotheism
upon the idea of the good life for man ?   First,
it should be noticed that no interest appears
to be taken in harmonizing the strong sense of
the omnipotence and omniscience of God, and
the idea of divine predestination in all human
history, with the correlative idea of human
responsibility, involving, as it does, the present
freedom of man to resist God, or, in the forcible
language of Isaiah, to " make God serve with his
sins."

The two correlatives are emphasized side by
side just as in Stoicism.   Though the obstinately
wicked may be regarded as finally " hardened "
by God and, so to speak, committed to sin, this
is not allowed to obscure the real freedom of
man.   " Behold, I have set before thee life

11

and death, blessing and cursing," God says to
the nation in Deuteronomy, " therefore choose
life " ; and the same awful freedom of choice
is emphasized for the individual will by Ezekiel
and in Ecclesiasticus—" Stretch forth thy hand
to whether thou likest."

The sense of the universal fact of sin, as
following from this freedom misused, and of
the disorder in God's world which it generates,
is everywhere evident. But the responsibility
for it lies with the sinners. When the idea of
Satan and other malevolent spirits comes to be
fully assimilated, as was the case before New
Testament times, it is accompanied and explained
by the conception of a fall of the angels from an
original righteousness. There can be no being
created evil. Moral evil is only lawlessness—
the violation of divine law by the rebel will of
man or of other spirits.

Physical evil, taken by itself, does not appear
to be felt as a problem, or to be in any way explained, except so far as it is identified with
divine judgments ; but the responsibility for
moral evil is wholly laid on the created wills.
Thus the world is viewed as a great scene in
which there is evident a divine purpose for good
destined at last to triumph, but at present
thwarted by human wilfulness—a scene, however,
in which man, made in the divine image, is
constantly called to co-operate with God. In
all this region the doctrine is the same as appears
in Zoroaster's Gâthâs. In both alike co-operation with God means specially moral co-operation.
There is no approach to God—no doing of the

work of God—except by keeping His moral commandments, which are the expression of His essential character.

From Amos downwards, as has been said, it is realized that God is the God of all the earth, and that all men, and not Israel only, are called to be just and merciful like God or to suffer punishment. But while Zarathustra shows no signs of a belief in a " chosen " people, that sense dominates the Old Testament. It expresses itself in the terrific requirements of extirpation for alien races, regarded as involved in hopeless wickedness ; and, within the circle of the chosen people, in the commands to extirpate such an evil family as the house of Ahab, which is akin to the external adversaries and has " made Israel to sin." It is, however, always represented that in proportion to the closeness of covenanted relation in which Israel stands towards God, is the severity of God's requirement and judgment upon her.

But what underlies all such terrible curses laid upon sinful man is the sense of the unchangeable righteousness of God, in conformity to which man must live or perish. Especially within Israel, the sense of the mercy of God, as a constant element in His righteousness, involving the like mercy in man towards his fellow-men, is very prominent. Nothing is more beautiful in the law and the prophets and the Psalms and the Wisdom literature than the requirement of mercy for the poor and helpless. There is no " respect of persons " with God, and God seeth the heart. No sacrifices, no devices of any kind, can shield from the judgment of God the " grinding of the faces of the poor." And a number of features in the law, such as the prohibition of usury or of the permanent alienation of lands, and the restrictions on slavery, are conceived simply in the interests of the poor and defenceless. Finally, as the result of painful experience of the effects of wealth on character, the idea of " the saints " comes to be identified with that of " the humble poor."

Thus associated with the prophetic demand for mercy is that for humility, and the accompanying horror of human insolence which the Hebrews shared with the Greeks. National and individual pride is mercilessly chastised. Unlike any other national literature, the Old Testament denounces from end to end the wilfulness and pride of the chosen people. They owe nothing to their own merits or their own power. They deserve nothing but evil. Insolent self-satisfaction or self-reliance is an abomination. No passages in the Old Testament are more splendid than the denunciations of pride, whether of intellect or will.

While the restraints laid by the law upon sensual lust are by no means up to the highest standard, and are framed in view of " the hardness of men's hearts," they seem in fact to have produced a people more moral in respect of sexual indulgence than can be found elsewhere. And the like may be said of the requirements of strict justice in the matters of buying and selling.

All the mass of prophetic exhortations and legal enactments and religious poetry is irradiated with beautiful touches which admit one to the inner life of the good man, who not only fears to do evil, but still more loves to do good and finds his delight in the loving fellowship of God; and though for the most part it must be admitted that the motive of the fear of God is more prominent in the Hebrew conception of the good life than the motive of love; and the sense of the inevitable divine judgment upon wickedness of all kinds is the keynote of the whole collection of the sacred books of Israel; yet this salutary fear is never (after the teaching of the prophets begins) expressed as if the terror of the Lord were the terror of something unknown, arbitrary and unintelligible.[1] Always, though " clouds and darkness are round about Him," His character and motive are known. What He looks for is righteousness, purity, justice, mercy, truth.

Viewed, then, as containing a presentation of the good life for man, the Old Testament reaches a very high level. It is imperfect. It is a religion for a particular nation rather than for mankind, though its broadening out into a religion for all mankind is contemplated. It is savage in its expression of the divine judgment on the enemies of Israel. But in considering its imperfections, it must be remembered that it is throughout presented to us as conscious of its imperfection. It looks forward to a better day— to a fuller light, and more perfect and spiritual covenant, a completer inspiration of the divine spirit.

[1] E.g. nothing is to be found like the earlier story of the " breach upon Uzzah " (2 Sam. vi. 6 ff.).

We may illustrate this by a more particular examination of the central document of Jewish morality, the Ten Words. They are obviously imperfect; they are, not exclusively but mainly, negative, and they were, in fact, drastically revised by the greatest of the sons of Israel, Jesus of Nazareth. But revised in His spirit, taken back behind the act to the motive and spirit of the action and converted from negative to positive precepts, they are found fairly to cover the whole realm of public and private morality; and in the highest ethical reaches of the Old Testament, this deepening and conversion of their meaning, such as appears more constantly under the " new covenant," is already in principle almost accomplished.

If the laws of the Second Table correspond with the commandments formulated by the Buddha for his monks and laymen, yet an essentially different spirit is introduced into the Ten Commandments in Israel by the First Table. The unique supremacy of the one God, the concentration of all worship on Him, and the exclusion of all idolatry, all attempts to represent God or worship Him in sensible forms, separate off the religion of Israel from all the non-moral religions around them, and from their spirit of indiscriminate toleration one of another. Israel's life is to be based, strictly and fixedly, on the recognition of the righteous Jehovah as the only God, the absolute creator of all that is, transcendent and unrepresentable by any earthly form. This positive side of the first two commandments appears in Deuteronomy as " the

first and great commandment " recalled by
Jesus. The third commandment, prohibiting
the taking of the sacred name in vain, is deepened
by Christ into the law of absolute truthfulness
in speech ; but it is found already so converted
in the Psalms and Wisdom books. The fourth
commandment consists of three laws—the law
of work, the law of rest in connection with the
Sabbath, and the law of fellowship in the recognition that all men and even animals are to share
the same privilege of repose. The generalized
law of work enunciated by St. Paul—" If a
man will not work neither let him eat "—is
quite in the spirit of the Old Testament. The
law of the Sabbath rest finds fullest expression
in the Christian association of rest with worship,
which again is anticipated in the Psalms ; and
the law of fellowship, deepened and expanded
in the New Testament, is found in fuller form
(again in Deuteronomy) in the " Thou shalt love
thy neighbour as thyself " which Christ found
sufficient.

Again, the law of obedience to parents, the
emphasis on which is as characteristic of Judaism
as of Chinese religion, is maintained and also
enlarged in the New Testament as a general
law of social order and mutual submission and
humility, and such enlargement can be found
already in the Wisdom books of the Jews. The
law prohibiting murder is already found deepened
to a requirement of positive goodness, in the
Psalms and elsewhere, in the spirit of Christ.
So the prohibition of adultery is already interpreted in the general sense of a requirement of

an all-round control of sexual passion—the prohibition of stealing as a general requirement of honesty and honour in mutual relations—the prohibition of false witness as a law which lies upon the tongue to allow no speech which is not kindly—and the final prohibition of coveting thy neighbour's good as a general condemnation of the acquisitive temper.

The Ten Words, then, no doubt represent an imperfect stage of moral education; but, deepened and enlarged in the spirit in which Christ dealt with them, they represent a remarkably complete scheme of moral requirements based on the profoundest motive; and the Jewish books show such deepening and enlargement already operating in the best minds of Israel. In a word, the ethical achievement of Israel cannot be justly disparaged; nor can any sacred book or collection of books in any nation rival the power and psychological insight with which the moral education of a nation and of individuals is exhibited, and illustrated with fascinating stories, in the Jewish Bible.

CHAPTER VII

As in the case of Zarathustra, as in the case of
Gotama the Buddha, as in the case of Plato,
so in the case of Jesus of Nazareth—for the
right understanding of this supreme teacher
of the way of life for man, we must pay
attention to the background on which He appears
and what He is able to take for granted. So
only can we appreciate His true originality.

§ 1

Jesus of Nazareth, then, was by origin and
training purely a child of Israel. It is true that
the Hellenistic civilization was near at hand in
Galilee, but there is no trace of its influence in
the Gospel story. Jesus took His stand wholly
on the Hebrew tradition about the unity and
character of God the Creator, and the nature of
man, and the glorious destiny of Israel.[1] One
important element in this tradition was, as we
have seen, the assurance that, at last, in spite
of the long-continued rebellion of man, God was
to come into His own, as in heaven so on earth.

[1] The Psalm of Zechariah (Luke ii.) is a summary of the hope
of Israel as it lay just behind the Mission of Jesus. Luke i. and
ii. describe the atmosphere of the pious homes whence Jesus
came. It should be noted that in i. 58 probably the true reading
gives us " shall visit," not " hath visited." The psalm has
turned from retrospect to anticipation.

This assurance appears in the Gospel in the phrase " the kingdom of God." But this does not mean merely the sovereignty of God, but the sovereignty of God as realized and perfected in Israel ; and generally as finding its centre in the anointed king of David's family, the " Christ," the final and adequate representative of God. The best minds in Israel had indeed foreseen that this consummation of the vocation of Israel was to have a world-wide effect—it was to enable Israel to become the evangelist of the nations, so that thus finally in Abraham's seed should " all the families of the earth be blessed " ; but still the perfecting of Israel was to be the first step, and that would require the moral and spiritual regeneration of that sinful people. That had been the constant message of the prophets ; and when they failed to find the response they desired in the mass of Israel, they turned to the faithful remnant—the group who had ears to hear—and declared them the true Israel. " Behold, I and the children whom the Lord hath given me." [1]

This was exactly the message by which John the Baptist prepared the way for the Lord. He was an inheritor of the old ethical spirit of the prophets, which after long years of deadness revived in him with a new power. Already in him the conflict between the prophetic spirit and the Pharisaic legalism is apparent. The only new point in his preaching was the announcement that the kingdom of God, the realization of God's rule in Israel, was immediately to be

[1] Is. viii. 18.

expected. The coming of the Lord to "visit" Israel in the person of the Christ was close at hand. But, as usual, Israel was found quite unfit to welcome Him. His coming could only be their condemnation. They were not good grain fit for the harvest of God, but rather chaff fit only for the furnace. Therefore they must repent. There was still opportunity for such repentance as would bring into being a new Israel, a people prepared for the Lord. And John used as his symbolic instrument in promoting this national regeneration a baptism or purification with water, accompanied with a public confession of sins. The ruling classes, Sadducees and Pharisees, paid no heed to John, as they "rejected the counsel of God for themselves"[1]; but he made a deep impression on the mass of the people, and it was into the fruit of his mission that Jesus entered. He took up John's message, "The time is fulfilled, and the kingdom of God is at hand : repent ye, and believe in the good tidings."[2]

And in the beginning of Jesus' mission in Galilee[3] it was only the goodness of the tidings which was in evidence. Here was a truly wonderful prophet who loved and cared for the poor and oppressed people, every one of them, who was endowed with an overwhelming authority alike over the diseases of men, over the spirits of evil and over the forces of nature, and who spoke, as no one had ever heard a man to speak, as

[1] Luke vii. 30 ; Mark xi. 31.   [2] Mark i. 15.

[3] I am leaving out in this necessarily brief summary the question of an earlier self-announcement of Jesus in Judæa and Jerusalem, as represented in the Fourth Gospel, which I am yet convinced we must accept as historical.

if He held from God the right to act in His name, even to revise the accepted tradition of the scribes, even to give a new law, or a new version of the old law, to the people of God.

But splendid as was the first impression made by Jesus, it soon became apparent, especially to Himself, that the situation contained the seeds of inevitable failure. The first enthusiastic faith in Jesus the wonderful healer was not deep enough for His purpose. If he had multitudes to listen to Him and to come to be healed, He made few real disciples. It was obvious why the wealthy and powerful classes, such as the Sadducean high-priestly family in Jerusalem, and the Herodians in Galilee, should be set against Him, for He had a horror of selfish power and of wealth, which He openly denounced and ridiculed. It was obvious, again, why the most respected class in the nation, the Pharisees, and the official scribes of their persuasion, should be up in arms against Him, for His criticisms of the official religion cut very deep. The " wine " He offered the people to drink was obviously a very " new wine," and the ecclesiastics in authority were bound to maintain that " the old was good." But it is even more important to notice that His absolute refusal to use or contemplate the use of force in the interest of religion set against Him all the " patriots " or nationalists in a people amongst whom, since the days of the Maccabæan rebellion, religion had been commonly identified with the hope of a military and victorious Messiah. Galilee teemed with rebellious spirits, and Jesus absolutely turned His back upon them, even when, in admiration of His seemingly boundless power, they would have come by force and made Him a king.

But neither Sadducees nor Pharisees nor Herodians nor Zealots made up the bulk of the poor and distressed people of Galilee. The common people heard Jesus gladly. But they were engrossed in getting their livelihood, and they soon found that the moral claim He was making upon them was something so profound, and so revolutionary in respect of ordinary ideas of the good life, that they had neither time nor inclination to entertain it. If they had " the faith to be healed "—that is, faith in Jesus sufficient to bring them to Him to be healed—they had not " the ears to hear "— the deeper faith such as could make them His disciples. So, though Jesus had many hearers, He had few real disciples ; and He knew it.

He acted then exactly like the old prophets and like John the Forerunner. He concentrated all His attention on fashioning a New Israel which, in succession to the Old Israel, was to be the true church of God, and which came in later days to be known simply as " the Church." He recognized that, though Israel in the mass had refused Him and would refuse Him, and was accordingly doomed under the irreversible judgment of God which would speedily follow, yet that God's purpose in Israel had not failed : He was sent exclusively to preach the good tidings to Israel. That meant, therefore, that He was to devote all the time that remained to Him on earth to evoking, instructing, and, in rudimentary fashion, organizing the New Israel, so that, after He was gone out of sight, it would be strong enough to stand against all storms of opposition and carry the Gospel into all the world. Jesus could not have identified Himself, as He did, with the figure of the Suffering Servant of Jehovah in the later Isaiah without knowing that He was set to be " the light of the Gentiles "; but of this world-wide evangelization Israel— not Israel as it stood in obstinate hardness of heart, but the true Israel which He was framing to take its place—was the divine instrument.

The Liberal Protestant school of critics, which has been so much in evidence, has taught us a valuable lesson in emphasizing the mission of Jesus as an ethical prophet—the preacher of the good life for man ; but they have often missed the very plain fact that His teaching was, with more and more intensity, directed to fashioning the " little flock " who were to be the heirs of the " kingdom," so that they might form, in a world which would fear them and hate them, an element as sharply distinctive, as luminously bright, and as unmistakably outlined, as salt is in food, as a lamp in a dark room, as a city set on a hill. Jesus was, as Sir John Seely long ago in *Ecce Homo* explained with such admirable penetration, before all things the " Founder." [1]

---

[1] *Ecce Homo* summarizes the mission of Jesus Christ as that of " a moralist speaking with authority, and perpetuating his doctrine by means of a Society " ; so also " Renan thought that the strongest proof of the originality of Jesus is not to be found in the novelty of the truths He taught, these having been for the most part anticipated by the prophets of Israel in the eighth century B.C., but in the society He created. In saying this Renan did

This same lesson has been missed by the Apocalyptic School. It is quite true that Jesus was apocalyptic. He was not merely the ethical prophet with wonderful gifts of healing. His vision was occupied with the divine climax. But He foresaw this " coming of the kingdom " in stages. In one sense it had already come in His coming among men—" the kingdom of God is come upon you "; in another sense it would come in the judgment on Jerusalem and that speedily, within the lifetime of men then alive ; but positively it was to find its expression in the New Israel which was to carry the Gospel into all the world ; so, only so, could the world be made ripe for the great consummation, which, alike in the case of those who should welcome the message and of those who should refuse it, alike for eternal fruition or eternal judgment, must close the vista of human history as Jesus saw it.[1] We are blinding our eyes to the evidence if we neglect any of these elements in the expectation of Jesus.

If Jesus was the wise founder of a visible society destined to play the central part in God's purpose for the world, we should naturally

less than justice to the originality of the teaching of Jesus, but he emphasized something which Jesus Himself regarded as of great importance—the creation of a society."—H. H. Scullard, *Ethics of the Gospel* (Student Christian Movement), p. 66.

[1] I am here leaving aside the question, which I have sought to deal with elsewhere (see *Reconstruction of Belief*, pt. ii, cap. v), whether Jesus announced the *immediate* coming of the End. The evidence, however, points to the fact that while He anticipated the immediacy of certain stages or elements in the manifestation of the kingdom, He refused to name any date for its consummation.

expect that He would occupy Himself greatly
with its organization. We find, however, that
He did this, in the sense which the words would
ordinarily carry, very little. In one important
matter, the matter of marriage, He appears to
have laid down an explicit law, as St. Paul,
St. Mark and St. Luke report [1] ; but in the
ordinary sense He was not a legislator. He
did nothing at all comparable to what Plato
did in his *Laws* for his ideal community. As
He refrained from dogmatic statements or
theological definitions, so He refrained from
legislative enactments. He proposed, it appeared, to inspire His church (in a most realistic
sense) with His Spirit ; and to leave it to the
church to deal with issues as they should arise
with the assistance of this divine Paraclete, the
agent or representative of God.

Nevertheless, a certain rudimentary organization He did give His society. He appointed
officers in the persons of the Twelve Apostles,
of whom Peter was the chief, and He gave them
authority such as the scribes had held in Old
Israel and had misused—to " bind " and " loose,"
that is, to legislate by prohibition or permission,
and to absolve or retain sins, that is, to exercise
discipline over individuals ; and He described
such a ministry as a permanent feature in His
household till He should " come again." Also
He gave His society two rites at any rate, a
rite of initiation (baptism) and a rite of fellowship (the Holy Communion). The evidence of
St. Paul's epistles and of the Acts raises it, it

[1] 1 Cor. vii. 10 ; Mark x. 11, 12 ; Luke xvii. 18.

seems to me, above all reasonable suspicion that the Church from the very beginning of its history believed itself to have been endowed by Christ with these institutions and authoritative commissions, and this gives us the best reason for accepting the narratives in the Gospels which record their institution or imply them.

We should notice that so deeply was it impressed upon the mind of the primitive Church that Jesus (if the expression may be pardoned) staked His all on the Church, that there does not appear the least suggestion in the New Testament that His great salvation or His covenant of grace is to be found outside it.[1] There is, in other words, no idea to be found there of a membership of Christ which is not also membership in the Church which is the New Israel.

§ 2

I have stressed at starting this idea of Jesus as the founder of a visible commonwealth, to be in the world but not of it, because it controls our thought of Him as an ethical teacher—a teacher of the good life for man. For Him, as for others among the great teachers we have been considering, the good life was contemplated as life in a specific community—Israel as it was to be. Let us pro-

[1] This is only rightly understood if we carefully distinguish the idea of the Covenant of Salvation from the idea of the final acceptance of the individual in the ultimate judgment of God. As to this, we are to judge nothing before the time. " Many shall come from the east and the west, and shall sit down with Abraham and Isaac and Jacob, and the children of the kingdom be cast into the outer darkness."

12

ceed now to consider its main features as Jesus taught it, and to obviate certain misconceptions.

The good life, as taught by Jesus, was wholly based upon a specific idea of God and His purpose, as made manifest in action in the history of Israel and as declared by His prophets. There is nothing resembling metaphysical argument on behalf of God to be found in His teaching. He appeals to Israel as already recognizing the one true God, and as having had in a long experience knowledge of Him and His will and ways—for example, both of His mercy and of His judgment, and of His good purpose for Israel, with which He expects them to correspond ; but also He would plainly have them understand that God has more to teach them about Himself and about His purpose, and that He, Jesus, has unique authority to speak this new " word of God." " No one," he said, " knoweth the Father save the Son, and he to whomsoever the Son willeth to reveal him."

The novelty in His teaching about God lay in the emphasis He laid on His fatherhood. The recent Jewish tradition, in awful reverence for God, had taught men to fear even to utter His name. They preferred to speak of " the heavens." Now, Jesus spoke of God as " transcendent " indeed—your Father which is in heaven —but He brought Him down nearer to common men, and He emphasized His " tender mercies," by the familiar use of the term " Father "— " my Father," and " your Father." " Father," then, was not a new title for God, but the emphasis Jesus laid on it was new. It brought into clear light the equal love of God for every individual soul and His care for every part of His creation. "Not a sparrow falleth to the ground without your Father." This did not detract from His awful justice. That which God cannot do is to tolerate sin, or take the obstinate soul into fellowship with Himself. The tremendous responsibility to save or to destroy his own soul must still lie with each individual, and the only legitimate fear remains the fear of a God who has —not the will but the power " to destroy both soul and body in hell."

But God's fatherhood means that He will do His utmost for His sons. He will search for each one, follow him, welcome him home. He gives no preference to persons of dignity or position. " It is not the will of your Father which is in heaven that one of these little ones should perish." He hates the pride of place, or the arrogant selfishness which leads any individual, powerful by virtue of his wealth or learning, to despise another or exploit him as an instrument for his own advantage. And the worst sins—such as the world count worst— are no obstacle to God's ready acceptance of the sinner, if only the soul will turn to Him and put itself in His hands.

In any established society a distinction grows up between disreputable and respectable sins. Disreputable sins are such as interfere with the seemly order of society, with property and the peace of the home. Such are theft or violence, or adultery and licence, or atheism and rebellion. But other sins, though they may be verbally acknowledged as such, are in fact connived at. They are quite consistent with respectability. But Jesus would destroy any such distinction. Plainly in His eyes, pride, avarice, contempt and selfishness are at least as bad as fornication or violence. He loved to show the friendliness of God to disreputable people and outcasts— publicans, Samaritans, harlots—to stimulate their repentance, and to welcome them with the freest absolution. He came " not to call the righteous but sinners." And there is irony in the word " righteous." It means " self-righteous." And His quite evident judgment was that these righteous people quite as much needed fundamental repentance as the sinners. Indeed, spiritual sins, such as pride, Jesus saw to be harder to repent of than the more scandalous. " The publicans and harlots go into the kingdom of heaven before you " highly respected Pharisees. Jesus also dealt with women, bad women and good women alike, as having the same spiritual worth and capacity as men, though He showed no sign of making any woman one of His official agents or apostles.

No one can deny that the ethical teaching of Jesus, based on His thought of God, was in the eyes of respectable society deeply revolutionary and " upsetting." Plato, in his *Laws*, con-templates a state of society in which the only legitimate " fear " would be the fear of the best public opinion, and that would be a sufficient protection. Jesus, on the other hand, shows a dread of public opinion as the guardian of the moral standard. " How can you believe," He

said to the Pharisees, who belonged to a class
in which public opinion was very strict—" how
can you believe which seek honour one of
another ? "   There is only one real ground of goodness, and that is free and absolute correspondence
with God as He has revealed Himself in the past,
and is now revealing His mind and character
in Jesus.

God therefore is to be put absolutely and
unconditionally first in the thought of each
man.   There will be times, Jesus intimates,
when He will seem a hard and unjust taskmaster,
" taking up that he had not laid down, and
reaping that he had not sown " ;   then as a
hard taskmaster men must accept Him, and
strain every nerve to obey Him, as those who
have no being apart from God and no rights
against Him, though they will assuredly find
out that the estimate of Him as a taskmaster
or a merely sovereign power is very far from
the true estimate.   This same sense of the
penetrating supremacy of God appears when
Jesus drives back the idea of the sinfulness of
sin behind the outward act, which is all that man
can see, and all which can claim and win human
applause, to the thought of the heart and the
motion of the will.   Morally speaking, the value
of right action and the guilt of wrong action lie
simply in the will—in " the heart of man."   In
the regard of Jesus humanity is undoubtedly a
fallen being, needing in every individual specimen
repentance and a new birth.   But the sin which
binds him and dooms him lies not in the body
or anything which properly belongs to his nature

as God made him (there is not a trace of dualism in the teaching of Jesus), but it lies simply in the perverted will—in " the heart of man." Let that turn to God—to the Father—and all will be well ; for the redemption which Jesus brought was redemption of the whole man.[1]

Perhaps there is no point at which whole-hearted acceptance by Jesus of nature, including human nature, as fundamentally good is more evident than in the parables which formed so large an element in His teaching ; for it would seem on reflection that the very principle of the parables proper—as distinct from such moral tales, miscalled parables, as Dives and Lazarus or the Rich Fool—is that if we get down to any fundamental law of nature or of human action, whether in bad men or good men, we get to something which is also divine, and can therefore suggest to us the ways of God.

Many of the world's teachers about God have been mystics ; and the great mystics of all ages and races—Indian, Jewish, Greek, Muhammadan, Christian—have always been occupied in emphasizing the " oneliness " of God ; and the mystic's quest has been union with or absorption into the One. But Jesus, though He is constantly spoken of as absorbed in prayer, spoke no word of the mystical quest. For instance, the mystics have talked much about prayer, but have generally tended to merge prayer in adoration, and to depreciate the asking for

[1] In His treatment of man as a whole, Jesus retains the Jewish psychology in which " the soul " is not in antithesis to the body, but includes it : see Pedersen's *Israel* (Oxf. Press), pp. 99 ff.

particular good things. Jesus, as befitted one
who recognized absolute dependence upon God
as the true secret of life, naturally insisted
much on prayer, and inculcated an unlimited
belief in its efficacy ; and He did, it is true, in
the pattern prayer which He gave to His disciples,
put first the petition, " Hallowed be thy name,"
that is, adoration.   But all His teachings about
prayer emphasize its primary sense of asking—
importunate asking—for the supply of a felt
want, that is, its petitionary meaning ; and He
taught that our power to win from God a favourable answer to our petitions depends in part
upon the fervour of our faith in God's goodness
and His power—which shows itself in importunate
asking—but also in part on the conforming of
our desires to the mind of God, as He, Jesus,
reveals that mind.   This is the meaning of
prayer " in the name " of Jesus.   It means in
conformity with His spirit or point of view.
Prayer therefore implies adoration of God for
His own sake, and meditation on Him, but it
remains true that prayer, as Jesus taught it,
is mainly petitionary, and petitionary especially
in the sense that we should ask for all that makes
men effective agents of the kingdom of God.
The " mystical quest " is markedly absent or
kept quite in subordination.   This subordination
leads us to consider the meaning Jesus gave to
the love of God.

§ 3

Jesus, as all the world knows, found the
summary of the divine law in two sayings of

the Pentateuch.[1] The first of all commandments
is, " Hear, O Israel ; the Lord our God is one
Lord ; and thou shalt love the Lord thy God
with all thy heart, and with all thy soul, and
with all thy mind, and with all thy strength.
This is the first and great commandment. And
the second is this. Thou shalt love thy neighbour
as thyself. There is none other commandment
greater than these." Mankind in general, when
it has thought seriously about the matter, has
been prone to complain that this teaching, though
given as elementary, is impossibly high and, in
fact, impracticable. This is in great part
because it has mistaken the meaning of the word
" love." It knows what love means in the
love of man and woman, parents and children.
This is a *feeling* or passion which cannot be
controlled or summoned at will, and which a
man can seldom experience towards God, or
towards men in general, whom often he " doesn't
like." But this emotion or feeling, which is
what we commonly mean by " love," is expressed
by a Greek word (ἔρως) which never occurs in
the New Testament. The Greek word for love
in the New Testament (ἀγάπη) does not signify
any sort of emotion, but a deliberate disposition
of the will—something which is within everyone's
control if he chooses to have it so. We can put
God indisputably first ; and we can care im-
partially for the interests of those we like and
those we don't like.

The two commandments mean in fact just
this—" As thou art absolutely dependent upon

[1] Deut. vi. 4 and Lev. xix. 18 ; see Mark xii. 28 ff.

God in all respects, and hast learned to recognize in Him a purpose of pure goodness towards every man, so do thou, as in reason and duty bound, enthrone Him supreme over thy whole being. Seek first His kingdom and righteousness, and deliberately dispose all thy faculties in response to Him. That is to love God. And to love thyself is to recognize that the gift of life (which most men so grievously misuse) is a good thing, and thou art bound to make the best of it for time and for eternity—that is to save thy soul ; and that can only be by ordering thy whole being in correspondence with God. And to love thy neighbour as thyself is to recognize absolutely that with God is no respect of persons —that every man counts in His sight for one and no man for more than one, for God has no favourites. Therefore thou wilt deliberately study to think of every man and to behave towards him as towards one who lives like thyself in the regard of God—God, whose burning indignation is kindled against anyone who fails actively to further His good purpose for every other man, as he has opportunity."

Love is, therefore, both Godward and manward, a deliberate disposition which can be made a matter of choice and effectively cultivated if we will. As in the long run our feelings follow our will, on the whole, so we may find ourselves feeling warm affection towards God, and towards those whom we set ourselves to love in intention and action. But the command concerns not the feeling but the will.

Here, then, we have a complete philosophy of

life—as being co-operation with the gracious
purpose of God, who has let us know His mind
towards mankind.   Its aim is to realize the fatherhood of God in the brotherhood of man.   But
mankind, as it is, is not fit for this divine sonship
or human brotherhood.   The function of the
Church, as being *the* brotherhood[1] of those
reborn to sonship, is to exhibit in the world the
true expression of humanity.   " By this shall
all men know that ye are my disciples, if ye
have love one to another."   " We [the disciples]
know that we have passed from death unto life,
because we love the brethren."   If Jesus'
teaching about God is, as we have seen, so
un-mystical (in the sense in which we commonly
use the word), it is surely because He would have
us deeply recognize that there is no other
expression of love to God which is acceptable to
Him except that of setting ourselves deliberately
to correspond with His gracious and universal
purpose for our brother man.

Incidentally, from this point of view we can
easily understand the sense in which Jesus was,
or was not, other-worldly.   Certainly He did
not speak as one who held that God's good purpose would be, or could be, consummated in the
world of our present experience.   He anticipated
judgment, particular and universal, on " this
world."   He steadily bids us be prepared for a
situation—the " last days "—in which the good

---

[1] The expressions " sonship " and " brotherhood " are used
in the N.T. almost only with reference to the Holy Community.
Perhaps Acts xvii. 28 and Matt. xxv. 40, are the possible ex-
ceptions, and both are doubtful.

cause shall seem infinitely weak.   Certainly He
bids us look to another world to rectify the false
values and restore the right estimates of things
and of persons—a tremendous reversal of this
world's judgments.   He treats as merely folly the
living for this life and its transitory goods.
He dogmatically affirms the resurrection of the
individual to the life beyond and judgment upon
him according to his works.   Thus in one sense
Jesus is utterly other-worldly.   This world is no
more than a place of probation or " soul-making."
For final achievement we must look beyond.

But in the history of the Christian religion
" other-worldliness " has taken another meaning
and character.   " The saints " have sometimes
appeared as satisfied in mystical absorption or
as ignoring this world as something merely doomed
to perdition—and thus have behaved as if they
had no call to remedy its abuses.   This, as we
have seen, is flatly anti-Christian.   The function
of the Church in this world is to exhibit the spirit
of brotherhood in action in present-day society.
It is this spectacle which is to win the world.
To tolerate misery among men, without feeling
the call to remedy it, is to fall under the final
reprobation—" inasmuch as ye did it not."   If
the final " city of God," the " New Jerusalem,"
is to be a new creation founded on the ruins of
the old, still the new and perfect world turns
out to be only this world remade ; all the
materials of the " city of God " have been
fashioned or have to be fashioned here.   Moreover, Jesus, as the revealer of the mystery (or
secret) of the kingdom, does nothing towards

satisfying men's greedy curiosity about the life
beyond. There is a life beyond, and what will
prevail there is God's goodwill and justice.
To know that is enough to keep faith firm and
hope radiant and love active. But our curiosity
concerning the nature of the future life is plainly
not to be satisfied. All our attention in this
life, as disciples of Jesus, is to be occupied in
corresponding here and now with the gracious
purpose of God in the building of His kingdom.
There is no real love of God which does not find
expression in the deliberate service of men.

There appears to have been, in fact, very little
speculation in the Early Church about after-
world problems, though there was a good deal
of " spiritualism " in the world about them.

§ 4

We observe in the Gospels that Jesus gave
kindly recognition to all sorts of good-natured
actions—" the cup of cold water only " given
to one of His disciples. He plainly did not
regard mankind as it stands as only bad. Nevertheless, He demanded something much more
than this natural goodness for the citizens of
His commonwealth. The demand He makes on
them both Godward and manward is extreme.
It is the extreme of self-devotion, the extreme
of self-control, the extreme of meekness, the
extreme of unselfishness, which He sets before
them. It is true that, speaking as He did in
proverbs, the proverbial instances He gives
cannot be taken literally and turned into general
laws. When He bids us pluck out the eye, or

cut off the hand, which has been the advocate
of sin, He is, no doubt, not to be taken literally.
But what He certainly does literally require
is complete control of the flesh by the spirit,
and He does literally assure us that to win this
complete self-control we must make even an
extreme sacrifice of exterior liberty. "Narrow
is the gate, and straitened the way, that leadeth
unto life and few there be that are finding it."
There can be no question that, while He represented the life to which He was calling men as
indeed a glorious and blessed thing—a "pearl
of great price"—yet also He bade them count
the cost of buying it, and the cost was everything that they had to give.

In one respect indeed we may dare to say
that the ethical claim of Jesus was an "interim
ethic." I refer to the absolute claim which
He made for the renunciation of all earthly ties.
This is especially evident in St. Luke, as when
Jesus is reported to have turned upon the multitudes who followed Him with strangely repellent
words—"If any man cometh unto me and hateth
not his own father and mother, and wife, and
children, and brethren, and sisters, yea, and his
own life also, he cannot be my disciple. . . .
Whosoever he be of you that renounceth not all
that he hath, he cannot be my disciple." Shortly
afterwards, we notice, He is not represented as
making any such claim on Zacchæus, whom He
accepts and blesses. Doubtless by the "disciples" He meant the little band who literally
followed Him, especially the Twelve. These,
however unfit at present, He was preparing for

the task which lay immediately before them, that
of being the first heralds of His Gospel in a hostile
world.   For this tremendous task He needed
absolute and literal detachment—absolute and
literal renunciation of everything that the world
values.   And, after the extraordinary experiences
of failure and recovery through which the Twelve
passed in the Holy Week, Jesus got in them what
He wanted.   He had for His agents a band of men
whose feet were planted upon a rock, wholly
without cares, ready for anything.

Later we find St. Paul giving high honour
to such complete detachment, the opportunity
for which he finds especially in the celibate life.
But the general tone of the epistles of the New
Testament is different.   They are written to
people who are assumed to be living the normal
life of husbands and wives, parents and children,
masters and servants—who are addressed as
possessing private property (though under an
obligation to dispose of it in trust for the community as well as for their own family), and who
are expected to have a judicial system of their
own to protect legitimate rights.   In all this
there is no real lowering of the moral standard
of Jesus.   The claim that a man must die to
the worldly world and all its notions, if he is to
live " the life that is life indeed," is as obvious
throughout the New Testament as in the Gospels.
But in the absolute and literal claim made in
the Gospels for renunciation of all worldly ties
there is something—I will not say temporary,
for the need of it is recurrent and the claim
has been constantly repeated in the call to the

monastic life—but at least special, and made in view of the special emergency of the moment.

But even when this concession is made, the ethical claim of Jesus remains tremendous in its depth and range. He was no ordinary reformer. The ordinary reformer fixes his mind on certain changes in the ordering of society which he sees to be necessary, and, to secure support for these, he is prepared to take men as he finds them and make the best of them for his own purposes. Jesus was a reformer indeed—essentially of the deepest and most revolutionary kind—of the society of Israel. But He was content with no piecemeal reforms. He would be no " judge or divider " in a society rotten at the core. He demanded a fresh start on a basis of absolute truth. He was not an "ascetic " in the narrower or technical sense of the term. He contrasts Himself with John the Forerunner, who was. But if asceticism means the heroic venture to recover the true meaning and value of life, and its true liberty, by absolutely exalting the spirit over the flesh and absolutely subordinating the spirit to God, Christ was indeed a teacher of asceticism.

Sometimes writers who have noticed the horror which Jesus showed of the proud pretentiousness of ecclesiastics and the selfishness of the wealthy and powerful, and His respect for " the average man " and for his intelligence, and His peremptory demand for justice in human life, have spoken of Jesus as a leader of democracy. But if democracy means, as it does, an appeal to majorities or a putting things to the vote,

the Commonwealth which Jesus was founding,
though there would be found in it some of the
characteristic features of democracy, cannot be
called by that name. Jesus had a profound
contempt for majorities. It was a *theocracy*
He was founding, though with God brought
closer to men than in the old theocracy of
Israel—something not based by any means on
the opinions of its citizens but on the word of
God, as spoken by one who was Lord and Christ.
And, in respect of the general society amidst
which it was to live as a kingdom within a
kingdom, it was to be an *aristocracy*, representing
the true humanity of sonship to God and brotherhood among men, and winning a reluctant admiration by the essential dignity and beneficence of
its common life—thus acting as a leaven in a
corrupt world, even when men would not pay
the price necessary for belonging to it. But
its power of being " the leaven " depended on
its being first of all " the salt," " the light,"
the " city set on a hill " in marked separation
from the surrounding world.

It is true—most lamentably true—that since
the days of Constantine, by the recognition of
indiscriminate baptism, by the abandonment of
discipline, by the reckless adoption of the
principle of established churches, the Church
of Christ has dared absolutely to reverse the
method of its Master, and thereby has lost its
ethical distinctness and its moral power as a
corporate body. But I am not now looking so far
forward. Throughout the period of three centuries
before what is called the " conversion of the

Empire "—throughout the period during which the unpopularity of the Church and its liability to persecution helped it to sustain, on the whole, its ethical standard—it was faithful to the method of Jesus ; it was a society of persons who had died to live. That was what Christian baptism meant, not symbolically only but really.

§ 5

The analysis which I have attempted to give of the teaching of Jesus, as it is recorded in the Synoptic Gospels, shows that a coherent and systematic vision and revelation concerning God and nature and man underlies His ethical teaching. And when this latter is reduced to something like systematic form, the question may be raised whether parallels to its every element and detail may not be found in other ethical systems.

In the next chapter I shall be insisting upon the unity of tendency in—if not all, yet most of the theories of the good life which we have been considering ; and I am not proposing to discuss in detail whether there are actually any ethical maxims which Jesus alone enunciated. Certainly there is no ethical system in which humility and charity hold so dominant a place as in His ; or in which " the expulsive power of a new affection " over all lawless lusts is so apparent. But the originality of Jesus lies not nearly so much in the substance of His moral instruction as (1) in its method. His proverbs, His paradoxes, His incomparable parables, His way of meeting men's " plain questions "

18

not by " plain answers " but by asking another
question, thus forcing the questioner to see that
deeper thought ought to have led him to ask
a quite different sort of question, and to ask it
not of Jesus but of himself—it is all these features
in His method which fascinate and astonish
any open-hearted enquirer and make him repeat
the old cry—" Never man spake like this man ! "
Never was any teaching given which was at
once so stimulating to the will, so novel to the
imagination and so self-evidencing to the reason.

(2) But justly to estimate His originality we must
look farther on : we must think in what form the
ethical teaching of Jesus went out into the
world—that is, we must study the Epistles.
They are all in larger part ethical, and this
ethical teaching of the epistles is beyond comparison lovely ; and it is in its whole substance
the teaching of Jesus.   It gives exactly the same
paramount place in the good life to humility
—Godward and manward—and to brotherly love.
It demands the same combination of unresisting
meekness with inflexible courage and audacity
in face of the world.   But if we ask what is
really new in all this, we shall probably find
ourselves reduced to the conclusion that it is
not—or not so much—newness of substance as
newness of motive and spirit.   What a world of
fresh motives and what an abundant source of
new power for living the good life the Christian
society had received !   That is the last consideration on which I desire to concentrate your
attention.

" The Gospels "—the four little written books

so called—were not the first literary output of the new Church, and their detailed memorials of Jesus do not represent the first gospel as it was preached. For that you must go to the beginning of the Acts and the fundamental assumptions of St. Paul's earliest Epistles. The first dominant note is that of the resurrection on the third day of the crucified Jesus. Under the strain of the humiliating experience of the Cross the vacillating faith of the Apostles had failed. But the experience of the subsequent days had driven their innermost selves, as it were, round a sharp corner to a wholly fresh outlook. They had been absolutely wrong and Jesus absolutely right. God had altogether vindicated Him. He was exalted as Lord and Christ to the supreme throne of the universe. There was nothing left to do but to obey His call. His was the one name of salvation, and though Israel had rejected Him the offer was still open, first to Israel and then (it appeared) to all the world. All that was needed was faith in His Name and the self-surrender of faith.

But it was something more than a glorified Christ in the heavens in which they believed. At the beginning John the Baptist had taught his disciples to expect from the Christ the baptism, not of water only as in his baptism, but of the Spirit. Before His death Jesus had sought to fill His disciples' minds with the expectation of this gift as the chief object of His coming. And that Spirit had come in sensible power upon them some ten days after Jesus had disappeared for the last time from their eyes, and after that first outpouring on the original group of brethren, He had come successively to all who had received baptism, normally through the laying-on of the hands of the apostles, so that the reception could be looked back to as an event at a particular moment of their experience. And this Spirit was the Spirit of God, but also and therefore the Spirit of Jesus. Jesus was not to them merely a past example, or a remote Lord, but an inward presence and power. A mere example in past history becomes in experience a feebler and feebler power, all the more if the example is that of a genius, of a more than ordinary man. But the example of Jesus was something much more than a memory. For He who had taught them in the past how to live was alive in the heavenly places, and was working within them by His Spirit, moulding them inwardly in conformity with the pattern He had shown them outwardly. They were individually very members of the body of Christ, instinct with His life— eating His flesh and drinking His blood. Moreover, as " members " they were never alone. The holy community both required their assistance and also gave them its strong support. The divine grace on which they depended they were taught to look for in sacraments of Christ's institution, which were ceremonies of the society, and bound the spiritual life of the individuals into its close fellowship.

I need not go on particularizing what in the gross will be apparent to every fairly open-eyed student of the Epistles and the Acts—that the real originality in the Christian ethics lies not only in the fresh light thrown on moral duties, but also, and much more, in the abundant richness of the motives and supplies of power newly opened to the believer in Christ. We may believe or disbelieve the " good tidings " ; but no one can read the Acts and Epistles and doubt what the good tidings were. They were tidings of a new self-disclosure of God and of new sources of spiritual power opened to man. It was only after the first Christians had received and believed the message, and had become members of the Holy Community, that they began to receive, first by word of mouth and then in written form, the apostolic memories of how Jesus had first appeared, and how He had taught and worked and lived and suffered and died and risen.

The joyful message centred upon what had come to be recognized as the new name of God —the name of the Father, and of the Son, and of the Holy Spirit. Later the doctrine of the Incarnation of the Son, and the accompanying doctrine of the Trinity in Unity, became a matter of theological and philosophical interest and of bitter controversy, with the result that, especially in the speculative East, after the (nominal) acceptance of Christianity by the Empire, the Christian religion tended to appear rather as a theological system to be accepted in faith than as a life to be lived.

I do not speak as one who doubts the intellectual value or validity of the Christian theology. But Christianity did not come into the world as a new theological system. It came into the world as a life to be lived by a community—a blessed life of union with God and fellowship among men. And the new theological terms made their appearance, not as abstract ideas, but as living motives or forces constraining and enabling men for the living of the good life.

APPENDED NOTE

THE AUTHORITATIVENESS OF JESUS

There can be no question that Jesus taught as one having authority, and that He assumed that those who had ears to hear, those whose inward light had not been allowed to become darkness, would recognize what He said for truth. But it strikes one with astonishment to discover how widely different was His method of teaching with authority from what has been commonly found in the dogmatic system of the Church. Faith has too often been allowed to appear as the mere willingness to receive the statements of ecclesiastical authority with passive acceptance. But it is plain that Jesus strove in every way to encourage enquiry. There is about His teaching no touch of obscurantism. He shrank from making dogmatic statements. Plainly He preferred to stimulate the minds of His disciples to discover the truth (e.g. the truth about Himself) for themselves. Occasionally He makes a dogmatic statement, as about the indissolubility of marriage or the reality of the Life Beyond. But it is very rare. The faith which He so urgently and constantly demanded was self-surrender to God, and to the Good Life which is God's will for man, and to Himself as " the way and the truth and the life " embodied. This faith was no doubt found to involve the acceptance of doctrines by the intellect and the recognition of historical facts. But the assumption is always that " he that willeth to do God's will shall know of the teaching whether it be of God." The primary adventure of faith is always the acceptance of the claim of the Life.

CHAPTER VIII

REFLECTIONS UPON THE HISTORICAL SURVEY

§ 1

WE have finished our historical survey, and the result—if for the moment we omit India from our consideration—is certainly impressive. In the darkness of a remote antiquity, almost three thousand years back, a clear light shines upon the ancient prophet Zarathustra, whom we find proclaiming substantially the same gospel of the good life and the kingdom of God, as we hear again later from the prophets of Israel. He is addressing his own Iranian tribe—an agricultural people exposed to the persecution of more powerful nomads. This to his imagination represents the world-wide struggle on behalf of the good life for man against the evil which would thwart and annihilate it. But he stands there conscious of divine appointment and divine enlightenment to assure his people that the good life of truth and peace and righteousness has behind it the will and power of the supreme God ; and that, however strong the forces of evil—the Lie with its attendant violence and malice— seem to be, they are infallibly destined to utter overthrow. The good God is to come into His own in a world beyond this. The good life for man, then, leads to ultimate victory, but for the present it is a life of constant struggle.

There is offered to every man the opportunity
of co-operating with God and taking part in
the struggle which is His and man's. Every
man has kinship with God, and may share His
attributes and His spirit.

In Zarathustra's teaching we discern the
fundamental assumption of a conscience in man
which can distinguish good from evil, and which
can recognize the claim of the good life as self-
evidencing and divine—as something different
from the pursuit of the pleasure or profit of the
individual. Goodness is correspondence with
the divine will. It is co-operation with God.
Zarathustra, like the Hebrew prophets, shows
no interest in metaphysical speculation ; moreover, he is no mystic occupied in the contemplation of the One, and no ascetic disparaging
the body and its activities. He is the plain man
set in the midst of the struggle of life, and fully
prepared to enjoy it, but he recognizes in his
conscience the clear call of the Good God, who is
supreme, and must, because He is what He is,
bring those who will accept His hard service to
true and final blessedness, and doom the rebel
spirits, and the men who do service to their evil
cause, to eternal perdition.

This is just the same clear and vivid message
as we find in Israel, though in Israel, throughout
the " classical " period of prophecy, the vindication of God is expected only in this world,
not in another " world to come," and (what is
much more important [1]) the message in Israel

---

[1] More important because the prophetic message in Israel also
culminated in the same belief about the world to come.

is not the message of a single individual, whose distinctive witness is speedily swallowed up in revived superstitions, as in the case of Zarathustra, but the continuous voice of a great succession of men whose authority, after long-continued rejection, wins a conspicuous victory and becomes ultimately enshrined in the whole literature and cultus of the people—a message, moreover, which, delivered " in many portions and many manners," reaches a sublime culmination in Jesus the Christ.

From Muhammad we heard what is fundamentally only an echo of the message of Israel prophets and of a debased Christianity, but delivered with astonishing power in a new atmosphere ; it is, however, on a much lower moral level than Christianity properly understood. Thus we shall lose nothing if we take Christianity, not only as the consummation of Israel's religion, but as the best and fullest representative of all the distinctive types of ethical monotheism which have appeared in history.

In China we found, deep in its confused traditions, the idea of the supreme Heaven " all-intelligent and observing." " The wise king must take it as his pattern." So he becomes " the fellow of God." And virtue passes down stage by stage to the whole of his people, whom " God loves." [1] Amidst a mass of non-moral superstitions, the idea of an ultimate divine sanction for morality appears in the teaching of the three Masters who are the boast of China —Lao-tse, Confucius and Mencius. In Lao-tse, although he took the Indian road of mysticism

[1] *Shu King*, iv, 8. 2 and 5. 3 ; *S.B.E.*, vol. iii, pp. 99 and 115.

and abstraction from the world, yet the root idea is that of the *tao*, the " way " or " order " which, like the " nature " of the Stoics, is the divine principle of the universe to which all things must conform ; and this same idea, in a much more practical and ethical form, under- lies the moral teaching of Confucius and his disciple Mencius. Confucius found himself in a world utterly disorganized, abounding in " religions " which had no moral force. He set himself therefore simply to restore morality —the essence of which he found in obedience to parents and just rulers, in reciprocity, chastity, honesty and truth. He assumes the conscious- ness of this " good " as inherent in man and as self-evidencing ; he is very shy of talking about spiritual beings and religious sanctions. Nevertheless, behind all human authority, he postulates a divine authority. Obedience and the other virtues have a divine sanction ; and these same assumptions, accompanied by the same reticence about religion, we found in Mencius—morality belongs to the divine ordering of the universe.

The great Greek moralists beginning with Socrates found themselves in the same position as the Chinese sages.[1] In restoring the moral standard among the Greeks they also could look for no help from the popular religions ; but they could appeal to the conscience of men

[1] And at approximately the same period of time. Both the Hebrew prophets and the Chinese sages, and the Greek moralists and the Buddha belong to (about) the middle of the first millennium, B.C.

as recognizing the absolute value of good—
τὸ καλόν as distinct from τὸ αἰσχρον. The good
life might turn out in experience to be the
happiest and the most profitable life, but it
was not to be reached by pursuing individual
pleasure or profit. Wisdom, justice, self-control
and courage have a self-evidencing claim on
man's allegiance, and their sanction lay in the
divine background. This divine background is
found in the Platonic doctrine of the eternal
principles or "forms" centring in the dominant
Principle of the Good, till Plato finally reaches
a positive theism—an affirmation of the one
God, the supreme creative soul, who is good,
and who cares for men, and demands of them
the practice of the good life in the fellowship
and service of the city-state.

In Greece we find the speculative and scientific
interest at its height. But not only in Socrates
and the Stoics, but also in Plato the moral and
social interest remains on the whole practically
supreme, and the mystical or contemplative
tendency is subordinated to the interest of ethical
and social duty.[1]

Platonism, then, may be our type of the ethical
philosophies which, without being so definitely
based on the belief in a personal God as Zoroastrianism or Islam or the religion of Israel or
of Jesus Christ, yet postulate and insist upon
the background of eternal principles or values
upon which the good life for man depends, and

[1] Aristotle more definitely exalts the speculative over the
practical life ; and in Plotinus and Neo-Platonism this tendency
triumphs.

which give it an absolute worth. I will call this the idealist doctrine as distinguished from that of the more definite monotheists.

One feature that must be noticed as common to all these ancient teachers is that, finding men degraded and discouraged by the haunting fear of hostile powers, seen and unseen, and piteously conscious of their own weakness, they sought to lift up their heads and inspire them with courage and a sense of their own dignity and worth by implanting in them a faith in the supremacy of goodness, and assuring them of the fellowship of the good man with what is invincible and divine. This gospel appears in its most appealing form, as based wholly upon belief in a personal living God, in Zarathustra and Muhammad, in the prophets of Israel and in Jesus Christ. It is the assurance that if men will fear God and keep His commandments they " have nothing else to fear." It is an assurance which is indissolubly linked with another—that the man who ignores the moral law has everything to fear—even ultimate ruin—so that " the fear of the Lord is the beginning of wisdom." It is impossible to exaggerate the extent to which mankind in most ages has been degraded and paralysed by the sense of weakness in the presence of formidable adversaries, visible and invisible, and equally impossible to deny that what has shown most power to ennoble him and lift up his head is this prophetic message about the will of God.

All the teachers we are considering would have men overcome the paralysing fear of evil powers by entertaining a nobler sort of fear. Plato

in this connection is sometimes content to
find this nobler and emancipating fear in the
dread of falling short of what the best of our
contemporaries expect of us—as Festus says
to Paracelsus, in Browning's poem :

> It should seem
> Impossible for me to fail, so watched.
>
> .   .   .   .   .   .
>
> If danger daunted me, or ease seduced,
> How calmly their sad eyes would gaze reproach.

But Plato at other times[1] and Zarathustra and
the prophets of Israel and Jesus Christ refuse to
let us rely upon even the highest kind of human
regard. Even the public opinion of the best
circle is not trustworthy.[2] Nothing avails to
emancipate us from the fear of the world and
of evil spirits except the fear of God—the sense
of His almightiness and goodness combined,
which can quiet our hearts in an immovable
courage even under the worst assaults and in
the most unsupported solitude.

The authority and influence of the teachers
we have been considering (still omitting India)
cover a vast area in the history of the world.
I believe we may go so far as to say that all the
world over, even among the most backward
tribes, the appeal to the moral law, as having
divine sanction—as a law laid on man by God

[1] See *Laws*, x, 904–6, addressed to young men who attribute
moral indifference to the gods.

[2] See John v. 44, addressed to the Pharisees, amongst whom
a very high and intense form of public opinion was the basis of
their moral blindness : " How can ye believe, which receive
honour one of another, and the honour which cometh from the
only God ye seek not ? "

—is responded to by the human conscience. Further, though the moral standards of tribes and periods have shown such startling differences as make it impossible to say absolutely that the conscience of man is the voice of God,[1] yet in the great teachers I have named there is a marked tendency to agreement in their conception of the *content*—as well as the authority—of the moral law ; and, if we may assume for the moment that the Christian conception of goodness is the completest and best, the general conscience of mankind seems to have welcomed it and responded to it wherever it has been proclaimed by evangelists who commanded respect.

At present, however, I only need to call attention to the impressive unity of witness among the ancient moral leaders and teachers of mankind, including those whose theism is not a distinct feature, to the doctrine that human life is a good and not an evil thing, though it involves an often fierce struggle ; and that though the good life may be, and indeed is, in the long run the happiest and the most advantageous, yet it is not to be measured by considerations of pleasure and profit as they present themselves to the judgment of the individual at any moment, for that mankind is " under authority," authority which is eternal and divine, but which, if men will open their hearts to it, they will find written also in their own consciences.

[1] The Jewish term Bath-Qol, " the Daughter of the Voice " (of God), is, as Wordsworth perceived, a better description of conscience—which man has the power to stifle or sophisticate till " the light that is in him " becomes " darkness."

There is in an ancient Latin collect (which in the English Prayer Book version [1] is found sadly weakened in force), a prayer that " we who cannot exist without God, may have strength to live according to God," which embodies this philosophy of human life. Man is prone to claim a false independence, as if he had the fashioning of his own destiny according to his own fancy. But this is a ridiculous claim to a sort of freedom which has no real existence. Man is dependent, whether he likes it or not, on the Power which encompasses and controls him. In it he lives and moves and has his being. And this Power is realized in the human conscience as holiness and goodness; and also as having given to man the perilous dignity of a conditioned freedom, whereby he must choose either to rebel against the moral law to his destruction, or to rejoice in its service to his salvation. This therefore is man's proper prayer—that, as he cannot exist without God, so he may live in accordance with God. That is the sort of prayer which is enforced upon us by the consentient voice of these great teachers of antiquity. I will add another testimony, as to the real character of moral freedom, to which again I would claim their unanimous assent. " That man is free whose flesh is controlled by the law of his mind, and whose mind is directed by the government of God." [2] Man's true freedom— that is his power to realize his true being—lies in the control of his passions by his reason or will; but this reason or will, if it claims for

[1] Ninth Sunday after Trinity.   [2] St. Leo the Great.

itself a false independence, becomes only a deeper source of disorder. It gains its legitimate mastery only in glad submission to the higher law, which it has the power to recognize with sufficient clearness as a guide for conduct.

It follows of course from what has just been said that these moral leaders of mankind, whose records are under our consideration, are unanimous in their utter refusal to put the moral question to the vote. They exhibit a contempt for majorities, and look to the faithful few to maintain the standard of the right with an assurance of final victory.

Lastly, it must not be left out of sight that the unanimity among the ancients is the unanimity of independent witnesses. That of course could not be said of Muhammad. He did undoubtedly learn his belief in the one God from the Jews and Christians, and Jesus Christ did of course take His stand upon the teaching of the Hebrew prophets; but it is in the fullest sense true that Zarathustra and the teachers of China and the teachers of Greece and the prophets of Israel were quite ignorant one of another; their teaching, with the practice which it inculcated, established itself in each case on its own basis without external assistance.[1] At later stages of development Zoroastrianism may have influenced the religion of Israel and the religion of Christianity become fused with the philosophic tradition of Greece; but in their earliest de-

[1] See De Burgh, *The Legacy of the Ancient World* (an admirable survey), pp. 24 and 40. This for Israel and Greece. No one would doubt the independence of Iran and China as represented in Zarathustra and Confucius.

velopment (and it is only that which we have been considering) they were wholly independent.

§ 2

In this review of the historical survey I have omitted India. For reasons which I have explained we can expect to find, neither in the philosophies nor in the religions of India, any consistent theory of moral obligation or any consistent doctrine of the good life. The highest religious level reached is in the idea of devotion (*bhakti*) to some personal incarnation of the Divine. In this a mystical rapture is attainable by the individual soul; but there is no ethical standard arrived at or proclaimed for the common life of man. There are immoral incarnations to be found as well as those that are edifying. In the teaching of the Buddha we do indeed get a moral way of the utmost severity proclaimed for those who seek enlightenment; but the secret which Gotama had discovered and imparted to his disciples was the secret that life itself is an evil, not a good; and that the way of wisdom is to seek escape from the wheel of life by the remorseless annihilation of desire—not merely of evil desires, but of desire as such—so that the individual soul may escape from the curse by extinction. Thus original Buddhism can supply us with no doctrine of the good life (properly so-called) for man and no idea of the redemption *of* human life, but only with a method of redemption *from* life. It turns its back on all the fundamental human interests and hopes. It is true that Gotama also

14

preached a lower doctrine for the laymen—that is, those who had not the courage to embark on the true quest—by which they could hope to win a better state in some future life, and that this is all that the Buddhism of other lands than Buddha's own has sought; and that, while it has merged itself, in defiance of its founder, in surrounding idolatries and forms of magic, and become a ritualistic religion, it has retained certain characteristics of quietism, mildness and gentleness due to his teaching.[1]   But its foundation in the teaching of Gotama disqualifies it from presenting human life as a good thing capable of redemption. We must then leave out India in our survey of the idea of the good life, as being disqualified by a fundamental pessimism or moral indifference.[2]

§ 3

Our review of the idea of the good life, as it presents itself in the history of mankind, leaves us

[1] " Wherever Buddhism is [in any measure] true to the spirit of its founder, it promotes the difficult art of meditation, and the kindly and compassionate spirit "—Kenneth Saunders, *Buddhism* (Benn). I have introduced the words in brackets because it would seem that Buddhism is nowhere true to the fundamental motive of its founder.

[2] I cannot resist the impression that if India is to find the principle of moral renewal, it must look for help to something outside its own tradition, whether of religion or philosophy. On the other hand, China presents a different picture. In the Classical doctrine of Heaven, in the idea of the *tao*, and even in ancestor-worship, there is a tradition, though at this moment of her history it may be sorely imperilled, on which moral redemption, individual and social, may be built. To phrase this as a Christian believer would phrase it, there is, in the Chinese tradition, as there was in the Græco-Roman tradition, a " tutor to bring men to Christ "

face to face with a deeply significant fact—that mankind has over a very wide area and through long ages recognized the reality of an absolute moral obligation—has acknowledged not only what is but what ought to be, and not only desire and power but duty. Mankind appears, of course, most obviously and most universally, as striving for its own maintenance and enrichment out of the store-house of nature, in obedience to the vital appetite which lies at the root of his being. In this struggle with external nature the interest of the tribe or family appears to precede the interest of the individual considered apart. The old idea, so prevalent down to the eighteenth century, that the interest of the individual was the primal motive, and the interest of the group a later restriction, has been abandoned. It is recognized that the interest of the individual is a later differentiation. But the struggle for the welfare of the group does not demand any other explanation than the motive of self-preservation. The sacrifice of the individual to the group can be explained by the absence of any clear sense of individual personality. The group is, to start with, the unit of selfish regard.

But the more clearly the individual comes to be distinguished, or to distinguish himself, from the group, the more clearly comes into view the contrast and conflict between his own pleasure or profit and that of the group that he belongs to ; and there accompanies this emergent contrast and conflict the sense of duty—that the individual *ought* to subordinate his own interest to the general welfare. Moreover, side by side with man's relation to his tribe, there has been developing his crude religion—his sense of spirits or personal beings good or bad, beneficent or harmful, to whose power he is more or less accessible, whom he must propitiate, or against whom he must defend himself.   In this direction also the sense of obligation—that he ought or ought not to do so and so—develops.   It might be supposed that this sense of obligation is no more than a reflection of self-interest—that at bottom it is no more than the feeling that, if he neglects his recognized duty towards his tribe or towards his gods, he will suffer for it ; and that as mankind grows in intelligence he will reinterpret this haunting feeling of obligation into its real constituents, and realize Epicurus' ideal of the emancipated man—emancipated from all the fear of gods, or any other restrictive sense of obligation, except the restriction which his own common sense or perception of probable consequences imposes upon his clamorous appetites.

But this imaginary construction of human development, which has constantly reappeared in philosophical speculation, is destined to receive a decisive check.   It is the history of this check that we have been considering.   The upward development of man—which is apparent in history side by side with the experience of the deterioration of individuals and the collapse of civilizations—shows the idea of duty, as something of absolute value, establishing itself under the leadership of the prophets and sages of mankind.   It establishes itself in two forms, as we have seen—in the form of a definite ethical

monotheism, as duty to the one good God. This
is the form in which it appears in the teaching of
Zarathustra and of Muhammad and of the
Hebrew prophets and of Jesus Christ—whose
teaching we are taking as the type of ethical monotheism. It establishes itself also in the form of
what we have called ethical idealism, in which the
law or principle of moral goodness is recognized
as an absolute value, while the personal God
is less definitely acknowledged, and of this
ethical idealism we are taking Platonism as the
type, in the vaguer use of this term. But both
schools agree in the recognition of the absolute
authority of the moral law and the absolute value
of duty, and appeal to it (in spite of the heedless-
ness, selfishness and rebellion of the masses of
mankind) as something sure to vindicate itself
in the long run—for its authority lies in the very
roots of being. This is the fact which confronts
us as the conclusion of our survey.[1]

It is also to be noticed that the absolute
valuation of goodness, as an end in itself, does
not stand alone. Beside it is the absolute
valuation of truth and beauty. Beside the
prophets stand the philosophers and men of
science, who seek truth for its own sake, and
without regard to whatever advantage may
accrue to mankind from their investigations, and

---

[1] Prof. Elliot Smith is surely right in forcing upon our attention
the enormous influence upon human development of individual
men. "The great events in Human History were provoked by
individual human beings exercising their wills to change the
directions of human thought and action, or by natural catastrophes
forcing men of insight to embark on new enterprises" (*Hist. of
Man*, p. 60 ; cf. p. 100),

also the artists who maintain the absolute value of beauty. It may be true that the desire for knowledge, wholly for its own sake, is secondary in time to the desire for knowledge in order that man's life may be thereby better protected and furnished, but it is equally true that it rises high above the utilitarian bed in which it has grown as an end in itself, something sacred and eternal which man is unworthy of his destiny if he refuses to worship. Perhaps even more obviously is this true of beauty. That, too, may be secondary to use in the historical record of man's quest, but it is secondary only in time. It has an absolute value. In this respect truth, beauty and goodness stand side by side, refusing to be analysed into anything other than themselves ; and all ultimately making the same claim upon mankind. In a measure they exist as realized objects ; in another sense they are unrealized ideals, but ideals demanding realization by our efforts. And this is pre-eminently true of goodness. Its claim is obviously, as things stand, an unrealized claim, both within us and without. If it be a claim inherent in the nature of things, then undoubtedly we must conceive of nature as the scene of an unrealized purpose, with which it is our duty to correspond, and which it is man's supreme privilege to further.

This gives mankind a unique position in the world. Alone among visible creatures he appears as a responsible being engaged in a struggle for divine principles or purposes, the realization of which appears as precarious and as dependent upon his efforts. Even in remote days the mind of a poet-prophet could be overwhelmed with the sense of contrast between man's grand and divinely given destiny and his physical smallness or feebleness. " What is man that Thou art mindful of him, or the son of man that thou regardest him ? " And in a much later day the increased knowledge of the inconceivable vastness of the universe has smitten the soul of a Pascal, and of many other men of more ordinary mental stature, with a chill of terror. To-day it is frequently urged as a plea for refusing to entertain the prerogative place assigned to man in the religious or classical tradition. But this is really irrational. The vast spaces of the stellar universe are unknown to us. What unseen hosts of intelligent beings may people the stars we cannot conjecture. What we are bound to entertain are the considerations forced upon us by what we can know; and within the compass of our possible knowledge man remains the sole being who can be recognized as the conscious vice-gerent of God or responsible co-operator with a divine plan and purpose.

I may quote the conclusion of Prof. Eddington's consideration of man's place in the universe : " I do not think," he says,[1] " that the whole purpose of the Creation has been staked on the one planet where we live ; and in the long run we cannot deem ourselves the only race which has been or will be gifted with the mystery of consciousness. But I feel inclined to claim that *at the present time* our race is supreme ; and not one of the profusion of stars in their myriad

[1] *The Nature of the Physical World,* p. 178.

clusters looks down on scenes comparable to those which are passing beneath the rays of the sun."

§ 4

I shall, of course, be reminded that the teachers of the good life for man, whose doctrine has been under review, all belong to a more or less remote antiquity, and that the modern man and woman will not be content to look back to such antiquated standards and authorities. Now I should in this respect draw a distinction between the standards and authorities which have been under review.

But may I incidentally raise a protest against the habit which seems to me to prevail to a lamentable extent (even among that portion of the reading public of to-day which studies serious literature) of reading almost nothing but books of the day? (I am leaving poetry out of the question, in which I suppose there is still more attention paid to the ancients.) Science progresses, and fashions change—in some ages like our own with great rapidity. To read the books of the day ministers, no doubt, to the extension of knowledge, and to the intellectual curiosity which desires a succession of fresh excitements.[1] But it does not commonly minister to the establishment of stable convictions for life. Yet behind all the changes in the human outlook and all the developments of knowledge, which produce such sharp contrasts between

[1] There is an admirable passage at the beginning of the Preface to Butler's *Sermons* (dated 1729) which is certainly as applicable to-day as it could ever have been two hundred years ago.

that it is only the developed product which can show us the real meaning of all that led up to it. We are bound to discern in nature a gradually emergent purpose which becomes evident only in rational man, and, within the circle of rationality, in the consciousness of " the values "— of truth and beauty and goodness—as having absolute worth, and laying men under an absolute obligation.

Ethical monotheism, as represented in Christianity and ethical idealism, which has no such definite embodiment, but which has been closely allied with Christianity, since its first promulgation in the days of the Roman Empire, are certainly still living forces, which no one has a right to call antiquated. It is true that the Christian Church, as an historical institution in East and West, both under Catholicism and under Protestantism, has at several periods of history and in many respects been tried at the bar of man's free moral judgment, and been found wanting as a practical guide in social and individual morality ; it is true that to-day, in consequence of this seeming failure of the Church, there is a strong feeling in our modern world against what is called " institutionalism " ; but for the most part the consequent outcry has not been against Christianity but against certain presentations of Christianity regarded as corrupt, and the appeal has been, not forward to some new standard of living, but " back to Christ."

The Church has been taken to task, not because the pattern set by its founder was shown to be at fault, but because it has misrepresented it or deserted it ; and the indignant protest has been largely justified. Those who have been most scornful in their rejection of the dogmatic authority of the Church have, till quite recently, insisted that they were still zealous to maintain the Christian ethical standard. It would be easy to multiply quotations from John Stuart Mill and Huxley and John Morley [1] and George Eliot to this effect. There has been, in fact, no great moral teacher since Christ who has propounded a new standard or moral law for human life which has entered into rivalry with His with any wide effectiveness. What has been effectively done is to convince a great body of deep-thinking people that modern civilization calling itself Christian is, in fact, by no means worthy of the name and needs very radical reconstruction if it is in the future to become worthy of it. But the appeal has been still to Christ.

There has, however, been a revolt, of which we feel the full force to-day, which is really a revolt alike against the authority of Christ, and against the authority of the whole idealist tradition, and which had its origin mainly in the influence of Jean Jacques Rousseau. This is what we may call the philosophy of emotionalism, or self-expression. Rousseau revolted against all moral standards and conventions and all types of intellectual or religious authority. He believed in the fundamental goodness of unsophisticated

---

[1] I would refer especially to his *Voltaire* (1872), pp. 149 ff. and cap. v. : " The worst church that has ever prostituted the name and the idea of religion cannot be so disastrous to society as can a gospel that systematically relaxes self-control."

man if he were only left to express his natural feelings without external restraint.[1]   Qualifications of this doctrine of unrestrained emotionalism appear in his writings (especially in his idea of " the general will " as a necessary restraint on individualism), but that the main drift of his philosophy is of this sort is undeniable.   The great Goethe in Germany, in his earlier writings, shows the same tendency, but later it is checked by the demand for self-control and self-limitation, or " dying to live." [2]

In effect Rousseau's philosophy of life has allied itself with the otherwise utterly alien movement of modern industrialism—in the sense that the latter has also claimed the complete emancipation of its activities from theocratic control.   It is in this sense that Rousseauism has found powerful expression in the thought

[1] See App. Note, p. 226.

[2] The reaction in Goethe's mind is to be seen in the poem *Selige Sehnsucht* (see *Gedichte in Zeitlicher Folge*, Bd. ii, p. 56):

> Und so lang du das nicht hast,
> Dieses—Stirb und werde !
> Bist du nur ein trüber Gast
> Auf der dunkeln Erde.

(In prose, " So long as the maxim *You must die to live* has not got hold of you, you are but a sad stranger upon the gloomy earth.")

There is another verse, cited in Irving Babbitt's *Rousseau and Romanticism*, p. 363 :

> In der Beschränkung zeight sich erst der Meister,
> Und das Gesetz nur kann uns Freiheit geben.

But I cannot run it to earth ; nor the following : " Anything which emancipates the spirit without a corresponding growth in self-mastery is pernicious."   But I have no doubt they are genuine Goethe.

of such men of wide influence as Nietzsche and Walt Whitman. It is still finding expression in manifold forms and on the widest scale in the post-war literature of almost all countries. It is fundamentally a rebellion against the whole intellectual and ethical tradition, both of Christianity and of Platonism. Both Christianity and Platonism meet it with what is substantially the same answer, in spite of marked difference both in emphasis and in intellectual presuppositions. The answer is in effect this. A man is born with no ready-made self or soul for which he is entitled to demand expression as it stands. He is born with a bundle of instincts, emotions, passions, with faculties of sensation, memory, reason, imagination, will, which are the materials of a self of infinite worth. But the free being is entrusted with the fashioning of his own self for good or evil out of these materials, both by industriously developing their capacities and also by bringing them under a unified control. For anyone to allow unrestrained freedom of expression to his emotions or passions, as he finds them, is disastrous alike to himself and to his fellow-men. It is to lose or destroy his own soul and to promote the ruin of society. On the other hand, in the process of self-realization by self-control a man becomes conscious that he is not his own master—he is under authority. This is in part the authority of human society, of parents or State or Church, which may be misguided. But there is a higher authority of which he becomes conscious, which is properly divine, and inheres in the nature of things and expresses itself (more or less perfectly) in the moral law—to repudiate which is to repudiate the noblest part of his human heritage. To lay the reins on the neck of his emotions will not lead any human being to true liberty. That man only saves his soul or becomes truly a free man who both seeks to bring all his faculties under the control of the rational will and also his own will under the control of the society, which has for its end the good life of man, and above all under the control of the divine law to which his own conscience and the social conscience bear witness.

§ 5

There are very few of us who can seriously contemplate the philosophy (if it ought so to be called) which has its roots in Rousseau's emotionalism, either in its intellectual presupposition or its practical consequences, without revolting from it—without a strong conviction that no good life for man can be built upon it. But if so, there is abundant need that the intellectual presuppositions of the classical and the Christian traditions, both as allied to one another or distinguished from one another, should be investigated not only by the professed philosopher, but by the man of ordinary intelligence. We need to confront the world not only with good intentions, but with intellectual convictions. We need reassurance that the foundations of the traditional ethic are really rational. But it is impossible for me in the four lectures that remain to me to attempt to cover the whole field. I do not repent of having spent so large a proportion of the time allotted to me in the historical survey; but I must accept the consequences. I propose, then, to leave to others the vindication of ethical idealism in its general sense. It has been done with critical precision and sureness of grasp by Dr. Sorley, in his work which I have already referred to, which should be considered a classic. I should like to refer also to the recent works of J. E. Turner[1]; but I will not enlarge the list, though we have many vindicators of the authority of "the Values" to-day.

But it is obvious that while the presuppositions of ethical idealism are also the presuppositions of the Christian ethical tradition, the latter go farther than the former. Christianity is not content to name the name of God in the vague sense in which it was used of old by Stoics and Platonists or is used in contemporary idealism. It insists especially upon His personality and His transcendence as creator of all that is. It is specially to the question of the intellectual justification of these Christian presuppositions concerning God that I want to apply myself, and to ask your attention, in the next lecture; for contemporary idealism largely rejects them.

Again, Christianity has its own distinctive presuppositions about man, his freedom and his sin, which lead on to a conception of human nature which may be called pessimistic, because

[1] See the *Basis of Moral Obligation* and *Personality and Reality*. In Walter Lippmann's *Preface to Morals* we have from a definitely non-theistic standpoint a powerful presentation of actual moral tendencies in America and (more or less) in Europe, and an attempted reconstruction of the moral standard.

it presents the world as it stands as largely in
revolt against God, and in result as something
utterly different from the world as God would
have it.   But the pessimism passes into a glow-
ing optimism through the conviction of a divine
purpose of redemption which is finally to take
full effect.   To these Christian presuppositions
about man and his relation to the universe, I
shall ask your attention in the tenth lecture.

There is also always apparent in Christianity
the assumption of a special divine self-disclosure
or Revelation—an idea distinguishable though
not separable from the idea of the world, as a
whole, as the manifestation of God—and against
this idea of a positive Revelation modern idealism
has deeply rebelled ; thus the rationality of this
conception will demand candid enquiries.   That
will be the subject of the eleventh lecture.

Finally, we shall find ourselves with a certain
conception of a reasonable faith as representing
man's proper attitude towards the world ;   an
idea which differentiates itself on the one hand
from the kind of intellectualism which will take
no step forward without positive demonstration ;
and on the other from the sort of faith which can
fairly be called uncritical credulity.   In the last
lecture, then, I shall seek to vindicate the position
of reasonable faith, as against scepticism on the
one side, and superstition or dogmatism on the
other, and to define the contents of the Christian
ethic and its implied theology as the expression
of this reasonable faith.

I proceed, then, to discuss the intellectual
validity of the specifically Christian presupposi-

15

tions on the basis of an assumption that as against materialism, hedonism or positivism, idealism has already won an intellectual victory, which can be taken for granted.

APPENDED NOTE

ON MR. H. J. MASSINGHAM'S " GOLDEN AGE—THE STORY OF HUMAN NATURE "

Rousseau believed in the glory of primitive man before he had been sophisticated by civilization, and argued that, if man to-day were liberated from the shackles of authority, secular and religious, the primitive nature could again assert itself in its pristine beauty and freedom. This same conception of primitive man is being revived in the school of anthropology represented by Prof. Elliot Smith (*op. cit.,* pp. 180 f., 199) and Mr. Massingham. I do not wish to argue as to whether there is evidence of this Golden Age of man in a præ-historic period, which has survived, among tribes which escaped the first rudiments of civilization, even to our time. But it appears that this beautiful and innocent original manhood could not endure the least tincture of civilization. The very beginnings of agriculture sufficed for its undoing. To-day we have to do with a humanity which has undergone the influences of civilization for many thousands of years, and it is of this humanity that we have direct and constant experience. To suggest, then, that man as we now know him can trust his undisciplined instincts to guide him aright is to suggest what is, I think, obviously false.

CHAPTER IX

THE CHRISTIAN IDEA OF GOD

THIS, then, is the complex question which now confronts us—the Christian religion, which is here taken as the highest type of ethical monotheism, postulates, as its heritage from the religion of Israel, the one personal God, eternal and self-complete, the absolute creator of all that is, immanent in the whole creative process, but also transcendent, perfect in goodness as in wisdom and power, and awful in holiness, the judge and rewarder of all free spirits, pervading His creation by His providence, and guiding all things onward to the assured victory of good. It makes this further postulate—that this one God, while never in His essential perfection fully comprehensible to finite intelligence, yet has been in gradual process revealing Himself in sufficient measure to the conscience and intelligence of men, until this self-revelation reached its climax in Jesus Christ, at once perfect man and the adequate "image of God."

On the other hand many modern idealists of different schools, while agreeing in maintaining the name and idea of God, object to the attribution to Him of personality, as being an anthropomorphic conception ; and also of such transcendence and self-completeness as is implied in the idea of the absolute creator.[1]   They would have us regard the world as being as necessary to God as God is to the world ; or if they shrink from going so far in identifying God with the world, they bid us think of God as the name for all the sum of ideal values—truth, beauty, goodness—which emerge in the process of evolution as elements in Reality, which is spiritual as well as material ; and, while thus regarding the universe as a whole as in some sense the revelation or self-expression of God, they would decline to ascribe to God any such particular intention to reveal Himself along a definite historical line, or any such particular redemptive action, or any such final disclosure of Himself in a particular historical person, as the Christian monotheism postulates.

Now, the latter part of this large contention between rival intellectual claimants is reserved

---

[1] The question whether God is to be identified with the Absolute seems to be, from the Christian point of view, a verbal question.   Undoubtedly the Absolute may be so identified with the totality of being as to result in a pure pantheism, so that whatever occurs in the universe must be ascribed to God, whether it be good or evil.   On the other hand a Christian philosophy, while it must identify God with the Absolute in the sense that whatever exists exists by His creative will and depends on Him for its continuance in being (" In Him we live and move and are "), yet must draw a distinction.   There is indeed no rival source or ground of existence other than God.   But He has willed to create and maintain in being free spirits, and in them at least there is a relative independence, and their actions may be, and in fact have been, in flat contradiction to the will of God.   And this may be regarded as a limitation on His absoluteness, though a self-caused limitation.   Thus whether God can be identified with the Absolute is a matter for the definition of terms.

for a later lecture (XI).   In this lecture we are
only concerned with the ideas of the personality,
the unity and the transcendence of the one God,
the creator; we are to consider, negatively, the
idealist objections to these conceptions, and
positively we are to enquire which of the two
groups of ideas has the juster claim to be called
rational.   The notions involved are those of
(1) the personality of God; (2) His unity;
(3) His absolute priority and self-completeness;
(4) the conception of absolute creation.

§ 1

But before proceeding to consider these four
points in detail, I must ask you to recognize how
intimately the recognition of the group of ideas
just enumerated, which find their best expression in the Christian religion, is associated
in history with the actual moral advance of
mankind.   The leaders of this advance, Zarathustra, Plato, the prophets of Israel and Jesus
Christ, have demanded the inseparable union of
religion with morality;   and this merging of
religion in morality or ethical conduct has always
involved—as we have seen even in Plato—
the giving greater definiteness to the idea of
God.

We are not here concerned with the origins
of religion.   Thus I need not argue the question
raised by Otto whether the " numinous sense,"
the sense of the tremendous mystery, at once
terrifying and alluring, which is, no doubt, a most
important element in religion, arose out of the
belief in personal spirits or was prior to it as its

ground [1] ; but we are bound to recognize that religion, when it appears in history, is not generally what we can call " ethical " in its ideas or effects.[2] The accompaniments and rites of primitive religion are mostly non-ethical. That is chiefly what we mean when we call them superstitions. Religion again, in its mystical form, as it appears in India, can develop itself to a high intellectual level, while retaining its ethical indifference—thinking of God as above good or evil. It is the moral prophets, such as those just named, who have demanded the inseparable union of religion with character, and the conscience of the best part of mankind has responded to their demand ; and, wherever the alliance or unification of religion and morality has been accomplished, it has carried with it a rationalizing and clarifying of the religious ideas. It has demanded the recognition of the personal and righteous God, and His unquestionable moral sovereignty, and the manifestation of His righteous will. The pantheon has been purged of pluralism, in being purged of moral indifference, or of the mixture among the gods of good or bad ; and the righteous God, whose authority is experienced in conscience, has been elevated absolutely above the world.

Recognizing in the Christian religion the example of this process carried to its highest

---

[1] *Idea of the Holy*, p. 15.

[2] If you include in the term ethical all that belongs to human conduct, then indeed all religions must be called ethical. But we rightly restrict the term ethical to what demands a particular type of character, and not merely particular actions conforming to " the manner of the God of the land."

level,[1] we must admit that there, as nowhere else, the best moral aspirations of men can find their satisfaction. They find it in the idea of God, the one, the creator, the judge, the father, manifesting Himself in His prophets and in His Son, communicating Himself by His Spirit, taking men up here and now into intimate fellowship with Himself and with His purpose in creation, and yet bidding them regard this tumultuous life as only the first stage of their experience, a place of soul-making and also of kingdom-building, whereof the assured fruit and fulfilment lies in the Beyond.

In this teaching about God the soul of man, as represented in its moral aspirations, finds at once profound encouragement and severe chastisement ; it gains at once the deepening of the sense of sin and also of the sense of freedom to move and vigour to advance ; it enters into possession of a wealth of motives and a storehouse of power ; and what, for the mass of mankind, is an incalculable boon, it has constantly before it the embodiment of the moral ideal and standard in a living person, Jesus Christ. Many of those who have stood outside the Christian faith on intellectual grounds have recognized all this, and have expressed in pathetic language their sense of loss in not being able, as honest men, to repeat this creed ; while others, more dangerously, have strained their intellectual conscience so as to use a language of devotion which is more than their intellectual convictions warrant.

[1] Otto, *op. cit.*, p. 146.

The late Dr. F. H. Bradley bade us freely take
for granted all " the ideas which best express
our highest religious needs and their satisfaction,"
for they " must certainly be true "—but " ultimate truth they do not possess." The ideas that
are to express the practical requirements of
religion " must be more or less inconsistent, and
in a word mythological." [1] Now, later on (Lecture
XII) we shall be recognizing that our knowledge of things terrestrial, and still more of
things celestial, is relative and not absolute.
We see at the best but " through a glass darkly."
But surely we are bound to keep our religious
creed on the highest level of truth that we can
attain to in our present state of existence.

It is lowering the standard of truthfulness to
suggest that we can use for the purposes of religion a language which we know to be less true
than it might be, or a language that we know to
be inconsistent with science or history or metaphysical enquiry. It seems to me to be wholly
impossible for a man, who is both a religious man
and also a scientific student, to use with sincerity
one language in his studies and a language
inconsistent with that in his prayers and professions of faith. Such inconsistency can only
result in his using the traditional language for
convention's sake or for the edification of others,
while he speaks to his own soul and to his more
intimate fellows in another non-mythological
language. I cannot but believe that Jesus
Christ would have called such duplicity of speech
and thought hypocrisy. Plato surely falls from

[1] See Bradley's *Essays on Truth and Reality*, pp. 430–432.

his highest level when he discusses the possibility of persuading the common people once for all to believe a " noble lie," just as he falls similarly in another direction when, in the organization of his commonwealth, he substitutes compulsion for persuasion, and institutes his court of inquisition to administer death or imprisonment to the heretics. What we are bound to consider with all sincerity is whether the ideas about God which our ethical aspirations postulate are, intellectually considered, also the most rational that we can form, and compatible with all that science, history and metaphysical enquiry can teach us. Prof. W. Wallace is surely right when he bids us remember that " in the long run a truth in theology indifferent to a truth in science is intolerable to humanity." [1]

And on this great problem we are bound to exercise our own minds. These lectures, as given under the will of the Founder, are to embody the principle of free thought ; and to think freely means that, while giving all due deference to the authority of philosophers—and they are very far from agreement among themselves—we must refuse simply to accept the verdict of a school among them in place of our own considered judgment, so far as we have the opportunity to form one. Free thought means this in the school of philosophy as much as in the school of theology.

§ 2

Now, I believe that we all have, in different degrees, no doubt, but really, the faculty necessary

[1] *Lectures on Natural Theology*, pp. 84, 563.

for forming a judgment in the matter now in question. I believe also that if my hearers will examine themselves they will find that the conception of absolute values, and especially of moral values, as an essential element in reality, independent of our personal realization of them, is a conception inseparable from that of mind and purpose in nature as a whole, which is (in part) what we mean by God. That Right can absolutely claim the allegiance of all men is an idea which only a responsible, thinking and willing person can entertain. If, then, there inheres in the nature of things this absolute claim, this must mean that in the nature of things there subsists a righteous mind and will— that is, something not less than supreme personality.

Speaking for myself, I find that I cannot extricate myself from this conclusion. I cannot attach a meaning to moral values except as values for a person. It is perhaps hardly less obvious that the conception of truth as an absolute value, making an absolute claim on every intellect, cannot be otherwise interpreted than as the claim of a supreme mind who knows and wills truth—that is, a personal being. Once more the conception and feeling of beauty is something which only a mind or spirit can entertain.[1] But though the minds of all men can, more or less richly, entertain it, it is not the product of their individual minds : it inheres somehow in nature. Nature provides the ma-

---

[1] If animals can appreciate beauty, that is only so far as they approach towards personality.

terials which evoke the latent sense of beauty—
materials on which the human mind can respon-
sively work and on which it absolutely depends
to enable it to work. In J. B. Mozley's famous
phrase, " Nature . . . in the very act of
labouring as a machine is also sleeping as a
picture." [1]   This means in other words that
there is that in nature which corresponds to our
sensibility to beauty—which *intends* beauty,
as it intends goodness and truth—though
alike goodness, truth and beauty are at present
mainly unrealized ideals ; and what can that
be but a personal spirit of beauty, as of truth
and goodness ?

Plato at one period of his thought certainly
imagined a world of self-subsistent universals—
the " forms " or models of all the objects apparent
in the world of sensible experience (of concrete
objects as well as of values such as the virtues)
centring in the Form of the Good—without
any definite theism. Later, as we have seen, he
subjected this imagination to criticism, and it
vanishes from his later dialogues ; and finally,
in the *Timæus* he becomes definitely theistic
and postulates the Supreme Soul, the one
creative God, who fashions the world in accordance with certain mathematical and ethical
principles. I suppose that we all, with Aristotle,
reject Plato's earlier and cruder imagination.
But I dare to say that we ought no less decisively
to reject the modern conception of values as
somehow inherent in nature without personifica-
tion. Truth, beauty and goodness are surely

[1] Mozley's *University Sermons*, p. 139.

not otherwise really conceivable by us than as qualities of a personal being.

This I certainly affirm to be true of myself, and I believe the vast majority of thinking persons will give the same verdict, if they can summon courage to give a verdict at all.

It is said, of course, that this is mere anthropomorphism. Now, it must be acknowledged that mankind inevitably thinks anthropomorphically, that is, thinks as man, and thus dangerously tends to make God in its own image. That was the fault of the Greek pantheon, and the fault which the Hebrew psalmist derides when he represents God as protesting, " Thou thoughtest wickedly that I am even such a one as thyself." Equally man thinks anthropomorphically about animals, and falls thereby into sentimental delusions—but nevertheless with a certain justification in so far as the animal soul appears to be akin to the human, and an anticipation of it. Dr. Streeter also truly remarks that science itself cannot avoid anthropomorphism, as in the expression " potential energy," which appears to be as really anthropomorphic as the term " force " which it was intended to replace.[1] The fact is that we cannot think at all except on the assumption that the mind of man corresponds to cosmic reality—to mind in the universe. But essentially, and as used by those who think and speak carefully, the language about the personal God presented to us by ethical monotheism is not anthropomorphic language about God but theomorphic language about man. It expresses the

[1] Streeter's *Reality*, p. 19.

idea that nature reflects God, carried up to the highest point. For physical energy must express or reflect God [1]; animal life also in a higher degree; but the best and fullest reflection or expression of God must be found in nature's highest product—moral personality. True it is that personality in us men is limited by external and internal conditions, and is an imperfect thing, only in process of realization; while the personality we ascribe to God is, if in any sense limited, yet only self-limited, and perfect from the beginning—you may call it, if you will, super-personality. But it remains true that the conception of a supremely personal being, though it certainly transcends human faculties of imagination, is as really a postulate of the reasoning man as it is of the ethical and wor-shipping man—if, that is, spiritual values are to be kept in mind as essential elements of the real.

The only way to escape this conclusion is, it appears to me, the way of pure subjectivism—by which I mean the doctrine that we know (if knowledge it can be called) nothing but the con-tents of our own private minds—a position which cuts at the root of any knowledge of objects in nature independent of us, or of our fellow-men, as much as of God—indeed, it cuts at the root of any knowledge of a real subsistent self. That is a radical agnosticism of which I shall have something more to say in my last lecture. It is,

---

[1] The old Christian hymn for the Ninth Hour begins by the invocation of God as " the persistent energy of things " (*Deus rerum tenax vigor*).

as I think, a denial of the fundamental faith which lies at the basis of all rationality.[1]

§ 3

Now we must pass to the conceptions of the transcendence, self-completeness, unity, and absolute priority of God.

As I have said, there can be no doubt that in proportion as religion among mankind passes to higher levels and joins in indissoluble association with morality, it postulates for the God whom it both worships and serves an unconditional supremacy. It finds in conscience an inner witness to such a supremacy—the supremacy of the one good God. We see this tendency at work in China and Greece, but more obviously in Zoroastrianism and in Muhammadanism and in the religion of Israel. But we find it as a settled conviction in its highest form in the religion of Christ. The absoluteness of God is not indeed there presented in so crude a form as in Muhammadanism—for His transcendence is conditioned by His immanence in nature and man : I mean especially that the recognition of the witness of God in the conscience of man prevents the ascription to Him of what violates the postulates of the conscience. " The being of God " to which conscience bears witness must be " a kind of law to His working." If His power is over and in all things, yet He cannot do everything.[2] He cannot be unjust. He cannot deny Himself.

---

[1] See below, pp. 323 f.

[2] Etymologically, the Latin word *omnipotens*, and the Greek παντοκράτωρ, mean " powerful in or over all things," not " able to do anything."

Thus in the Old Testament the drama of the Book of Job, culminating in the final approval of Job by God, is a magnificent vindication of the right of man to challenge the divine justice in the light of his own conscience ; and elsewhere in the Old Testament God is represented as appealing to man to recognize that He has behaved towards him both justly and mercifully. In the Gospels nothing is more impressive than the reserve of Jesus in the expression of sheer authority, and His constant appeal to the conscience and reason of common men to recognize for truth what He is telling them. There is a famous passage in the Epistle to the Romans where St. Paul appears to speak of God's omnipotent will as if it were arbitrary and absolute,[1] but it is commonly forgotten that he goes on to correct such an idea in the argument which follows. It must be found ultimately conformable to justice as man at his best conceives it.

There are passages in the writings of two contemporary German teachers who are exercising a great and widespread influence—I mean Otto and Karl Barth—where the emphasis is laid so heavily on the " otherness " of God as to suggest that they have overlooked that the voice of God from without or from above must correspond with His voice from within the heart of man in his conscience and reason. But while this misunderstanding of God's transcendence is corrected by the recognition of His immanence, it remains true that Christianity, and the higher monotheism generally, postulates the one

[1] Rom. ix. 19 ff., modified in x. and xi.

supreme God, as in Himself perfect and also self-sufficient, containing in Himself the fullness of being—such as is expressed in the words of Emily Brontë, which the late Lord Haldane used to repeat with such enthusiasm :

> Though earth and man were gone,
> And suns and universe ceased to be,
> And Thou wert left alone,
> Every existence would exist in Thee.

The most obvious objection to this exalted and thorough-going monotheism lies of course in the portentous and enormous fact of moral evil in the world, which seems to suggest, at times almost irresistibly, that we cannot believe in a God who is both powerful in all things and also perfect goodness.   It is this momentous objection which will confront us in the next lecture.

Apart, however, from this menacing difficulty, monotheism, such as the Christian scheme postulates, finds itself still confronted in our modern world with a fundamental pluralism [1] —including the always seductive form of fundamental dualism—and on the other hand with a monism which (in some sense) identifies God with the world and affirms the world to be as necessary to God as God is to the world, and also with various theories of a finite and emergent deity who (or which) is gradually coming into being in the process of development.

Using, then, my own reason, to the utmost of my capacity and with the utmost freedom, I

---

[1] Such as was represented in the thought of the late Dr. McTaggart.

cannot but find all forms of ultimate pluralism inferior as regards rationality to monotheism. I do not speak of monotheism as demonstrably true, because I cannot (as will appear) eliminate an element of faith from our most fundamental convictions. There does not seem to be any theory of the universe based on absolute demonstration possible to man. Thus I am content to claim for monotheism as compared with pluralism or dualism a superior rationality. There is a certain kind of pluralism indeed which is inherent necessarily in every theory of the world which includes a belief in free spirits ; for in a world where free spirits exist we must be prepared for evidences of their independent action ; and there is a certain dualism inherent in every ethical theory which postulates the rebellion of free spirits, and sees in this world, at least over a prolonged epoch, the conflicts of rebel wills with the supreme will. The creation of free spirits *ex hypothesi* involves on the part of the supreme God a real and voluntary, if only a temporary, self-limitation. Of this more hereafter.

But the rational spirits of whom we have experience are a late production in the development of the world ; and they are not the creators (as far as we can discover) of either organisms or values. There is no sense in calling them " gods many." The question is whether the ultimate creative energy in the universe, which alone can be rightly called by the name of God, is one or many. And in answer to this question, I contend that it is not only the moral conscience

16

which postulates the oneness of God. Physical
science also has surely wiped out polytheism by
its progressive disclosure of the essential coherence of the universe in all its parts—as one
universal system. This leaves no place for the
conception of physical nature as the scene of
conflict between two rival powers or between
many spirits. It is too closely knit to admit of
any such idea. Again, whatever explanation is
to be found of the apparent moral conflict between hostile wills, that must be recognized
as lying only in the upper stratum of nature,
i.e. in the moral world with which we shall be
concerned later. Throughout all its vast physical
bulk we find only one coherent system, one
process, one law or system of laws, and, if
there be a divine energy there revealed—then
one God.

This essential inter-relatedness of all the elements of nature modern physics carries back to
its very foundations. There is no room left for
any ultimate atomism. Clerk Maxwell taught
us long ago that " the atoms have all the appearance of manufactured articles." But more recent
physicists go behind the atoms. We are not
allowed to think of them as ultimate entities,
having each an independent existence, and sub-
sequently entering into relation and combination
with other similar and self-contained entities.
The protons and electrons which are constituents
of the atoms already belong to the larger world.
The whole, we learn, is already implied in all the
parts. Organization is found in the very basis
of nature as well as throughout its whole bulk.

" The stellar system," says Eddington, " is one great organization." [1]

But can we conceive organization apart from mind ? A universe organized on a rational plan from its foundations upwards, as modern physics represents it, surely involves the priority of one rational mind.[2]

The monotheism, however, the reasonableness of which we are considering, attributes to God not only unity and consciousness and priority of existence, but creative will and purpose ; it can find, for instance, no satisfaction in the Aristotelian conception of the supreme being as pure intellect contemplating itself, without interest in the world of things below it, or in the kindred Neo-Platonic conception of the One which is beyond good and evil. It demands one God who made and cares for all things, who has a purpose in His whole creation one day to be realized, and is calling us to co-operate in its realization.

[1] Nature, vol. iii, p. 18 ; cf. his work referred to in the next note, pp. 103 f. ; cf. W. McDougall, *Modern Materialism and Emergent Evolution*, p. 72–73. McDougall, however, denies that Whitehead has the right to say that " the whole of Nature consists of organisms " (p. 131). " Organization pervades nature everywhere " (p. 72), but " organisms " do not appear in inorganic nature.

[2] Some mathematical physicists of to-day (see Eddington, *The Nature of the Physical World*, pp. 75 ff., 220 f., 309 f.) are demanding from us the recognition of a certain indeterminateness at the very roots of the universe, which would apparently conflict with the old-established idea of the " universal reign of law." I am not enough of a mathematician to understand the grounds of this demand. But it is surely too early to take this bewildering conclusion for granted. May not the layman be satisfied for the present with the recognition that there is that at the very basis of the material world which cannot at present be brought under any conception of law ?

It is sometimes said that it is only in the moral and mental region that the idea of purpose or design in nature presses itself strongly on the mind. And it is true that only there do we get any indication of what the purpose or design in nature is. But I am not at all disposed to admit that the whole bulk of physical nature is capable of rational interpretation without the hypothesis of plan or purpose. As to the nature of that purpose, I am not arguing at present. I am postponing therefore to the next lecture what are called the evidences of *dysteleology*—that is, the evidences that the purpose in nature is not at any rate wholly good or effective— I am arguing only that when physical nature as a whole is contemplated, we cannot eliminate from it the evidences of directive purpose either in detail or in general.

The evidences of directive purpose in the details of biological evolution are very strongly brought out in what has been, I think, an unduly neglected work—J. N. Shearman's *Natural Theology of Evolution*—and in a more recent book—J. H. Best's *From the Seen to the Unseen.* We cannot reasonably say that the stricter adherents of Charles Darwin have succeeded in eliminating from nature irresistible evidences of a positive design in the details of its structure. There is indeed a general trend in the world of recent thought to acknowledge some positive tendency in evolution towards specific forms not yet realized, which cannot really be distinguished from design,[1] to which Dr. Whitehead

[1] See McDougall, op. cit., p. 152.

gives the name of " the principle of concretion,"
which he finds it necessary to postulate throughout nature, and to which he gives the name of
God.[1] This " principle " does not seem to me
to be rationally conceivable as anything less
than a presiding purposeful mind present from
the beginning.

This sort of argument has recently been stated
in a new form and with fresh force by **J. E.
Turner**, in his *Personality and Reality*.[2] His
point is that, in our experience, the increasing
dominance of mind over external conditions,
which we should all agree to be the mark of
civilization, manifests itself, and cannot but
manifest itself, in the construction of mechanisms
—not only material machines of increasing complexity and perfection, but also social institutions
whereby human society realizes and maintains
itself ; further, that the more perfect the
mechanism, the more " autonomous "[3] it becomes—the more it " goes of itself," and the
less, or less frequently, any interference of
the inventing or directing mind is required ;
with the result that to the " untrained intelligence of a savage " the machine is mistaken for a demon or God, that is to say,
for something really autonomous. This sort
of apparent autonomy applies to social arrangements, where they are successful, as well
as to machinery.

[1] *Science and the Modern World*, p. 216, but see below, p. 257,
n. 1.

[2] Published by Allen & Unwin. See chap. vi, onward ; cf.
Streeter's *Reality*, pp. 10 ff.   [3] But see below, p. 260.

With this indisputable and constant experience
in his mind, then, the philosopher looks out upon
the material world of nature.   What is presented
to us there is a whole of which the unity, in-
tricacy and apparent automatism are indisputable.   It is the very perfection of these
qualities which seems to render unnecessary
for scientific purposes the postulate of a creative
or directive mind.   But such a conclusion is
contradicted by our whole experience of mechanism.   The perfection of the machine always tends
to the apparent obliteration of its designer or
operator ;   the thing appears to go of itself ;
but to the competent intelligence it is obvious
that the creative or inventive mind is not the
less but the more to be postulated, because he
is so effectively concealed.   Now, designing mind
is an essential element in the highest stage of
developing nature—that is in man ; and when
it appears, it begins to dominate the material
world in which it finds itself by way of increasing mechanization ;   that is the characteristic
of mind.   Is it not reasonable, then, for the
mind of man, if, as it grows to know more
and more of the world, it finds it more and
more clearly to possess the characteristics
of an organized machine of vast range and
intricate coherence, which appears to go of
itself, to argue—not "there is no God," but
"verily thou art a God that hidest thyself "?
And this designing mind, which partly con-
ceals and partly manifests itself in nature, we
cannot but think of as prior to a universe
which, as we are bound to acknowledge, exhibits,

with gradually increasing clearness, a rational purpose.

But there is a further consideration to be entertained.[1] The humanly constructed machines (leaving out of account social machinery) are not plastic. It belongs to the very nature of such mechanism that it is absolutely impossible for it ever to alter its own structural arrangements, except of course destructively through wear and tear : thus mankind must be continually scrapping old machines and devising new ones ; on the other hand, the better the mechanism of human society, the more plastic it is ; the more it can improve and adjust itself. The more self-adjusting machinery is, the more clearly it reveals mind ; and it is just this sort of plasticity which the mechanism of nature tends to exhibit. It is an evolving machine, such as suggests all the more inevitably the action of the mind which has conceived the whole.

To quote Turner's conclusion : " The material universe being in itself a mechanism which, as mechanism, cannot evolve, while at the same time it actually does evolve—and evolves farther on the vastest of scales which seems to possess no final limitation—necessarily implies the real existence of a mind which so dominates the whole realm of matter as progressively to embody therein, by means of perfectly definite, unalterable, and indestructible mechanisms, its own constructive—if not indeed creative—ideas. Such a mind therefore is a supreme self—the

[1] See J. E. Turner, *op. cit.*, p. 156.

personal factor of the psycho-physical universe within which it is omnipotent." [1]

§ 4

There is, as I have said, a widespread tendency in the current philosophy of science to recognize purposefulness of some sort in nature as a whole. The intellectual atmosphere appears to be freeing itself from theoretical materialism. But some sort of monism is still largely dominant. By monism we describe all the theories which are pantheistic—that is, which identify God and the world ; or which bid us find God in the world (immanent),[2] and not prior to it or transcendent ; or which declare the universe to be as essential to God as God is to the world.

But all monistic theories seem to me, pondering as deeply as I can, to have such fundamental weaknesses as give to the monotheist doctrine an evidently prerogative claim to rationality. Perhaps the primary objection to all identification of God with the world—such as Spinoza's

[1] J. E. Turner, *Personality and Reality*, p. 158. To the whole of Turner's argument cf. F. R. Tennant, in the *Journal of Theological Studies*, Oct. 1929, p. 76 : " If Nature's manifold interlacing adaptations (vastly more suggestive than the adaptiveness within organisms) bespeak design or wisdom, and otherwise are inexplicable marvels and mysteries, it is hardly the case . . . that it is a matter of indifference whether we say that Nature, or that God, has wisely arranged things so ; for the simple reason that Nature has no wisdom to arrange anything."

[2] But the word " immanence " is in truth misapplied where it is used as not implying " transcendence." " As a pantheist, Spinoza could not hold the idea of God's immanence, properly so called, in the world or in man ; His so-called immanence is really identity " (F. R. Tennant, in *Journal of Theol. Studies*, Oct. 1929, p. 78).

—lies in its inability to give any explanation of moral evil and the existence of sin.

Any realization of what sin is, such as we find under monotheism, refuses to let us be content with minimizing interpretations; we can see in it nothing less than rebellion against God. But sin is a vast fact in the higher developments of nature. It seems to postulate a rebellion within nature against God; thus it postulates a distinction between nature and God. But with this we shall be dealing in the next lecture. All the monistic theories, however, seem to me to fail on the field of metaphysical argument also.

We can legitimately find in nature, taken by itself apart from any idea of God, no consciousness or conscious purpose till we arrive at the higher animals, or more clearly at man. Hence it is that some of our contemporary philosophers have enunciated the theory of the gradually emergent God, who first in man becomes conscious of Himself and of the values of truth and beauty and goodness which it is man's destiny to realize. But either these values had their origin in the mind of man and have no validity outside his mind—an idea which this school of philosophers repudiates, for they feel bound to recognize the values as properly inherent in nature, or in reality as a whole—or we are driven back upon our previous conclusion that the gradual development of nature as one grand organization culminating in rational man postulates an original Creative Mind in which the idea of the whole was already in conscious existence before ever the gradual development of the universe began.[1]   If, then, it is to reason that we appeal, it must be acknowledged (so I have argued) that reason cannot accept the idea of unconscious purpose.

I cannot but think that Matthews and McDougall are right in their idea that the theory of emergent evolution is not more than a convenient halting-place in the passage of contemporary philosophy from mechanistic materialism to the general recognition of design or purpose throughout nature—which surely involves the idea of God the Creator.[2]

§ 5

Epistemology again seems to point to an original Creative Mind. The man of common sense postulates both the self which knows the world and the world of natural objects which he comes to know through his senses, including people like himself who share this knowledge. As soon as the scientific analysis of knowledge begins, it appears that the verdict of common sense requires profound correction. The world of natural objects appears not to be a direct product of sensations, but a mental construction upon the basis of sensations. As a result of this analysis, a series of famous philosophers have formulated a subjective idealism which declares

[1] I have elsewhere examined in detail what seem to me to be the inconsistencies in Dr. Pringle-Pattison's article on " Immanence and Transcendence " (in the volume entitled *The Spirit*, edited by Dr. Streeter). See the *Reconstruction of Belief*, pp. 69 ff.

[2] McDougall, *op. cit.*, p. 156, quoting Dr. W. R. Matthews.

that all is mind ; and they appear to the plain
man to be denying that the existence of a world
external to the individual mind, or of other
individuals external to himself, is more at best
than a precarious conjecture. This is from the
point of view of common sense, with its age-
long experience of the verification of its instinctive assumptions, a ridiculous conclusion.

Now, common sense, in making this protest
(in the manner of Dr. Johnson), is in part " kick-
ing against the pricks," and will find itself
obliged to give in. The subjective contribution
in our knowledge of external objects is too evident
as a result of analysis to be denied. It must
be admitted also that the world, as known to
the common sense of mankind, is not absolutely
the real world. The world which we can imagine
that a dog or a dragon-fly, with its very different
faculties, knows is not the same as our world ;
nor is our world of common experience the same
as the world which the imagination of the
physicist strives to realize—the world in which
apparent solids are really almost entirely empty
spaces. The common-sense knowledge of the
world, then, is a relative knowledge—but all
the same it is the knowledge to which experience
has always corresponded and continues to correspond. As Dr. Eddington reminds us, the
physicist has quite to forget his physics if he is
to walk into a room comfortably or transact
the ordinary activities of the living man. And his
physics must somehow construct such an appara-
tus of " strains and stresses " as shall account
for a " complex of nearly vacant spaces," be-

having as if it were a solid body, which can inflict summary vengeance on that other complex of nearly vacant spaces, which we call his body, if it presumes to behave as if solid bodies were not actually what they appear to be. Thus the common-sense knowledge of external Nature is proved to be, if not absolutely real, yet the conception of reality which best conforms to the requirements of common experience. So common sense protests against both the scientific and the idealist analysis.

In face of this justifiable protest, the idealist explains that in saying that " all is mind " he is not speaking of the mind of the individual considered apart ; the construction of the individual mind is a very partial thing. Relative to the universe we are to conceive of the universal mind. The process which we call sensitive experience is the process through which the universal mind gradually communicates itself to the particular mind which is only its fragmentary representative. Thus philosophers have proposed, as substitutes for the conception of permanent natural objects external to us the experiencers, the conception of " permanent possibilities of sensation " or " permanent possibilities of experience." But such phrases seem utterly ridiculous to common sense, which, it protests, " knows " that the objects in the external world are subsisting quite independently of the experiencing selves, and were there before they were born, and whether they are awake or asleep.

The independent existence of natural objects,

moreover, is really borne out by the best analysis
of sensation which we are able to make.   For if
this analysis reveals the constructive action of
the mind upon the data of sensation, it also
reveals the absolute dependence of the action
of the mind upon the sensations not only for
the supply of its material, but also for the
supply of the material in such constant and
regular order as force upon it a particular construction.   The sensations of pressure, colour,
smell, sound, taste, arrive with a constancy of
order and relation, over which the knowing
subject has no control, which give it no alternative but to construct an image of a particular
kind and an image of an enduring object.   Thus
the sensations dictate the mental result, quite as
truly as the " synthetic unity of apperception "
constructs the object.

Is not the rational conclusion from all this,
that the reality of both the perceiving subject
and the object perceived is involved, from the
beginning, in all experience—that common sense
(granted the relativity of its knowledge of
reality) is quite right in its instructive assumption
that it is living in a world of real objects, and
is itself an intelligent person surrounded by
other intelligent persons ? [1]   This is, in fact,
the formula best suited to express the reality
for man in his present world of experience ;
and philosophy only makes itself ridiculous when
it seeks to gainsay it.   But, granted this sort of
realism, is it not necessary to go farther, and to

[1] See Eddington, *The Nature of the Physical World*, pp. 226,
285–286.

affirm that the conception of God as the creator alike of natural objects and of men, each fitted to each and dependent one on the other, but having each its own independent reality, the most rational conception, because the one which corresponds best to experience and best interprets its meaning ? No doubt this belief about God was in its full force the outcome of (what claimed to be) God's own revelation of Himself. With that we are not yet concerned. But is it not also the conception which rationally considered is best able to reconcile the postulates of common sense with the demands of the analytic reason ?

§ 6

There is, however, one grave objection to the conception of the one personal God, the absolute creator, as prior to all His creations, and self-complete, which must be faced. Any strictly unitarian conception of God appears to be rationally impossible. What is postulated is a *living* God independent of and prior to His creatures. But life, and especially personal life, involves relations. It appears to be essentially relative and social.[1] There can be no thought which is not thought of something other than the thinking subject. There can be no effective will without the production of some effect. Still more obviously there can be no love which is not the love of person for person. This necessity appears to inhere not in any of the limiting conditions which belong to human personality, but in the essential nature of the thing in itself.

---

[1] Wilfrid Richmond's *Essay on Personality.*

Neither Zarathustra, nor the Jewish prophets, nor Muhammad, show any consciousness of this difficulty. They were not the least metaphysically minded. And Jesus touched on no such difficulty. But the effect of His teaching—of the language He used about the Father, and Himself as Son of the Father, and about the Spirit of God— was such that we find the first Christians recognizing the Name of the Father and of the Son and of the Holy Spirit as the new name of the one God in whom their fathers believed ; and this primitive recognition of the threefold Name came to explicit expression in the doctrine of the Triune God—three " persons " in one God. (The terms used for " persons " in Greek and Latin were elaborately apologised for as having a necessary inadequacy, but as being the best that could be found.) This trinitarian theology was developed, quite independently of any philosophical considerations, under the necessity of maintaining the Christian experience of redemption by the Father, through the Son and in the Spirit. But later, considered philosophically, and with due recognition of the relativity of all human thoughts about God, there was found in this theology the resolution of the formidable difficulty which we are considering.

God was living and personal ; but He was not to be thought of as one eternally solitary or atomic person. The supreme One involves relationship and reciprocity within Himself. Prior to all creation He is alive with the full life of Will and Thought and Love—the Father eternally generating His Word or Son, and knowing Himself in Him as His adequate image, and loving Him in the Spirit who is His life. It was never pretended that such a thought of God could have been arrived at *a priori* by human insight. What was claimed was (and is) that this thought of God as triune was implicit —necessarily implicit—in the actual experience which the apostles had of the divine redemption through Jesus Christ; and that as made explicit (though human language could never do justice to the reality) it did relieve the Christianized intelligence of a formidable difficulty.[1] It did suggest how, prior to all creation, the fullness of life could be in the one God : and it found in the unfathomable depths of the divine being the ground and principle of that fellowship which is of the essence of personal life as we know it.

The idea of the " triunity " of God is, then, I contend, if not discoverable by reason, yet satisfying to reason. It corresponds to the requirement of Hermann Lotze. " If reason," he says, " is not of itself capable of finding the highest truth, but on the contrary stands in need of a revelation, still reason must be able to understand the revealed truth, at least so far as to recognize in it the satisfying conclusion of those upward soaring trains of thought which reason itself began, led by its own needs, but was not able to bring to an end." [2]

But here I am anticipating the question of

[1] Perhaps Marius Victorinus Afer, the Christianized Neo-Platonist of the fourth century, was the first to perceive this (see *Dict. of Christian Biography*, s.v. Victorinus).

[2] *Microcosmus* (English Trans.), vol. ii, p. 660 ; cf. S. Thomas Aquinas, *Summa Theol.*, i, qu. 32, art. 1, ad. 2.

revelation.   In this lecture I have been limiting my argument to one point—that the idea of God presented to us in Christian monotheism, the idea of His personality, His unity, His absolute priority and self-completeness, and His creativity of all that is, is strictly more rational, or more acceptable to the enlightened reason, than the various substitutes for it suggested by divers schools of modern idealism.[1]

---

[1] I feel the great importance of the cosmology which Dr. A. N. Whitehead is expounding, but I find him very difficult to understand. I suppose him to give strong support to the interpretation of nature as one vast organization, and of the creative process as involving a rational purpose. Every step in the process, every " event " or " occasion," looks before and after : it embodies the old in a new " concretion," which again prepares for a further step. Throughout the entire process Dr. Whitehead postulates God as " the principle of concretion." But though God is eternal, and though His nature embodies the whole sum of " eternal objects "—a phrase which seems to be almost equivalent to the Platonic " forms "—which are gradually to be realized in the process of evolution, yet He Himself is conceived of as unconscious and merely " potential " apart from the world, so that if " God creates the world " it is also as true to say that " the world creates God," both being alike dependent upon " creativity," which is the ultimate power. (See *Progress and Reality*, pt. v, cap. ii.) I cannot but feel that all that Dr. Whitehead is seeking to express might find better expression in the terms of Trinitarian theology. But this is obviously not his intention. I can only refer to an article in *Theology* (of August 1930) by Dr. E. A. Taylor which both respectfully interprets Dr. Whitehead and also criticizes him.

17

CHAPTER X

WE were occupied in the last lecture with questions concerning the nature of God—His personality, His unity, His transcendence, His relation to the universe as creator. These are postulates of ethical monotheism which were not generally arrived at by any process of reasoning, but by a certain kind of prophetic intuition, the value of which we shall be considering later. But our contention has been that these postulates, however arrived at, are found to provide an interpretation of the data of experience, both ordinary and scientific, not less but more rational than the theories of pluralism or monism or emergent evolution. Now, we are to make our start from those postulates of ethical monotheism which concern the nature of man, that is, first of all from the assumption of his moral responsibility and absolute obligation to do what is right, the right being conceived of as the will of the Good God who made and governs all things, although, as a being endowed with freedom, man is capable of disobedience as fully as of obedience. First, then, we must carefully scrutinize this conception of moral responsibility and moral freedom with a view to its definition.

§ 1

There is, as Dr. Sorley has said, no logical road from the sense of *what is* to the sense of *what ought to be*, that is, *what need not occur but what can occur, if I do my duty.* But we cannot hesitate to say that this latter sense is characteristic of mankind. It belongs to its very essence. It exists equally under very varying conceptions of the content of duty—for instance, as between the traditional Indian and the traditional Christian conceptions of the rights and duties of a widow, or the Stoic and the Christian attitudes towards suicide. And this sense of responsibility for doing one's duty is the correlative of another equally universal sense—that of rights—of what one can legitimately claim of others in their conduct towards oneself. The idea of rights and the idea of duty are inseparable ; but the idea of duty, as Mazzini insisted, is the prior idea.

No doubt, the sense of responsibility varies indefinitely in different persons, and is found to be very weak in a vast number of individuals. The same must be said of the sense of beauty or of the value of truth. But they exist probably in some measure in all. One who had no such senses would be called hardly human ; and just as we look to the few among us who are artists or poets, if we wish to appreciate the sense of beauty, so we look to the pre-eminently " good " men if we are to understand the idea of duty ; for there we see it dominant and luminously clear.

It is also, no doubt, the case that the emergence of the sense of duty in the development of life on our planet is buried in obscurity. We may argue, but it must be inconclusively, as to whether it is to be found at all in the sub-human world of animals. Such argument must be inconclusive, because we cannot put ourselves in the position of horses or monkeys so as to see things through their eyes, or to think their thoughts. Thus the stronghold of the sense of duty lies in the inner consciousness of man ; and in the language of contingency and responsibility in which that inner consciousness inevitably expresses itself. It seems to me somewhat misleading to speak, as Mr. J. E. Turner speaks, of the increasing " autonomy " [1] exhibited in the animal world as it advances to its higher development. Increasing complexity of organization and increasing centralization in the nervous system is not properly called autonomy ; and Mr. Turner himself shows this when he speaks of the increasing " autonomy " of machines made by man. A machine may be made to " go of itself " with less and less of human interference ; but it can go only in one way. The most elaborate machine is not really more " autonomous " than a spade or a flint knife. We blame the maker, not the machine, if it fails. Thus again we do not seriously blame a plant or an animal if it fails to correspond to our requirements, we only try to get one of a better breed. The fact remains that first in man do we clearly find the inner sense of moral obligation, and we can build no logical bridge between " I am " and " I ought."

However certainly, then, we believe that the evolution of the world was gradual, we must recognize that when the sense of moral obligation

[1] See, e.g., *Personality and Reality*, p. 123.

dawned upon the world, there was a new stage reached in the development of life, even though we cannot fix the point of its emergence ; and if we cannot but see in the process of world-evolution the realization of a divine purpose, we must say that God created a new thing when a being appeared conscious of obligation, and of the alternatives of " right " and " wrong " open to him.   That is the real difference, or an important part of the real difference, between " he " and " it."

There is a sense in which no " ultimate of experience " can ever be explained, for explanation means the interpretation of the more complex or difficult by the more obvious and simple.   Thus you cannot explain either the beautiful or the good.   They both represent ultimate states of consciousness and ultimate elements of reality. The suggested explanations of them always turn out to be assuming the thing to be explained. Thus Henry Sidgwick was surely right when he finally refused to " reduce the notion of ought to terms of anything else " because it is an " irreducible datum of moral consciousness." [1] But we can make these elemental ideas more luminous to our minds by contrast with other ideas. Thus Mr. Turner helps us when he contrasts the idea of moral obligation with that of urgent desire, which presents itself as equally imperative. For " the imperiousness of desire," he says, " seems to rise solely from ourselves, while moral commands appear to come to us from without,

[1] J. E. Turner, *Philosophical Basis of Moral Obligation*, p. 251, referring to Albee's *History of English Utilitarianism*, p. 14.

and to be as it were foreign to us.   Still, we feel
that the moral claim upon us is indefeasible, so
that we are really ourselves only in recognizing
and obeying it." [1]   That is to say, that we
recognize ourselves as belonging to some larger
spiritual world in which a moral law is somehow
necessarily inherent.

Again, the sense of duty sharply distinguishes
itself from the appetite for pleasure (one special
form of desire).   It presents itself as something
which has to be done irrespective of pleasure
or pain consequent to the doer upon the perform-
ance of it—even though in the long run it may
seem to us that the path of duty is the way to the
truest and most enduring pleasure.

Once more, it helps us, passing from contrasts
to resemblances, to observe that the sense of
obligation attaches itself not only to what is
commonly called moral conduct, but to all other
values, believed to be part of the larger reality,
the promotion of which lies equally within the
sphere of our voluntary action ; we thus recognize it as a duty to make our world beautiful,
and a duty to submit ourselves to truth, as such,
though these forms of duty are less widely
acknowledged than the duty of right conduct.
But all recognized " values " become alike imperatives upon the will.

§ 2

The idea and reality of moral obligation is
essentially bound up with the idea and reality of
freedom.   There can be no meaning in penitence

[1] Turner, *op. cit.*, p. 222.

and the sense of shame on account of having done or omitted to do this or that ; there can be no meaning in ascribing to a person responsibility for any particular occurrence, except on the assumption of contingency—that he need not have done what he did do—that its occurrence under the circumstances was not inevitable. If all occurrences are in truth equally and absolutely determined in the physical sequence of events, it cannot be denied that the whole language about responsibility and guilt, about penitence and shame, is the language of illusion.

I am of course conscious that even so clear-thinking a moral philosopher as Hastings Rashdall was ultimately disposed to be a determinist,[1] while still maintaining not only practically but theoretically the principle of moral obligation. But I can only regard this as a conspicuous instance of the way in which an excessive regard for what is called logical consistency has led clear-thinking men to the denial of a patent element in experience. It is undeniable that if any man were genuinely convinced that his every action was absolutely predetermined, so that he was no more justly to be blamed for anything he might do than a cabbage or a sheep, and were to allow this conviction to dominate his conduct, he would cease to be a fit member of human society. Thus, Bishop Butler, in his famous chapter on the " Opinion of Necessity," is content to leave the determinist theory out of discussion, though he calls it absurd, simply because no man

---

[1] The same appears to be true of Mr. Shebbeare, in *Problems of Providence* (Longmans).

can behave as if it were true without becoming less than a man and being treated as such.

Of course, ordinary observation and scientific enquiry severely limit the just idea of human freedom. The laws of nature, the latent forces of heredity, the strength of habit, and so on, limit the freedom of the individual. It may be that, as acts form habits and habits character and character stereotypes, it is possible for an individual actually to cease to be free, and not to have any longer the alternatives of good or bad open to him. This may be the truth latent in the phrase that we all have the making of our own heaven or our own hell—that actual freedom to become this or that belongs only to a temporary " state of probation." We can leave these questions aside. We are now concerned only with the present condition of the normal man. Our argument also is not affected by the fact that a vast number of human beings have a ridiculous idea of freedom, as if it meant independence or " the right to do as we please." This is ridiculous, because we must all strenuously seek to live " in accordance with nature," as the Stoics phrased it, or " in accordance with God," or else inevitably suffer disaster. The true nature of freedom lies in our action being contingent on our will, not on its wilfulness. But it does not matter to our argument how broad or how narrow are the limits within which freedom obtains, so long as, within its limits, freedom really exists, as the instrument alike of our moral development and moral probation. Nor does it destroy freedom to recognize that it never means independence of motives, but only the mysterious faculty for choosing the motive we will act upon, and thereby giving it preponderant strength.

For here we get to the root fact, which subsists and must be recognized in the centre of our rational being, that the various motives, which are relatively to be judged good or bad—pleasure, acquisitiveness, ambition, pride, the love of God, the love of man, the fear of hell, the hope of heaven—present themselves to our consciousness at crucial moments, and are estimated at their relative value by us, and that we can, by a deliberate act of choice, so attach ourselves to one or the other, as that our resultant action becomes decisively this or that, the other motives being ignored ; indeed in cases of violent temptation, it may even happen that the consciousness of the strong pressure of some motive contrary to that which we actually choose only seems to increase the vigour we put into that which we have chosen. If freedom of choice in this sense is denied to be possible for all normal men and habitual in good and thoughtful men, it appears to me that such a denial is simply a refusal to face the facts, as revealed directly in human consciousness.

What takes place is something unique indeed, but unmistakable in quality.   It is totally different from what takes place when distinct and opposing physical forces are acting simultaneously upon a physical body.   The motion of the body is then the mixed resultant of the different forces. In the case of a variety of " motives " acting upon the will, the will surrenders to one and ignores the others, as has just been remarked.

They are neutralized, or the very pressure of the rejected motive seems to add intensity to the one to which surrender is made—so that the man does the right all the more vigorously or the wrong all the more impulsively, because of the strong pressure he experienced to do the contrary.

Before considering the implications of this essentially human consciousness, there are certain considerations to be entertained.

(1) That in proportion as the physical sciences are coming to recognize the " abstractness " of their subject-matter—or in other words, since the dominance of a mechanical materialism has been relaxed—in that proportion science is ceasing to ban the idea of real freedom as the quality of spiritual beings. Thus Prof. Hobson, in his admirable *Survey of the Domain of Natural Science*, strongly condemns the attempt on the part of science to ban the idea of real freedom. " The assertion of this view in its absolute form is then merely a dogma resting on nothing but an illegitimate extension to the whole of what may have been shown to be true of some part. It is in direct contradiction to the immediate deliverance of our consciousness as to the real efficiency of the will." [1]

Prof. Eddington similarly would restrain the dogmatism of physical science from the denial of free-will.[2] " Meanwhile," he writes, " we may note that science thereby withdraws its [*moral*]

[1] *Op. cit.*, pp. 355, 367.

[2] See in *Science and Religion* (The Sheldon Press)—a composite volume—pp. 208, 214–216, and more recently in the *Nature of the Physical World*, p. 295. In my quotation I have bracketed the word " moral," which I do not understand.

opposition to free-will. Those who maintain a
deterministic theory of mental activity must do
so as the outcome of the study of the mind
itself, and not with the idea that they are thereby
making it more conformable with an experimental
knowledge of the laws of inorganic nature."
Prof. Eddington's words imply a repudiation of
determinism which is very far-reaching indeed.
For he finds indeterminism in nature at its very
basis. I am incapable of estimating his argument on this point. I simply note a widespread recognition on the part of distinguished
men of science that it can legitimately claim no
right to exclude the conception of free-will.
This is a very important withdrawal. No one
now can hesitate to accept the verdict of our own
consciousness on the ground that science declares
that it must be an illusion. But it should be noted
that what the conception of human freedom
requires is not that the action of our will results
in any augmentation or reduction of the physical
energy which passes into the human body and
passes out of it in action. All that is required
from the ethical point of view is a certain (confessedly restricted) control over its direction, as
in this or that kind of activity.

I must dissent altogether from a statement
quoted from Dr. Inge by Mr. Turner,[1] that the
claim of moral freedom involves that " the self
that is free must be outside the flow of events and
itself timeless." On the contrary, it is within the
flow of events, and as incarnate, that the moral
personality emerges, essentially limited by the

---

[1] Turner, *Basis of Moral Obligation*, p. 95.

flow of events, but not so limited as that a new quality does not appear which sheds its light on the whole flow of events by revealing a new meaning and purpose in the universe.

(2) I must also call attention to a similar withdrawal of antagonism on the part of theologians. Christianity, in the days of the Greek Fathers, distinguished itself by its enthusiastic insistence on the reality of free-will and moral responsibility. Under the influence of Augustine, however, in his extremest moment of antagonism to Pelagianism, the Western Church in part adopted an idea of divine predestination, the logical implication of which did no doubt cut at the roots of any real sense of moral responsibility. The late Master of Balliol—Benjamin Jowett—was right, I think, in calling attention to the fact that this doctrine of predestination was so deeply involved in the clouds and darkness of inscrutable mystery, that it was much less calculated to paralyse the sense of responsibility in fact, than the plainer form of scientific denial that any action of the human mind could interfere with the determined flow of physical events. But to-day the extremer Augustinianism, and its daughter Calvinism, are being frowned out of court by theologians from all quarters—even from Scotland. There is a much more general readiness to admit that the recognition of the creation of free beings does involve a conception of God as having thereby imposed a limit upon Himself, at least temporarily, in that while He solicits human beings through their moral consciences, He refuses to compel them. This also, to many minds,

carries with it the implication that to know precisely what we are going to do cannot lie in the prevision even of God—that though He keeps control over the consequences of our actions He cannot foreknow them in particular. But this profound problem will recur for consideration later.

(3) We must recognize a permanent ambiguity in the use of the words " freedom of the will." It expresses the idea that a choice lies open before the will, not only between good or bad, but more generally between this or that kind of action, within certain limits, whatever motive finally governs the choice. But it has always suggested to the wilfulness of mankind a kind of liberty to follow its fancies which is wholly unreal. The Stoic hymn of Cleanthes was quite right in warning mankind of the folly of wickedness, since, inasmuch as the moral life is the life according to nature, nature will revenge itself on immorality as surely as on the violation of any other of her laws. We used to hear the same peremptory warning from the lips of Thomas Huxley. It is expressed, in diverse religious traditions, in the idea of divine judgment on sin. Inside, and widely also outside, Christianity rebellious sinners are warned that, though they are " free " to ignore the will of God, such freedom does not deserve the name—so short-lived is it and so disastrous.

Mankind, in fact, is balanced between two worlds. If he yields himself to the flesh— the lower world—he changes his freedom into slavery, and a slavery which ends in destruction. But the only escape from such slavery is by

surrender to the higher will of God. Man is
bound to lose his balanced independence, in the
one direction to his destruction, or in the other
to his redemption and real self-realization.
God's service is the only real freedom. This
doctrine is found widely in the moralists of
many nations. For the same moral consciousness which assures us of freedom assures us also
of responsibility to One Above. We are men
" under authority." Surely one of the most
impressive elements in Butler's moral philosophy
is his insistence that to gain a true idea of human
nature it is not enough to examine its constituent
elements separately—their relation to one another
is still more important ; and that in " the
economy and constitution of man " the principle
of reflection or self-judgment, which we call
conscience, has by inherent right a supreme
authority. " This is a constituent part of the
idea, that is, of the faculty itself. . . . Had it
strength as it has right, had it power as it has
manifest authority, it would absolutely govern
the world." [1]

§ 3

Taking it now for granted that we find in
mankind generally, as history presents it to
us, and especially in the men whom their fellows
have venerated as the best, this consciousness
of an absolute moral obligation to observe a
law of conduct believed to be divine, and
corresponding to this obligation a sense of freedom to obey the law, which is also a freedom to

[1] See *Sermon II*, and *Preface* to Sermons.

rebel, we have to ask ourselves what are the implications of this belief ?

I do not say this twofold consciousness cannot exist without the belief in a personal God, but I would say that it strongly suggests it, and that nothing else satisfies it.   For instance, the Stoics theoretically did not believe in a personal God, but only in an impersonal Nature.   But their strong sense of personal moral obligation forced them to equate Nature with Zeus, and to use such strongly personal language about him and his judgments as we hear in the Hymn of Cleanthes,[1] and forced upon them also a manner of conceiving the indwelling divine spirit, which, though it is based on a materialistic pantheism, suggests strongly a spiritual theism.[2]   Again, I would not say that this consciousness of moral responsibility cannot co-exist with polytheism or dualism.   But I do maintain that the consciousness of a sovereign moral law does forcibly suggest the idea of the one and only personal and holy God ; so it is that in Zarathustra we see this consciousness of moral obligation lifting him out of a traditional polytheism into a practical monotheism.   Hardly anyone would, I suppose, deny that the moral consciousness is shown in its fullest assurance and highest development in the monotheism of the prophets of Israel and in the religion of Jesus Christ.

It has been argued above that the sense of absolute values inherent in the nature of things is for most of us not separable from the con-

See above, p. 137, where it is quoted at length.

[2] See below, p. 286.

ception of God as personal; also that the sense
which science develops in us of the close-knit
unity of nature is incompatible with any ultimate
pluralism or dualism; and once more that the
sense of purpose in the whole process of nature,
which we cannot get rid of, almost forces us
to think of the priority of mind and purpose,
that is of a God who knows and purposes, to
the whole time-process of natural development.
If this be so, the belief in the one, personal,
Creator—God, does not depend wholly on moral
considerations. But there is no doubt that it
is there it has its strength. It is the teaching
of the great moral prophets which has purged
the traditional pantheons, and bade men feel
themselves under the eye of the Holy God who
wills the morally right. Certainly it is in the
developed moral consciousness of man that we
first get a glimpse of *what* the divine purpose in
the development of Nature is. The universe
is incredibly vast, and of what is going on in its
infinite spaces we know little indeed; and in a
large part of our own world, so far as we can
trace its history, it is hard indeed to detect any
indication of " what it is all for." Is it not true,
then, to say that it is first in the developed moral
consciousness of man, when we find him conscious of himself as a willing co-operator with
God for the realizing of a divine kingdom of
holiness and love, that our hungry search for the
nature of the purpose in creation first gets any
real and sufficient, even if still partial, satisfaction ?

It has been very well observed by Pringle-

Pattison that Kant, who had so firmly refused to accept the argument from design in the physical universe to God the Creator, found that argument irresistible when he turned to contemplate the world of man's moral consciousness. There at least he found himself unmistakably in a " realm of ends."

But here we are confronted with an astonishing difficulty. The obvious suggestion of our moral consciousness is that God wills goodness and has brought rational man into being, endowed with a glorious freedom, so that he might co-operate with the divine purpose of goodness and build the kingdom of God in the world. But, in fact, the human world seems at first sight to offer us a spectacle in even startling contradiction to such an idea. Humanity, broadly considered, presents itself as very generally ignoring moral obligation, even when it is formally acknowledged. This pessimistic impression finds utterance in all languages at all times both in the confessions of individuals, such as " video meliora proboque —deteriora sequor," and in judgments on mankind in general—" the whole world lieth in wickedness." Granted that the dismal spectacle has sometimes overthrown sanity of judgment even in wise men, and produced exaggerated statements of human depravity, such as ignore the average good in mankind, yet the fact remains that the wisest and even the kindliest of men have expressed the severest judgments on mankind as they have known it in experience.

What can be more impressive than the evidence that is presented to us in the plays and sonnets

18

of Shakespeare, if we seek to read them chrono-
logically, that he passed from a genial acceptance
of the spectacle of humanity, " good and bad
together," to a profound gloom as he gazed
deeper and deeper into it, and found himself
confronted with some fundamental incapacity
in men to be the thing they would be—some
fundamental victory of passion and circumstances
over feeble good—a mystery of ruin baffling
all power of speculation to extract a meaning
out of it ? [1]   Surely a light-hearted optimism
about human nature is not wisdom.

There are two explanations of the tremendous
problem of moral evil—the one ancient and the
other modern—which can be set aside.

The first is the proposal to find the source of
contamination to the pure spirit of man in the
material body, viewed as the prison from which
it hopes to be delivered.   This was part of the
Orphic tradition,[2] whencesoever derived, but
the earlier and nobler thought of Greece did
not surrender to this pessimistic estimate of
the body and of matter generally.   It obtained,
however, a great hold upon the later Hellenistic
world, so that the popularity of the mysteries
was largely bound up with the hope that the
initiate could find in their sacred rites the promise
of purification for the soul from the contamination of the body and its redemption at death.

---

[1] The last " romantic " plays may seem to contradict this
interpretation of Shakespeare's mental development.   But it is
truer to say that in these last plays he " invents a new mythology "
expressly to rescue his characters from tragic issues (see Walter
Raleigh's *Shakespeare*, pp. 210–214 (*English Men of Letters*)).

[2] Burnet, *Essays and Addresses*, p. 147.

And it cannot be denied that there are phases of experience which seem to support such an indictment of the body ; yet for all that it is fundamentally and normally false. The seat of sin lies in the will—" from within, out of the hearts of men," as Jesus said,[1] arises all that defiles human life. There is nothing fundamentally evil but the evil will, as Kant affirmed.

I am speaking now of moral not physical evil—of sin, not pain. But it is good to recognize how deeply true it is that of the mass of evil which we call physical—which has depressed and does depress mankind—by far the greater part is the result of the wilful refusal of mankind to obey the moral law. It is good to reflect how easy would be the redemption of man, economically, socially and politically, if only mankind in the mass would set itself to be unselfish and self-controlled, honest and just. It is, in fact, the doctrine that sin lies ultimately only in the will—whether its apathy or its rebellion—that is the secret of the hope of human progress in this world. If sin lay in the material body, there would be no legitimate hope. We cannot become dis-embodied except by death. But if sin lies in the will—so that when once the will is right, all the whole nature can be restored to order also (at least in normal man)—there is boundless hope for the individual and so for the society.

There is another explanation of moral evil which has been popular in modern times—that evil is only good in the making—a defect which

[1] Mark vii. 21.

is to be, and is being, progressively overcome. But surely it does not in the least correspond with the facts. Progressive moral deterioration in individuals is certainly a fact of experience as widespread as moral improvement. Men's characters tend to become fixed for evil as surely as for good. And if we consider man corporately and not individually, while there is clear evidence of a real tendency in mankind to advance in civilization, in spite of catastrophes and collapses, there is no evidence of any general tendency among men to become morally better as they become more civilized. The sins of civilized man are different from the sins of barbarous man, but it is really wilful to say that the roots of sin—selfishness, or lust, or acquisitiveness, or pride—show any tendency to be outgrown.

Thus we come back to face the problem presented by the fact of the immense prevalence of moral evil in humanity. The awakened moral sense cannot reconcile itself to the idea of making God responsible for the creation of bad man or for the world as it stands. What, then, is the theory which ethical monotheism propounds? It is simple, and intelligible enough, and conceived in the boldest outline—viz. that God was not satisfied with the creation of a merely mechanical or unintelligent world. He chose to create a world or worlds of free spirits whose destiny was glad co-operation with His good and gracious purpose. But the creation of free beings capable of voluntary correspondence, by a necessity lying in the nature of things, from which

God Himself could not be exempt, involved the possibility of a refusal of service. Mankind could not be capable of free service without being capable of rebellion. Nevertheless, God, if we may so say, ran the great risk. He preferred that there should be free beings, even though that involved the awful liability to a dominion of sin as a result of human perversity. A little steady consideration will show us (as has been said already) how vast a proportion of the misery of the world, physical as well as moral and social, is due to human perversity. It is amazing to think how gloriously transformed a world would come into being, even in a short time, if mankind in the mass would steadily set itself to cease to do evil and learn to do well. The mystery lies in the fact that mankind in the mass does seem steadily to refuse to learn this lesson, and for this reason lies under the adverse judgment of God. The responsibility lies not with God but with man.

At this point passionate human reason rises up in its wrath—at least in the more pessimistic moods of the human spirit—and exclaims, that if such were to be the consequences of the creation of free spirits, it were better for God not to have created any such, or indeed not to have created anything at all. But, in fact, such challenges addressed to the supreme wisdom are not wise. The human reason cannot hope to put itself at the point of view of God or generally to answer the question *why* things are as they are. Let me quote Robert Bridges' *Testament of Beauty*,[1] which

[1] P. 7.

was his own last will and testament to his contemporaries.

Wisdom will repudiate thee, if thou think to enquire
why things are as they are or whence they came : thy task
is first to learn *what is*, and in pursuant knowledge
pure intellect will find pure pleasure and the only ground
for a philosophy conformable to truth.

.   .   .   .   .   .

We come back, then, to the facts of the moral
conscience and its postulates, as they are presented to us by Christianity, which is being taken
as the type of ethical monotheism.

It cannot of course be denied that, in fact,
these postulates were not arrived at by speculation, but were believed in as the outcome of God's
own disclosure of Himself to man.   But with that
we are not yet concerned.   We are taking these
postulates of ethical monotheism, and we are
asking about their rationality.   Face to face, then,
with moral evil—that awful world-wide spectacle
—we listen to this bold and simple theory.

God is good, and the author only of good.   His
purpose in His whole creative activity—so far
as we can judge it within the narrow limits of our
observation—is first clearly seen to have been
good when we observe its culmination in man—
that is, in man as he was capable of being and
was intended to be.   The culmination of nature
was to be a world of free but embodied spirits
capable of the intellectual appreciation of goodness, beauty and truth, capable of sonship with
God and glad co-operation in the fashioning of the
kingdom of God which is the fellowship of love.
What this kingdom would have been we can

observe and hold in clear conception if we fix our attention on that portion of mankind who are " the men of goodwill." But the world as it is is not the world of God's intention. For the freedom given to man involved the opportunity not only for glad service but also for rebellion, and, generation after generation, man in the mass has rebelled against God through pride and lust and selfishness, and reduced the world of our experience to a mere parody of the divine purpose. Clear thinking will show us how vast a proportion of all human disease, misery and degradation is due to the way men have treated themselves and one another. God still abides in the world and sustains it in being; but over the human world He stands also as its accuser and its judge.

As its accuser and its judge—but Christianity, which we are taking as the best type of ethical monotheism, will not suffer us to think of God as the just judge without also recognizing in Him the saviour. As He sees His work marred under His eyes, the creator becomes the recreator and the redeemer; and this work of redemption pursues a course as gradual as the work of creation, and has its culmination in Christ, and His divine society of the redeemed. Moreover, we see but a beginning of His work, for He has eternity to work in. What is to be the final issue does not fall under our observation. It may well be—it must be if God is really good—that the lives which seem to us merely neglected or crushed by circumstances or needlessly tormented in this world would, could we see them in their full extent beyond the veil of death, appear in a quite different light.   Our first judgment upon them would be wholly reversed.   The most crushing affliction would be seen as no more than a necessary stage of education.

But here we are in a region of belief which depends directly upon the idea of divine self-disclosure or positive revelation, to the consideration of which we have still to address ourselves.   What we have done is to work out the implications of the direct consciousness which belongs to man of his moral responsibility and His freedom.   We have analysed its postulates both as to the character and purpose of God, and as to the way in which it compels us to regard the world as it exists—as we can observe it in human experience.   What I desire to represent to you is that this theory or general view of the world, which the postulates of ethical monotheism lead you to form, is a view of the world which embraces the whole of experience better than any other view, and has therefore a better right to call itself rational.

Men, according to their dispositions, are apt to become optimists or pessimists ;   in either case, they tend to become irrational and one-sided, through refusing to do full justice to the facts which conflict with the feeling to which their disposition and their circumstances incline them. But the optimism of the genuine Christian, based on the conviction that God is at last to come into His own in His whole universe, is the most truly rational optimism, because he has been forced by his religion to face so steadily and take into such full account all that ministers to pessimism, and to base his emergent optimism only on the solid ground of the ultimate purpose of God— solid ground, that is, if the Christian faith in a divine self-disclosure is justified.

§ 4

Leaving aside for the present this question of Revelation, to which we are to proceed in the next lecture, and leaving aside also the consideration of the limits of human knowledge, which remain even if divine revelation is recognized as a reality, which will be the subject of my last lecture, there is only one other point on which I wish to touch, which is a subject of constant discussion—that is, the actual variety of ethical standards which we find among men in different countries and ages; for the actual variation is so great that it appears to dispose of any idea of an identical moral law, ascertainable by all men, a " law of nature " such as the Stoics spoke of, and indeed taught the Christian Church to speak of also.

Certainly the moral standards current in different nations, and in the same nation at different ages, are greatly unlike one another; and it must be admitted that the conscience of the average man in all countries and ages is mainly determined by this public opinion round about him. We have also to take into account the unevenness or partiality in the moral standard of individuals and classes at all stages of history. For you find in history conspicuous individuals who, while they are content with the prevailing moral standard in general, rise high above it

at some specific point.   Thus in semi-civilized
kings, such as King David, according to the
remarkably frank picture of him given in the
Old Testament, or Baber, the first Moghul
Emperor of India,[1] we find a remarkable spiritual
sensibility coupled with a remorseless brutality
in his treatment of his enemies.   Again, among
people for whom the highest moral illumination
is at any rate available, you find an extraordinary
deadening of the conscience in some particular
direction.   The   deadening   of   conscience   in
Christian communities over a long period as to
religious persecution, or the iniquities of the
slave trade, or the gross injustices of the industrial
system, or the administration of the criminal law
are obvious instances.   And constant experience,
internal to ourselves and external, warns us of
the lamentable possibility of sophisticating conscience till the light that is in us becomes darkness indeed.   Certainly we cannot speak of the
individual or social conscience absolutely as " the
voice of God " or of a specific moral law sounding
in the spiritual ear of mankind.

But when all this variability in the conceptions
of the good, which may be found among men,
has been recognized, it must be noticed that there
is a very noticeable tendency to unanimity in
the utterances of the great moral leaders of
mankind whose records we have reviewed.   To
a great extent they all inculcate the same virtues,
and agree in their conceptions of right and wrong.
It is also noticeable that their high standards
are appreciated and recognized by their con-

See in *Theology*, Sept. 1929, " David and Baber."

temporaries, even if the homage given to the ideal is largely lip-service, and has little effect upon the average level of conduct. There is, moreover, noticeable evidence of progress in many nations towards a similar ideal. It is remarkable how widely—for instance in India— the Christian moral standard is hailed as the best by public opinion, even where the specific Christian doctrines are rejected and ridiculed. The evidence as to the unity of the moral ideal among men is plainly of a complicated nature, but on the whole it indicates a tendency towards unity.

There is a remarkable notion in later Jewish literature of the Bath-Qol—" the daughter of the Voice " [of God]—which is intended to express something in which some divine quality can be recognized, but which falls short of directly divine authority. Consciously or unconsciously Words-worth repeated this notion when he called con-science the " stern daughter of the voice of God." This is a good description, as has been already suggested, of what the conscience in man may be if it is allowed to speak freely.

We must grant that the Stoic account of the law of nature, such as is given in the passage from the *De Republica* of Cicero which I read to you in an earlier lecture, is an exaggeration. There is no such explicit law, constant and uni-versal, to be found in history. Nor among the Jews can the Ten Commandments be properly spoken of as its republication. Growth in moral perception is recognizable both in Israel and in the world at large, and men and nations may also lose what they have gained, and may deteriorate as well as advance.   Such is certainly the verdict of history.   Nevertheless, a tendency towards unity in the moral ideal is recognizable, even if it be a broken tendency.   And the great moral prophets of humanity, though they have spoken independently,   have   spoken   with   a   certain approach to unanimity.   Moreover, it is the moral prophets who have had the supreme in- fluence in human history, not only in elevating but in fixing the standard of the good life, so that, as Aristotle said, for the settlement of disputes, we must look to " the decision of the good man." [1]   And here certainly Christianity has a supreme advantage.   In spite of all the moral failures of its chequered history, even in the judgment of most of those who have rejected its doctrines, the moral ideal embodied in the character of its Master, Jesus Christ, stands out as the best expression of what all races and generations of men can recognize as the good life.

[1] ὡς ἂν ὁ φρόνιμος ὁρίσειεν.

CHAPTER XI

WE are taking our stand upon the ultimate fact of the moral consciousness of mankind—the sense of " I ought," and the idea of the good life founded upon this sense of obligation. We have found that this fact and this idea receive two kinds of interpretation among the moral leaders of mankind—which we have called the idealistic and the theistic—which differ, as in other respects, so especially in respect of the emphasis laid on the personality and transcendence of God. The course of our argument has been directed to vindicating the superior rationality of the latter, the theistic, interpretation—both its interpretation of God and its interpretation of human sin as rebellion against God. We now proceed to another point.

§ 1

It cannot be denied, if we consider the history of Zarathustra, of Muhammad, of Israel's prophets, and of Jesus of Nazareth, that the strongest and highest convictions concerning God and His will for mankind which have appeared in human history, and have transformed the imagination and conduct of individuals and peoples, have been unhesitatingly ascribed by the prophets who propounded them, not to their own thought or discovery, but to the direct action of God disclosing Himself to the individual prophet and sending him to deliver His message to mankind. And the prophet has assumed that there exists in the souls of his fellow-men at least a faculty for recognizing the authority of the message, as Adeimantus in Plato's Republic is represented as welcoming Socrates' dogmatic assertion of the pure goodness of God with the words, " Now you say so, I give my assent." [1] Thus the well-disposed part of mankind, when listening to the prophets, has, whether enthusiastically or reluctantly, made the prophet's conviction their own in virtue of their common moral consciousness. Indeed, man in general recognizes in his conscience at least " the daughter of the voice " of God. " Man's conscience is the lamp of the Eternal, flashing into his inmost soul. So Dr. Moffatt brilliantly renders a verse in the Book of Proverbs.[2]

This estimate of conscience is widespread among mankind. It was especially vivid among the Stoics, from whom it is true to say our popular idea of conscience is largely derived. Thus Seneca speaks of conscience as " a holy spirit residing in us, the guardian and observer of our good and evil deeds." [3] It is reported again as existing, in a striking form, among savage people, as when an individual is seized with a mysterious terror at the thought of doing or having done something wrong. But besides this haunting sense of God as speaking in the common conscience of man, the prophetic sense of a positive inspiration to speak a particular

[1] *Rep.*, 382 E ; see above, p. 11, n. 1.   [2] Prov. xx. 27.
[3] See quotations in Lightfoot's *Philippians*, p. 278.

message from God, or from some particular god, is also widespread—it is by no means confined to Israel. It is impressively presented to us in Zarathustra ; and though Muhammad appears clearly enough in his later career to have sophisti- cated his conscience and produced " oracles " dictated, in fact, by nothing better than his sense of political expediency or his passions, yet those who accept the claim of Israel's prophets to divine inspiration can hardly refuse to recognize genuine inspiration in Muhammad at least at the beginning of his prophetic career. It was a Jew who bade us recognize that " the spirit of the Lord filleth the world," and that " from generation to generation " His wisdom, " passing into holy souls, maketh them friends of God and prophets." [1]

It is true that the common belief in messages from gods given through inspired individuals, as we find this belief in popular religions, in China and India, in Egypt and in Greece, is not generally impressive intellectually or morally. We feel that as we read such a book as Edwyn Bevan's *Sibyls and Seers*. Indeed, among the Greeks, where we find this belief increasingly influential in the Hellenistic age, both in con- nection with the mystery-cults, and along a different line in the Hermetic books, it is asso- ciated with the decay of that clear and confident rationality which is part of what is highest in the Greek genius. Still, we reverence in Socrates his belief in his divine vocation to teach the Athenians to " care for their souls," and in his " demon," which restrained him when he was

---

[1] Wisd. i. 7 ; vii. 27.

going astray ; we remember also Plato's enthusiastic recognition of the " inspired " men who,
without argument, have enlightened their fellows ;
and, what is in the highest degree moving, the
desire which he attributes to Simmias in the
Phaedo, when he recognizes the unconvincing
character of human arguments on behalf of
immortality—even of Socrates' " swan song " just
before his death—for some " word of God "
which should be able to give fuller assurance.[1]
Let us have this fact, then, clearly in our minds,
that of what we esteem most valuable in our
human heritage a great part comes from those
prophetic souls, who would have repudiated
altogether having invented or discovered what
they announce, and with the deepest conviction
would have ascribed it to the self-revelation of
God in their own souls—the word of God.[2]

§ 2

Psychology has been occupied recently in dis-

[1] " Well, Socrates, then I will tell you my difficulty. . . . For
I dare say that you feel as I do, how very hard or almost impossible is the attainment of any certainty about questions such
as these in the present life. And yet I should deem him a coward
who did not test what is said to be uttermost, or whose heart
failed him before he had examined them on every side. For he
should persevere until he has obtained one of two things: either
he should learn or discover the truth about them ; or, if this is
impossible, I would have him take the best and most irrefragable
of human words, and let this be the raft upon which he sails
through life—not without risk, as I admit—if he cannot find some
word of God which will more surely and safely carry him "
(Plato, *Phaedo*, 85 (Jowett's trans., slightly altered)).

[2] That it is not only religious prophets, but poets and artists
also, who must be recognized as in some sense " inspired,"
see below, p. 306.

cussing whether we can recognize in our human nature any distinctive faculty which can be called the religious faculty, or any immediate experience of God as an objective reality. Dr. Tennant,[1] sternly refuses to recognize any such faculty or experience. " There is no ' higher faculty ' than those involved in ordinary knowledge." " If the ' truth of religion ' or ' the validity of religious experience ' is to be established at all, it must be as reasonable inference from discursive ' knowledge ' about the world, human history, the soul with its faculties and capacities ; and above all, from knowledge of the interconnections between such items of knowledge."

Now, I think we are right in entertaining a hearty dislike of the " faculty psychology " as it was current among the Greeks, and has reappeared from time to time in generations nearer to us, because it has tended to separate emotion, reason and volition from one another in our souls, as if they existed in separate compartments, and were really distinguishable entities. We put it to the credit of Tertullian that he should have striven to make it a feature of Christian philosophy that it should emphasize the unity of the soul of man, which feels when it reasons and reasons when it feels [2]—and, we must

[1] *Philosophical Theology*, vol. i, cap xii, pp. 306, 325 ff. ; see also vol. ii, pp. 225 ff. It is a disappointment to me to confess that one to whom I owe so great an obligation as I owe to Dr. Tennant deserts me here ; but, in spite of qualifications and hesitations expressed, this seems to be his conclusion.

[2] Tertullian, *de Animâ*, c. 18. John Henry Newman's real contribution to recent philosophy seems to me to have lain in his strong insistence upon this principle, against the rationalism of his day.

19

add, wills both in reasoning and feeling. But Dr. Tennant seems to suggest that the alternative to recognizing a separate faculty for religion in man is to acquiesce in the position that his belief in God must ultimately be the outcome of his reasoning faculty, a conclusion which he draws from the evidence supplied ultimately in sensible experience. Yet, as we have just been saying, the most impressive figures which religious history presents to us would surely refuse this estimate of their knowledge of God. Without denying that the existence of God may be a valid conclusion of reasoning, they would say—Not so have we known God or felt able to speak of Him to our fellows.

Zarathustra never appears as reasoning at all. He experiences directly, amid the desperate straits of his people, a mighty call of God in his soul, summoning him to co-operate in His redemptive purpose. So it is with the prophets of Israel. We hear them talking with God—that is, strongly representing their own inclinations and thoughts to God, and finding them overruled by His constraining authority and commission. Most obviously of all, it seems quite impossible to place ourselves face to face with Jesus of Nazareth and listen to His utterances about God, spoken in such a tone of infallible authority, and then to say, " I dispute this conclusion of yours as based on insufficient evidence " ; for it is not uttered as a human conclusion based on an estimate of evidence at all. It is something coming from above, conveying a divine certitude so impressive that almost any man, however sceptical, will find it hard indeed to bring himself to say, " I do not believe that you know more about God than I or any other man with a reasoning mind."

The real question, it seems to me, is not whether man has a special religious faculty, but whether his soul, or conscious self, is accessible to God, and whether God is a being who can make such an impression of Himself upon the human spirit as cannot but utter itself in communicable propositions for the intellect and directions for the will. I suggest that our contemporary psychologists and philosophers not only commonly fail to find a satisfying answer to this question, but fail to put the question in its proper form, which is an important part of philosophy.   I remember visiting Edward Caird on his death-bed in the Master's Lodge at Balliol, and finding him reading St. Augustine's *Confessions* ; and he said to me, " Whatever philosophers may say about this man's answers, at any rate he knew how to ask the right questions."   There is a great deal in that.   The right question in this case is : Can it be denied that, at very different stages of intellectual progress, and therefore with very different capacities for intellectual formulation of their impressions, certain men at any rate have received such overwhelmingly vivid impressions of God " speaking " directly to them as that they could not doubt the objective reality of their experience, and could not but express it in propositions for the intellect and directions for the will of their fellow-men ; and that the reception of their teaching as " the word of God " has had such surprising and permanent results in lifting the lives of their disciples to a higher moral and spiritual plane that we can hardly refrain from saying that their claim has received a kind of verification in experience? [1]

It is true that when we survey the records of revelations, supposed to be divine, given in different ages among different peoples, the evidences of crude and unspiritual ideas in the minds of the prophets, who have claimed to have received these divine communications, often force us to recognize in the human subject a medium which at least deeply colours and distorts the supposed word of God. It follows that if God is really to be recognized as " speaking," it is through an integument, often a very thick integument, of human material. One chief interest in the Old Testament is to observe how this thick and disturbing integument is gradually refined so as to become the pure vehicle which it is in the higher reaches of Hebrew prophecy, while yet these higher reaches are obviously continuous with its lower levels. But still the area of such supposed communications is so wide, and the effect of them on the whole in the noblest instances tends to such agreement, that it seems unreasonable to doubt that, responding to the efforts of man's struggling thought and passionate prayer— " seeking after God, if haply he may feel after him and find him "—God Himself has moved out towards man to assure, to strengthen, to guide and to enlighten. For myself, I profess,

[1] On the validity of such argument from religious experience see below, p. 313.

I cannot read Zarathustra and the prophets of Israel or listen to the words of Jesus without receiving the conviction that so it has been. " God who in many portions and many manners spake in old times unto our fathers by the prophets, hath in these last days spoken unto us by His son "—one who is more than any prophet.

It is exactly this *question* which many of our contemporary philosophers or theologians seem to me not to be willing to put to themselves. And I ask, " Why should it be thought a thing incredible with you " that God should so disclose himself to men ?

I will mention only one instance of this ignoring of the real question. I read many critical studies of St. Paul which trace the development of his theology—especially his doctrine of the person of Christ—in which he is described as sitting down, like a philosopher, and producing a " first draft " of his theory in one of his epistles and a considerably different version of the theory in another. Now, as a critic I read the evidence differently. I think the whole theory of what is called the cosmic function of the Son of God before His incarnation, and His eternal life in God, as you find it in Colossians or Philippians, is already substantially present in such phrases of the earlier epistles as " one Lord, Jesus Christ, through whom are all things, and we through him," or " our Lord Jesus Christ " who " though he was rich, yet for your sakes he became poor." [1]

I see no substantial difference in meaning

---

[1] 1 Cor. viii. 6 ; 2 Cor. viii. 9 ; assumed to be earlier than Col. i or Phil. 2.

between the four passages. I think the critics
have a far too acute eye for differences, and are
far too insensitive to substantial unities. Their
method is too microscopic when applied to such
untechnical language as that of St. Paul's epistles.

But to examine this question is not our present
business. I do not dispute that St. Paul had
to find words to express what was in his mind,
and found this a difficult task, and in finding
expression for his thought drew upon the existing
intellectual furniture of his mind. I think that
in all, even the highest, utterances claimed to
be divine words, must be recognized the human
element of representation. But what the critics
ignore is the fact, which seems to me indisputable,
that St. Paul, from the time of His conversion,
recognized the divine sonship of Jesus as a
revelation of God made to himself personally,
which it was his urgent business henceforth to
propagate, and which did not leave him much
choice in his manner of propagating it. " It
pleased God," he says, " to reveal his Son in
me," or rather " through me " [1] ; for the phrase
implies not only the fact of the veridical revelation in his own soul, but the stringent obligation
to impart it, and to claim its reception as not
the word of man but the word of God. Our
contemporary critics of the Bible and our philosophers seem to me neither to estimate at its due
importance this psychological fact witnessed
to by " the goodly fellowship of the prophets,"
nor to connect it with the general significance
of the testimony of conscience as (when not

---

[1] See Lightfoot on Gal. i. 16 ; cf. 12.

deliberately sophisticated) bearing witness to
a word of God vaguely conceived, which the
specific revelations presuppose and render more
explicit. It is upon the importance of this idea
of divine self-revelation, general and particular,
explicit enough to be expressed in propositions
for the intellect and directions for the will,
that I want to concentrate your attention.

It is not the only road by which men have
believed themselves to reach the knowledge of
God. There has been also the method of reasoning from premises supplied by experience to
conclusions reached by logic. That is the
characteristic method of philosophers. Greece
is the central home of philosophy, and of this
kind of philosophy, though it must never be
forgotten that the whole Platonic theology rests
upon certain moral assumptions which Socrates
felt as God's word to mankind. But this is not
the only method by which man has seemed to
himself to approach God. To man's quest
there has been God's response, or God's spon-
taneous act has preceded all man's enquiry.
God has revealed Himself; and of the consciousness of this we find the most conspicuous witnesses
in the prophets of mankind and the supreme
type in the prophets of Israel and in Jesus.
The fact on which I want to concentrate your
attention is not only that so the prophets and
Jesus believed and spoke, but that their testimony
has been believed through the subsequent generations as true, and has been acted upon, and that
the best of mankind have found their faith confirmed in experience by the vast enhancement of

moral capacity which their faith has generated in them. To refuse to give serious attention to this immense volume of testimony seems to go contrary to what appears to be a fundamental canon of human reason; namely, that what greatly augments human powers, and lifts mankind permanently to a higher level than it had shown signs of being able to reach before, must be rooted in reality.[1]

§ 3

What is called the " otherness " of God [2] has been much emphasized in Germany and Northern Europe lately, under the influence of Dr. Otto and Dr. Karl Barth. These powerful teachers, very different in their points of view, agree in a determination to make us realize that God, as He presents Himself to the human conscience, and as He appears in the records of revelation, is wholly other to man, overwhelming his consciousness by His inconceivable majesty, thundering upon him with His judgment, and leaving him utterly prostrate and passive. There was, no doubt, an immense need for this reassertion of the " numinousness " of God and of the " tremendous mystery " : we recall, in illustration of this numinousness, not only scenes in the Jewish and Christian Scriptures, but the terrible theophany in the Bhagavadgita.

[1] At the end of James B. Mozley's essay on Blanco White (in his collected Essays *Historical and Theological*, vol. ii, Rivington's, 1878), there is a grand presentation of the contrasted ideas of discovery and revelation.

[2] A phrase which appears in St. Chrysostom ($\theta \acute{a} \tau \epsilon \rho o \nu \ \tau o \hat{v} \ \theta \epsilon o \hat{v}$); see Otto, *The Idea of the Holy*, p. 184.

But we must never forget that though there are moments in the Old Testament where God appears as a mere terror, this is not the impression we are allowed to retain. We are not allowed permanently to forget what is involved in the conception that man is created in the image of God. It means that he has within him, in his conscience and reason, something which testifies to the character of God ; something to which God must justify Himself, and by which man must judge of what is divine. It is this which gives its tremendous force to Job's protest against the seeming injustice and cruelty of God. It is Job's conscience and reason which give him the right to make his almost blasphemous protest against God's apparent conduct to himself. He is appealing against the apparent God to what he feels must be the real God. When God answers Job out of the whirlwind, He seems at first hearing only to appal him by His majestic power ; and Job appears to be satisfied merely by having wrung an answer from God, though it is an annihilating answer. But that is not all. Job's previous protests against God are justified in the great drama by the voice of God. Job spoke, it appears, well after all, while his more pious-seeming friends spoke ill. And more than that, the seemingly trivial conclusion of the story, with the restoration to Job to more than his former prosperity, is really essential. It represents, though it be in a childish form, the conviction that God is bound by His very being to justify Himself to the human conscience. He must finally *appear* to have behaved justly.

The same ultimate principle appears in the passage
of St. Paul's Epistle to the Romans, where first
he appeals to the merely numinous—to the
irresistible authority or absolute determination
of God—" Who art thou, O man, that repliest
against God—the clay against the potter ? "
But the argument goes on to give a very different
impression—that behind God's temporal judgments there lies a mercy which is both ultimate
and universal, and a wisdom which must finally
justify itself to man.

So it is that in Old Testament and New Testament alike God makes His appeal for justification to the human conscience—" O my people,
what have I done unto thee ? and wherein have
I injured thee ? testify against me." [1]   " Why
even of yourselves judge ye not what is right." [2]
" True and righteous are God's judgments." [3]

This consciousness restrains the Christian from
ever justifying an irrational faith, or an idea of
revelation which leaves the human reason and
conscience merely passive before it. Not even
miraculous power is to convince us against our
conscience. Nothing, in fact, is more striking
in the Gospels than the sense they give of a
divine authority in Jesus which consistently
refuses to terrify and overwhelm the conscience
and reason of those who listened to Him. He
refuses utterly to stun men into acceptance of
His word by mere power. He must both win
their hearts and convince their consciences and
reasons. This is the tone of the whole New
Testament.

Mic. vi. 3 ; cf. Moffatt.   [2] Luke xii. 57.   [3] Apoc. xix. 2.

Thus, if we are agreed to take the New Testament as presenting to us the highest type of ethical monotheism, and if we recognize, as we are bound to, that it presents to us a " word of God " and not a " word of men," a divine revelation and not a conclusion of human reasoning, yet we can never allow ourselves to isolate and exalt the supernatural, as if the natural were of no account, or as if it were possible for God, who made us in His image, to crush either our reason or our conscience.

§ 3

I have just used the word " supernatural," and contrasted it with " natural," but it is a word very liable to lead to misunderstanding. When we contrast the laborious attempts of the human reason to interpret experience with the brilliant illumination thrown upon experience by the mere word of God, spoken by the prophets, we cannot help distinguishing the results as natural and supernatural ; or when, like St. Paul, we contrast the failure of man's best efforts, as he struggles by the exertion of his own will to realize what he recognizes to be right, with the triumphant power felt in the converted life, consciously inspired by the Spirit, it is irresistible to express the contrast as that of nature to supernatural grace. We cannot, as things are, do without this contrast of natural and supernatural. But this cannot be pressed to the point of dualism. It is the same God who works within us as an influence, and from without us as the giver of objective messages and objective gifts, perhaps embodied in visible

sacraments.   What is recognized as truly a divine
word must be found to correspond to, and crown,
the best intimations of human reason ; and the
most objectively conceived gifts of divine grace
must be estimated as only co-operating with the
responsive movement of the human soul from
within.   We cannot, then, do without the word
" supernatural," whether as applied to revelation
or to grace, but if we seek, with Aquinas, to draw
the line between the elements in our belief which
are natural and supernatural, we shall probably
find ourselves baffled in the attempt, and if we
seek to draw the same line between grace and
nature, we shall find ourselves compelled to
acknowledge, as even Augustine acknowledged,
that grace is not contrary to nature, but is the
restoration of nature.   God as transcendent and
acting as from without must never even for an
hour be separated in our thought from God as
universally and in all men immanent and inwardly
operative.[1]

It cannot be denied that there has appeared
in the Christian Church again and again a
tendency to put the supernatural in violent
contrast to the natural, and in particular so to
exalt revealed truth as to delight in the dis-
paragement of reason. Impulsive individuals
like Tertullian and Luther will be found guilty
in this respect as well as hosts of lesser men,
and the tendency dominates whole periods, just

---

[1] E.g., can we say that the word of God through the prophets
is supernatural and the clearest intimations of conscience merely
natural ?   Or can we dare to limit grace—which means only at
bottom the activity of the Holy Spirit—within any specific
channels or limits ?

as, from widely different motives, what we may call anti-intellectualism dominates certain periods in literature ; but we must put it to the credit of the Christian Church, that it has not, at its best periods and in its best representatives, shrunk from the appeal to conscience and reason. Thus, when it went out into the Hellenistic world in its first period of conflict, all the time that it was claiming the position of a society entrusted with an authoritative word of God, meant for all men and demanding " the obedience of faith," it was proclaiming also the rights of the human reason as reflecting the reason of God, and showing its power to assimilate, even while it inevitably modified and corrected, the Platonic tradition in philosophy, and in particular the moral philosophy which was both Platonic and Stoic. The resultant synthesis you see in the theology of the Greek Fathers and of Augustine, and in respect of morality in Ambrose and his followers. A second magnificent synthesis followed the revival of philosophical thought in the thirteenth century. There has been no like synthesis effected since the period of the later Renaissance, and it is not likely that the present generation will enjoy the spectacle of a commonly recognized alliance between religion and science or religion and philosophy.

For the thought of mankind, alike theological, moral and scientific, is in a condition of too great unsettlement to admit of such an immediate hope; and the Christian tradition, both Catholic and Protestant, had wedded itself, as indissolubly as it could, to an antiquated science of nature and to the idea of " the infallible book " ; and the progress of the natural sciences and of historical criticism has demanded a readjustment of religious ideas which goes very deep, and is difficult for a broad and divided society like the Christian Church to accomplish. But it cannot be denied that a large number of our best and ablest Christian thinkers—not least in Scotland— have recognized with a whole-hearted allegiance the divine rights of science and criticism, and have found their way, in their own minds and in their writings, to a synthesis between the Christianity of the New Testament, undiminished in force, and modern knowledge, such as is worthy of the name—a synthesis which satisfies their own reason and that of others. Elsewhere, I have tried to go into the details of such a synthesis, but it would be beyond my scope in these lectures. It is, however, much to be lamented that those who stand out in current literature as the critics and repudiators of the Christian tradition, so often appear to have confined their study of Christianity to the theology of a hundred years ago, or to that of their grandmother Lois or their mother Eunice. This is a criticism which applies to really distinguished men. They exhibit an ignorance of Christian thought at its best, whether ancient or modern, the like of which in the treatment of science would expose a theologian to well-merited ignominy.

§ 4

But we must pay special attention to one method by which it is proposed to destroy the impressive force of the appeal to a divine self-disclosure.

It is proposed to explain, or explain away, the impression to which the human conscience has so widely surrendered itself, of being in contact with a God who knows it and would communicate Himself to it, by psychological considerations. Thus the experience of answers to prayer is resolved into self-suggestion, and self-revelation of God into " uprushes from the subconscious." Now, we have admitted, and shall shortly be considering the meaning of our admission, that there is no demonstrative evidence *a priori* to confute the absolute sceptic who declares we cannot possibly know anything except the content of our own minds. But we can recognize that the whole of the human advance, alike nature-ward, man-ward and God-ward, has been based on a fundamental faith natural to man, that his instinctive assumptions are not purely delusive but bring him into contact with reality ; and it is very difficult to affirm the reality of nature and the trustworthiness of natural science while refusing to recognize the reality of the spiritual values inherent in nature and the divine activity upon the soul of man, to both of which the human conscience bears convincing witness.[1]

But we may go farther than that : we may point out that the subconscious region of man's

[1] It is satisfactory to notice the recovery of modern scientific thought from pure subjectivism : see Whitehead's *Process and Reality*, pp. 102, 106, 159, 210 ff. With reference to spiritual realities, see Eddington's *Nature of the Physical World*, p. 332 (4) and elsewhere.

mind, while it is or may be the depository of a
vast amount of animal and subhuman instincts
and " racial memories " and mental experiences,
which prudence or pride has forced us to sup-
press, has provided no evidence at all worthy of
the name to show that it can be the source of new
knowledge or fresh disclosures such as have
advanced and ennobled mankind. Inheritances
from a subhuman ancestry, or from early man,
may be latent within us, and be capable of re-
emerging. Forgotten memories may be renewed
and latent forces reawakened. Thus there is a
great deal in the history of debased religion and
in the records of frenzied prophecy which may
rightly be laid to the credit, or discredit, of the
subconscious ; but there is very little to lead us
to believe that there is anything stored in man
below the line of consciousness which does not
belong to the past of the individual or his pro-
genitors. It is the active conscious mind or
will or heart which appears to have the credit
for the ideas and discoveries which have advanced
mankind. There is no justification for attri-
buting to " the subconscious " the thoughts or
utterances of Amos or Isaiah or Jesus. There
was nothing in their past traditions to account
for such thoughts. It must be acknowledged
that they have all the appearance of being down-
rushes from the superconscious rather than
uprushes from below the level.[1] Philo, indeed,

---

[1] I believe H. S. Holland to have been the first to use this
phrase ; see the *Philosophy of Faith*, edited by Wilfrid Richmond,
p. 102. On the whole subject I may refer to *The Reconstruction
of Belief*, pp. 102 ff.

the Jewish philosopher who sought to co-ordinate
the religion of Israel with the current philosophy
of the first century, adopted the pagan idea of
inspiration, as something which must first dispossess the human reason before it could enter
into possession, and could only use the human
being for its organ of expression as the pipe-
player uses his pipe. But the Christian Church
repudiated this idea of inspiration and prophecy.
It was the fullest and most-awakened human consciousness which, in Amos and Isaiah and the
rest, it believed to have responded to the coming
upon them of the divine Spirit.

It does not seem to me that we can prove by
any absolute demonstration either the reality of
God's revelation of Himself or indeed any other
of the normal conclusions of the human reason.
We cannot dispense with faith. But in the
lecture which concludes this series I shall be
contending that there is a fundamental faith
which is so far from being irrational that it is a
primary constituent of reason. My point at
present is that the normal man, if he will dare to
think freely, and will place himself deliberately
face to face with the great prophets of history
or especially with the prophets of Israel and with
Jesus Christ, will find himself strongly constrained
to believe that they were divinely inspired.

Certainly, if we take into account the whole
range of human enlightenment, we cannot easily
escape the conclusion that, much as mankind
owes to scientific records and to the logical
reason, it owes at least as much to what we
cannot but call inspiration—and I am not only

20

thinking of the inspiration of prophets, but also of that of the poets and musicians and artists. The materials on which these masters of men worked are nature and human kind—the sights, the sounds, the experiences which are common to all men. When we common men read or hear or behold their " creations," we can appreciate them, and in some measure assimilate them, for we have a sensibility like theirs. But what they possess—what constitutes them masters of our souls—is not any superiority in the reasoning powers, but an immense superiority in the power of their intuition. Beauty is an important element in reality, and it is discovered by intuition not reasoning. The poet's or artist's soul is extraordinarily receptive of this reality. We cannot really express what we feel about him so well as by saying that the spirit of beauty in nature (which is the spirit of God) has inspired the man, and enabled him so to express this spirit of beauty in words or musical sounds or artistic symbols as that the souls of commoner men can feel it with him and rejoice with a joy unspeakable. He is an inspired man, and the vehicle therefore of a revelation. It seems to me absurd to deny how large a proportion of human enlightenment we owe to inspired men.

But I return to the special kind of inspiration and revelation which at present is occupying our attention. I am conscious of what appears to be an almost irresistible antipathy in many of the leading representatives of the " modern mind " to the very idea of such divine revelation as is claimed for the Christian religion, and I will endeavour to analyse this antipathy into its intellectual elements.

§ 5

(a) There is first the fact that the supposed divine self-revelation, especially as it culminates in Christ, is associated with the occurrence of miracles. A generation back it was supposed that science was in a position to repudiate the miraculous as such. But that appears to be no longer a maintainable position. It is hardly too much to say that Dr. Tennant has demonstrated its untenability[1]; and Prof. Hobson, in his *Survey*[2] has stated plainly and forcibly that "it is a piece of *a priori* dogmatism, quite incapable of substantiation on scientific grounds." Science does not know nearly enough to exclude the possibility of the miraculous from its idea of nature, any more than to exclude the "free determination" of human actions.

It is the truth, I think, that the question of freedom in man and the question of the possibility of the miraculous are one and the same question. If we cannot deny that man can deliberate, and within certain limits choose and determine his course of action, and that the very evidence of rationality in man, by contrast with instinct in animals, is that he can and does under exceptional circumstances act exceptionally, it is impossible to deny to the supreme Spirit, if such there be, the same freedom for exceptional action, or perhaps I should say, of something higher

[1] Tennant, *Miracle and its Philosophical Presuppositions.*
[2] Hobson, *op. cit.*, p. 490.

and less expressible in human language, of which this freedom in man is the best analogue.

If we turn from science to history we find the same prejudice among the historians (though by no means without exception) against the admission of the miraculous. It is quite true that most of the stories of the miraculous which we find in human tradition are such that human credulity and self-hypnotism or crowd-hypnotism can easily account for them. There is nothing in literature less impressive than hagiology in the mass. But history is very far off the position of being able to profess such a knowledge of the ultimate laws of nature or human action as to deny that some miraculous events have in fact occurred. Logically, the recognition that human imagination has so craved the miraculous as to imagine it freely where it has not really occurred, is no sort of justification for saying that it never has occurred in fact.

Nor is it to the point to argue that the Christian faith would be all the better for discarding the miraculous.[1] Speaking for myself, I wholly dispute this position. I feel sure that, as Christianity could never have got its start without the miracles of Christ and in particular without its confident proclamation of the miracle of His resurrection, so I believe it could not retain its hold without these elements. They supply the certificate human nature so greatly needs, that the God of Nature is also the Saviour.

[1] This idea is not so modern as is supposed. Rousseau exclaimed: " Ôtez les miracles de l'Évangile, et toute la terre est aux pieds de Jésus-Christ " (*Lettres de la Montagne*, iii).

But this question is really irrelevant. The point is, how, in fact, did Christ present Himself ? And I dare to say that, after a century of drastic criticism of the Gospels, nothing has become more evident than that, if you repudiate *a priori* the miraculous element out of the original tradition, you so destroy its foundations as to leave very little that is coherent or trustworthy behind ; but that, on the other hand, anyone who admits the possibility of a divine self-disclosure will find the record of Jesus as a whole, both of His teaching and His miraculous working, historically convincing. I say " as a whole," not meaning to demand any infallibility in detail for our records, but only such trustworthiness as is asked for in ordinary history believed to be circumstantially credible. What I ask of you, then, is that, when you demand free historical criticism, you should take care that the presuppositions of your criticism are not arbitrary.

(*b*) Nor is it reasonable to seek to *substitute* a general for a particular self-disclosure of God— to say that one can in a general sense believe that God is manifested in the universe of things and in the universal thought of man, but that one cannot reasonably believe that a revelation of the truth most needed by man could have been given through the narrow channel of one little race and reached finality in one person. This is not a protest which can be based on general observation. For, so far as the story of evolution lies before us, it is a fact of frequent occurrence that things most needed for man, physically and mentally, appear and are developed in one place and among one race, and thence spread to become a universal inheritance. No one, I trust, wishes to deny that there is truth in speaking of a universal self-revelation of God. But you must recognize that particular races appear as " chosen races " in the sense that they have some special aptitude, as for government, or for the expression of beauty in art, or for science, so that some universal need of mankind found satisfaction first among them and spread thence to mankind at large. Does not Israel, then, including the Christ, in fact display a special genius for religion ? Is there anything of value in any national tradition of religion or any individual message of any human prophet, which is not either already comprised in the religion of Christ as you find it in the New Testament, or such that it cannot easily and naturally be assimilated ? Is it not true that Christianity supersedes all other religions by its very nature—not by excluding but by including the elements of truth which they all contain ?

Certainly Christianity, in virtue of its essential idea, claims to be final. There is no relation of God to man or of man to God which can be imagined closer and completer than the Christian faith assumes to exist in Jesus and by Him to be made available for mankind. The language of finality is essential to Christianity. But the consummate thing, at that point in history finally given, whether as it concerns God or as it concerns man, is so rich that it must take all nations and periods to exhaust its significance. The final object, which we are bidden to contemplate in the New Testament, is only the starting-point of a new creation, which is a process as gradual as was the old.   A man who believes the fundamental Christian creed as valid for all time, must still look round on the world to-day, and wonder whether mankind can even be said to have begun in earnest to estimate and exhaust its implications.

(c) It is an objection of a quite different kind which rejects Christianity, not because it is so ancient and conservative, but on the contrary because it presents such a bewildering variety of churches and creeds.   But, again, it is not worthy of a rational mind to make this fact (so far as it is a fact) an excuse for a refusal to give serious consideration to the central claim that the Christian Church is, in spite of all its faults and failures, the carrier of the truth about God and man.   You must take the facts of human history as they are.   We find the best elements in humanity, such as liberty or justice, strangely misrepresented and abused by their official organs.   Grievous faults and excesses and exaggerated claims and resultant revolts and conflicts are lamentable facts in the life of the Christian Church ; so much so that the surface of its history does often appear to discredit it, just as the surface of human history discredits any lofty claim of any kind made for mankind. But it is the negation of wisdom to refuse to hunt for the spiritual treasure, because it is hid in a field thick with weeds.   It is childish petulance to say that I will only welcome truth if it is easily discovered.   It cannot be denied that human unfaithfulness has, in the tradition of the centuries, grievously mishandled Christian ideas, and has often tied them to some transitory phase of human science so that it is a laborious task to disentangle essential Christianity. But those who cannot undertake this task for themselves can at least fix upon some teacher who seems to be both morally worthy and intellectually capable, who has devoted himself to the task of presenting essential Christianity in a form which does not present needless hindrances to the modern spirit, and can make a frank study of his presentation, and compare it with what he reads for himself in the books of the New Testament, and think again before he comes to the conclusion that Christianity is antiquated.

There is an objection, as deep as any which hinders men from welcoming the Christian Gospel, which is in effect that it is too good to be true—that the Christian optimism cannot be reconciled with the grim and repulsive aspects of nature, so as to let us believe that the God of nature is really the Father of Jesus Christ; but this shall be left for consideration in the lecture that follows.

It is obvious that in the latter part of this lecture I have been compressing into a very short compass considerations which need to be much more fully developed, which, in fact, I have endeavoured to develop elsewhere.[1] But it is not my object in these lectures to present an apologetic in detail. What I have attempted is to re-draw the various pictures of the good life which have prevailed among men, under the influence of great prophets and seers. I have

---

[1] In *Reconstruction of Belief*, B. i, capp. vii–xi.

pointed to the divine background which they all in common postulate. I have sought among their diverse creeds to vindicate Christianity as the noblest form of ethical monotheism, to bring out into distinctness its intellectual postulates, and to establish their rationality as superior to anything which is offered us by any other faith or philosophy. I have not claimed to be able to *demonstrate* the truth of Christianity or to *demonstrate* the fundamental postulates of idealism. I believe that when we get down to the foundations, or back to the ultimates, of human thought or life, we are confronted with the necessity of a fundamental faith. And it is the place of faith in reason—I do not say over against reason but in reason—which must be our last subject for consideration.

APPENDED NOTE ON THE ARGUMENT FROM RELIGIOUS EXPERIENCE
(See above, p. 292)

Religious experience shows that certain specific beliefs have permanently and greatly elevated human nature and augmented its capacity. It is therefore, I think, legitimate to argue that the beliefs in question must have " something in them " or must really have brought the believers into fresh touch with reality. There is, therefore, a legitimate argument from effectiveness to truth. But it is only legitimate so far as it rids our minds of prejudice against the " evidences " of some particular creed. Christianity, for example, as being a religion profoundly based on historical events, can never appeal to spiritual experience as if that could be a *substitute for* historical evidence, if it be admitted that this has been weakened or destroyed by criticism.

For (1) there can be no " verification " of past historical

events by subsequent spiritual experience comparable to the verification of scientific hypotheses or discoveries by subsequent experiment. I am sure that Tennant's criticism of Mr. Spens's *Belief and Practice* is justified on this point ; see *Philos. Theol.*, vol. i, pp. 331 f.

(2) Subsequent religious experience can provide no *substitute* for the original historical testimony, if that is supposed to be inadequate. There again Bishop Arthur Chandler's criticism of Mr. Spens in *Christian Religious Experience* (Longmans), pp. 17 ff., is fully justified. The Christian experience is always based upon and conditioned by a postulate of historical truth.

(3) No spiritual idea or practice can gain a right to become an authoritative part of the Christian creed or system merely because it shows spiritual effectiveness. In fact ideas and practices of the most contradictory kinds have shown spiritual effectiveness.

All that it seems to me even widespread and long-continued spiritual experience can do is to open our minds to give a welcome to whatever evidence is forthcoming for the doctrine or statements of fact on which the experience is based.

CHAPTER XII

As a lecturer on Lord Gifford's foundation, I have stood before you to give account of the idea of God and of man and of the world which, after a lifetime of serious thought, I have found the most satisfying—that is to say, to give an account of what the Germans would call my *Welt-anshauung*—my general outlook upon the world. It is, in fact, no novel vision, but the Christian outlook—as you find it in the New Testament. In each settled epoch, however, the Christian creed has become involved in contemporary assumptions, which do not really belong to its original substance, and which need to be discarded when the fashion of thought and volume of knowledge have changed. Owing to the conservative prejudices and the intellectual indolence of the great majority of mankind, this disentanglement of essential Christianity becomes a laborious and a difficult process, which in our day rational theologians are struggling to bring to effect, not without success. The Christian creed, then, which I stand here to profess, is a purged or reconstructed creed, which in the truest sense can be called " catholic." But I am not appealing to the authority of the Church, or of any church, on its behalf. That is an appeal which Lord Gifford barred. I am standing before you simply as one rational being speaking to other

rational beings, and giving my reasons for holding
that the Christian view of the world is the most
rational view which we men can entertain.

§ 1

I have not scrupled to appeal in part to its
moral effectiveness. A man seeks to live the
good life ; he cannot live by bread alone ; and I
cannot doubt that the spiritual nourishment
offered by the Christian creed has proved itself
to be in the highest degree effective. That is to
say that its conceptions of God and man are such
as supply anyone who believes them with the
grandest and strongest motives, and the deepest
and most efficient succours, for living the good
life. They most effectively help him to face all
that in human experience—and it is a large *that*—
which makes for pessimism and discouragement,
and to penetrate through all such discouragement
to a ground of final optimism. I do not hesitate
to say that one of the deepest reasons for believing
that Christianity must be true is the evidence
of the lives of those who throughout the centuries
have shown themselves to be real and whole-
hearted Christians. This is a never-ceasing
evidence which appeals to us all. We cannot but
believe that a creed which can produce such a
result, on such a scale, and over such a length of
ages, must be in some deep correspondence with
reality. Let me enlarge a little on this superior
moral effectiveness of Christianity.

The idea of history as a whole given by
Christianity—its account of the redemptive purpose and action of God, and most of all the record

it gives of the manifestation of God in Jesus Christ
—gives it an enormous advantage. The idealists
of the past behind Christianity talked of a
" moral law," and Christianity adopted this
element of " natural religion." I read to you in
an earlier lecture a magnificent panegyric, from
Cicero's *De Republica*, of this permanent and
universal law. But what is it in fact ? What
are its provisions ? Where are they to be found ?
Christianity has here an obvious advantage.
It tells us indeed that there was a positive law—
the Ten Commandments of the Jews—which
expressed the divine will in a rudimentary form
for a temporary purpose and for a particular
people ; but it tells us also that these definite
prescriptions proved inadequate. They do not
indeed lose their value ; but they need to be
deepened and enlarged.

Christ gave His Church some such detailed
laws, though very sparingly. But He gave what
is infinitely more valuable and more applicable to
all times and states of life—He enunciated
intelligible moral principles and, more than
that, He set a perfect example, in which the
principles of the good life are plainly to be
seen, and which illustrate His moral teaching
with a force that no merely positive laws could
have.[1] This revelation of the moral ideal in a

[1] He also is recorded to have endowed His Church with an
authority to translate the principles of living which He enunciated
and illustrated into detailed injunctions binding upon its members
—that is, to " bind " and " loose "—with a heavenly sanction.
He did this in spite of the misuse of a like authority which He
had noted in the contemporary scribes. That He really did so,
the Acts and Epistles supply convincing evidence.

perfect human life, in a person worthy of the absolute faith which He claimed, and capable, as He proved, of supplying by His Spirit inward power corresponding to the outward example— this embodiment of the ideal in a person who is richly and fully human—gives to Christianity an enormous practical advantage—something of which the philosophers felt the need [1] but which they never could adequately supply. It is, in fact, by its emphasis on personality—the personality of God, the person of Christ, the divine and personal Spirit, the undying personality of each man—that Christianity vindicated its right to claim to be the supreme expression of ethical monotheism. This is the argument from effectiveness—to many of us the most effective of all arguments.

§ 2

But we cannot be content with this appeal. We are concerned with the rationality of this creed, alike as regards God and man and his place in the universe of things; and it is its superior rationality, in view of human knowledge as a whole, that I have been chiefly arguing. Practical issues of the most important kind for the individual and for society depend upon the attitude of each of us towards this faith in God. It is not enough to be vaguely interested; and it is practically and in the long run impossible to be neutral. If there are materials for decision, we must decide. We are not perhaps philo-

[1] Aristotle, as we have seen, can find no other criterion of doubtful cases than " as the wise man would determine."

sophers ; and the variety of philosophical opinions reflected in current literature is so bewildering that there is a special temptation, experienced by persons of a more or less intellectual disposition, to abandon all hope of forming a decision of our own, and to be content to find all opinions interesting. But this is ignoble. We cannot stand out of this responsibility for decision. As Socrates warned humanity, each man's gravest responsibility is the care of his own soul, and indissociable from the care of his own soul is that of the souls of others. We are bound to exercise our own judgment on questions which so vitally concern the welfare of mankind.

Thus I have presented to you the reasons which appeal to me for finding the Christian belief the most rational of all the intellectual interpretations of the world. But I have not presented it to you as capable of absolute demonstration, so that in making it your own there should be no need of the faith which goes beyond proof. I do not believe that there is any theory of the world which, in claiming acceptance, can dispense with faith—for the absolute scepticism which is content to proclaim the world and human life wholly meaningless enigmas is not a theory but the negation of theory. And it is this idea of a rational faith which I am now set to justify.

If you contemplate the spectacle of human development on this earth, so far as history and anthropology can spread it out before your eyes, it is obvious that a vast deal of experience preceded the advent of philosophy. On this enough was said at the start of these lectures as a reason for preferring the type of philosophy which is the least *a priori*. A vast experience of nature and of mankind and (as was believed) of divine beings who influence man's lot preceded the rise of speculative thought. This long-standing experience was based on a fundamental kind of faith. Man began his career with the animal instinct urging him to survive and propagate his kind. Illuminated by dawning reason, this instinct becomes a faith—that life is good and can be made better—that the nature which surrounds us is trustworthy in a measure, and will respond to man's efforts—and that our fellow-man is also on the whole and within limits trustworthy. This faith in its later forms becomes the consciousness of values which it cannot question—of goodness and beauty and truth, and it feels itself subject to some divine influence which must be treated with awful respect, and to spirits which must be propitiated.

Thus a vast experience had accumulated—scientific, humanist, religious—before the philosopher appears on the scene. We can watch his appearance best in Greece, and interest ourselves in his attitude to all this common experience and belief. He exists of course to criticize, and to take account of things as a whole. He is confronted at once with the great problems—the difference between appearances, which are obviously largely deceptive, and reality—the problem of the one and the many—the conflict of opinions, which are so many, with truth, which can be only one. The first utterances of philosophy sound childish in their simplicity—

" All is water," " All is air," " All is motion—
there are no fixed things." " All particular
things are unreal—there is only the one."   But
these early explanations were destructive of
familiar beliefs, and especially the traditional
beliefs about the gods suffered at the hands of
the philosophers.   To them they were ridiculous
myths.   But then, what is the worth of the moral
maxims on which the state and the social life
of man seem to be based ?   Is it not all a mere
matter of custom and expediency ?

In this atmosphere of general and fundamental
scepticism we see Socrates seeking to steady his
contemporaries by an appeal to what we call
moral values.   There is something certain—
that is, the distinction of good and evil and the
absolute obligation of doing the right.   This,
he implies, is something which does not admit
of further analysis.   It is an ultimate datum.
On this basis it was that the fabric of Platonism
was built.   It is an appeal to a fundamental
faith which does not admit of argument.   It is
on such an appeal that the argument of these
lectures rests ;   only they have shown that it is
an appeal which is not only made by Socrates
and his followers.   It appears in the claim made
by the prophets of all nations—it is the basis of
humanism and of the sense of the worth and
dignity of human life all the world over.

It is not to be denied that the appeal to this
fundamental faith is more obviously necessary
in the moral region than in any other.   There is
no *a priori* evidence that existence is a good
thing and not (as Gotama thought) an evil thing

21

or a mere illusion. Logically, pessimism or
nihilism [1] is an equally possible conception. But
it is contrary to the ultimate instinct of life.
That life is good and is to be made the most
of, is the ultimate act of faith. And, as appears
in human experience long before the advent
of the philosopher, this does not mean merely
that pleasure is good and pain is evil; it recognizes
other values such as are analysed later on as
virtue and truth and beauty. They as well as
mere physical satisfaction constitute the good,
and rank indeed as higher goods than physical
life itself. That this is so is the ultimate act of
faith for which neither Socrates nor any of the
wise men or prophets can give any further reason.
It is their unanalysable ultimate. They therefore
show no scruple in making it the dogmatic basis
of the education of each fresh generation.

The famous passages in the *Republic* and the
Laws, in which Plato emphasizes the supreme
importance of the education of children, before
they are of an age to appreciate rational processes,
is based quite frankly on the idea that they should
go out into the maturer stage of life with one
supreme prejudice, which is both æsthetic and
moral, embedded in the emotional and volitional
basis of their nature—that there is a right way
of living—that there are divine principles which
must not be violated, and that obedience to
these is duty—it is to obey God rather than
men. I am taking my stand on this principle—
that the idea of the absolute values on which

---

[1] I.e. the refusal to believe in any ascertainable truth or
reality.

the good life is based is an ultimate act of faith,
to refuse which is to repudiate both religion and
humanism. It is this faith alone that can make
life worth living.

It is, I say, no doubt the case that it is in the
moral or spiritual life of man that the necessity
for this ultimate and continuous act of faith is
most obvious, but it is really quite as true
that the basis of natural science also lies in
a similar or identical act of faith. No would-
be rationalist can flatter himself that he has
got rid, or even can hope to get rid, of this
fundamental necessity. The basis of science
lies in a certain trust in nature—that nature
will prove " reasonable," or will behave in
such a way as corresponds with the demands of
reason for a certain order or uniformity. It is
obvious that this could not and cannot be proved.
It is obvious that there is a great deal in
experience—in the experience of primitive man,
or even in that of developed man—which cannot
be accounted for, and which appears to be
arbitrary. This appearance might well have
overwhelmed the consciousness of primitive man,
and cut at the root of progress. It was his
faith in nature which prevented this ; and Dr.
Tennant is surely quite right in saying that,
however deeply and permanently scientific experience has justified the primitive faith, and
even overlaid it so that its existence may be
ignored, it cannot really be denied, and must
not be forgotten. The uniformity of nature (or
whatever phrase you choose to express the fundamental assumption of science) never can become a

self-evident proposition.   It is a venture of faith
confirmed in experience, but not so confirmed
as that the practical proposition that " the future
will resemble the past " can become anything
more than an act of faith.

As Dr. Tennant says, the definition of faith
given in the Epistle to the Hebrews, " the
substantiation of things hoped for, the assurance
of things not seen," is also the definition of the
assumption on which science works.   Bishop
Butler's famous maxim, that " probability is
the guide of life," admits of extension.   " It
can be broadened into the assertion that probability is the guide of science.   Scientific
' knowledge ' rests on indemonstrable belief ;   it
is not in the strictest sense ' knowledge ' unless
certain beliefs are valid ;   which, in turn, and
again in the logically strongest sense, are not
' known ' to be valid.   In science, as well as
in other fields of thought, we have to purchase
rationality—i.e. reasonableness with belief, which,
used in all proving, is itself incapable of being
proved :   *credo ut intelligam* is an attitude which
science did not drop, when it put away the
childish things of man's primitive credulity."
To-day, " the majority of the representatives of
science would not be perturbed at hearing . . .
that science walks by faith and cannot give a
' rational ' (i.e. demonstrable) but only a ' reasonable ' reason of the hope that is in it."   " Without faith, that in essentials is akin to that of
religion, there is no scientific ' knowledge ' possible as to the Actual."   So far Dr. Tennant.[1]

[1] *Philosophical Theology*, vol. i, pp. 278, 285, 290, 296.

I am leaving out of sight—what would of course add much emphasis to what I have just been saying—the recent affirmation of mathematical physicists, such as Prof. Eddington, that there is a random, indeterminist, element at the very basis of nature; and the assertion that we have no right to speak of *laws* of nature, for the so-called laws are only formulated descriptions of the experienced behaviour of nature under accurate but partial observation—because I cannot but wonder whether these novel representations are to be taken as " assured results " of science. We laymen are not yet convinced that the *quanta* may not turn out to be only examples of *apparently* random phenomena which will some day be found to exhibit some sort of law. I am working rather upon the scientific assumption of thirty years ago, which was the basis of the older rationalism such as now appears to be vanishing, and I am affirming that it could never substantiate its claim to take for granted only self-evident propositions and proceed from them only by rigorous proofs. The ultimate assumption which science was bound to make at starting, and is bound to abide by throughout its course, is purely an act of faith which goes far beyond what can be demonstrated or can be regarded as self-evident.

Let me repeat that I am not denying that the need of faith is both more evident and more constant in the moral sphere than in that of science. Science, strictly speaking, has its sphere of operations in the region where ocular verification is possible. It is true, of course, that scientific imagination, which cannot claim verification up to the present or even can never hope to claim it, has held a large place in the scientific equipment. Yet on the whole verification by experiment takes a much more tangible form in scientific enquiry, and a form which appeals much more readily to every man, good or bad, idealist or cynic. Whereas faith is not only the concealed basis, but the overt glory and boast of the moral and religious life. Thus the faith which religion postulates is much more obviously a " faith that rebels " (as Dr. Cairns calls it). It glories in triumphing over apparent fact and reaches out to a yet unapparent vindication. That is obviously the case wherever the good life is struggling to maintain itself against lower ideals, which dominate the world about it.[1]

But if you compare divergent moral systems which exhibit this same fundamental faith—if you compare ethical idealism, as it appears in the synthesis of Platonism and Stoicism which constituted " the religion of sensible men " when Christianity came into the world, or the ethical idealism of to-day, with the ethical monotheism of which the faith of the Christian Church is the supreme type, I should not admit that the latter

[1] This is the meaning of the famous phrase " credo quia impossibile," for which Prof. Eddington confesses a weakness. Really, of course, it only means, " I believe because the apparent impossibility of my creed at the present moment only emphasizes its essential necessity." It is a moral rather than a logical proposition. It is attributed constantly to Tertullian *ad invidiam*. His actual phrase (*De carne Christi*, 5) is " certum quia impossibile." It is one of a series of rhetorical exclamations meaning that the immensity of the divine condescension in the Incarnation constitutes its attraction.

lays a greater strain on pure faith than the former. Also I cannot allow any antithesis between faith and reason; for no satisfying account can be given of the soul or self of man which does not recognize in faith a primary function of reason. Let me enlarge this point.

§ 3

Recent psychology has reacted strongly against the older rationalism—sometimes into an excessive irrationalism—but I am safe in saying that our present-day knowledge of the soul or self shows that its conscious thought depends upon a subconscious region, which from the first exercises a determining influence upon it. Conscious reason is never pure reasoning. The adventure of the conscious self is an adventure on which it starts heavily conditioned by a sub-consciousness which is largely the product of heredity. Moreover, the self is very far from starting as a realized unity. It starts as a bundle of faculties or impulses very loosely unified, but yet not so loosely as that the self should not be from the start conscious of its own unity as soon as it is conscious of anything. It becomes conscious of self in becoming conscious of the world in which it lives. And its consciousness is not a passive consciousness. At the root of self-hood is the will to live, which is an implicit faith that life is good and an implicit love of the good. This vital impulse is volitional, emotional and rational— all in the germ. Reason as it develops is first of all a calculating faculty brought to bear upon all the crude material of experience so as to dis-

cover how best to live—how best to preserve the
good and avoid the evil. But it has its motive
in the will to live, and the sense that life is good
is its implicit faith. Nor can any evidence be
produced to make it probable that, as the idea
of what is good developed, the spiritual ideals—
the ideal of duty, or the ideal of beauty, or the
ideal of truth—were merely derivative motives,
mere offshoots of the motive of pleasure.

Without attempting to do what lies beyond our
knowledge, that is, to give the order of
time in which these distinctive ideals emerged,
we must be content to recognize that they emerge
as existing in their own right. Man must be
defined as recognizing the satisfaction of the
desire for pleasure, and of the sense of beauty and
of the sense of the value of truth and the obligation of moral duty as all fundamentally and
independently elements of the good. Reason
is the minister of satisfaction to all these fundamental claimants. The soul of man must be
recognized as by its nature not only susceptible
of the satisfaction of the senses, but also as
endowed with certain susceptibilities—the susceptibility to beauty, truth and goodness—which,
all in some measure, present themselves to it as
imperatives, claiming its allegiance ; but this
imperative authority must be recognized as, in
an especial sense, belonging to the idea of moral
duty. It is in this respect that man appears as
most obviously haunted by the sense of a superior
authority under which he lives, and thereby
deeply susceptible of God. It is in special men—
the prophetic souls—that the susceptibility be-

comes striking. They know God as dealing with themselves.

But what is remarkable is that in the history of mankind the prophet's declarations of God awaken the susceptibility in the souls of their fellow-men, so that their witness to God (whether cruder or purer in character) is accepted for undoubted truth. This susceptibility is most apparent, then, in the prophets—not only the prophets of Israel—and the supreme example is in Jesus Christ. But it exists in all men as a fundamental natural endowment—or if anyone appears to be totally destitute of it, he must be pronounced as in that respect less than complete man, as much as one who is totally destitute of the sense of beauty or of truth, or who is deaf or blind.

I have ventured into this slight incursion into psychology only in order to indicate that, while we give glory to reason, yet when we find it attempting to discard faith as something alien to itself, we must remind it that it belongs to its very essence, for neither in science nor in any other department of its activity can it do without it. It is rooted and grounded in faith. And when we find reason repudiating the very idea of a divine helper who can reveal Himself to man and has in fact revealed Himself, we must remind it that it is repudiating one of those fundamental human susceptibilities which, like the susceptibility to beauty or to truth, belongs to the nature of man as he appears in experience.

§ 4

But if arrogant reason, scornful at the very idea of faith, needs chastisement, there is no more effective chastisement than to force upon it the recognition of human ignorance.

That is a favourite theme of the wise man of the book of Ecclesiastes. Four times we hear him deploring the utter impossibility of making sense of the universe—of detecting any rational purpose which it subserves from end to end. " For the mind of man God has appointed mystery, that man may never fathom God's own purpose from beginning to end." " Reality is beyond my grasp : deep it lies, very deep, and no one can lay hands upon the heart of things." " I found that man is unable to grasp the truth of all that God does in the world." [1] This is the lamentation of the sceptic all the world over. And neither religious nor scientific illumination can wholly contradict this verdict.

" We know," St. Paul says, " but in part " or " bit by bit " ; " We see, but in a glass darkly "— that is, but a blurred reflection of ultimate reality, as in a dark saying which both informs and baffles. This is not the whole of St. Paul's feeling about our relation to ultimate truth. No one exulted more than he did in the clearness of the knowledge both of the mind of God and of the nature and destiny of man, which was conveyed to the souls of men in the revelation of Christ. But if a man seeks to reduce this illumination, which

---

[1] Eccles. iii. 11 ; vii. 24 ; viii. 17 ; xi. 5, Moffatt's trans., which at least gives the general sense.

for the practical purposes of life is so abundant, to a complete science, he finds its baffling incompleteness. He looks forward to a future state, when he shall know even as he is known. But for the present he finds knowledge fragmentary or unsatisfying—a sadly baffled vision. That is again the verdict of Bishop Butler. This world is not a place of intellectual, any more than of moral, satisfaction. It needs faith to discern any " scheme of things." And the bright lights which faith welcomes in this " state of probation," if they are enough to give a glimpse of an ordered scheme, yet leave it at the best " a scheme imperfectly apprehended."

And science tells us the same humiliating story. " Nowadays," says Prof. Eddington, " whenever enthusiasts meet together to discuss theoretical physics, the talk sooner or later turns in a certain direction. You leave them conversing on their special problems or the latest discoveries, but return after an hour, and it is any odds that they will have reached an all-engrossing topic— the desperate state of their ignorance. This is not a pose. It is not even scientific modesty, because the attitude is often one of naïve surprise that Nature should have hidden her fundamental secrets successfully from such powerful intellects as ours. It is simply that we have turned a corner in the path of progress, and our ignorance stands revealed before us, appalling and insistent." [1] It would be easy to multiply professions of ignorance from the stu-

[1] *The Nature of the Physical World*, p. 179.

dents of other branches of human science. Thus when we are comparing the claim of science and the claim of religious faith, it is important to recognize that both are agreed that the " scheme " of things to which they admit us is a scheme very " imperfectly comprehended." Here, in St. Andrews, I would remind you that your famous philosopher, Prof. Ferrier, who invented the word " epistemology," intended that we should couple our recognition of this branch of science with a parallel recognition of "agnoiology." Certainly we need a theory of ignorance. For science may remove part of it. But it will not remove what is the cause of the greater part of our ignorance, namely, the relativity of human knowledge which, though it does not restrain the enquiring mind from seeking to become " a spectator of all time and all existence," does seem effectually to bar him from attaining that vision in his present world of experience. He cannot reach the absolute or divine point of view, even if he can dimly perceive that there must be such a one. And those who believe in the Christian revelation are bound to recognize that, while it gives an abundant light, so far as our practical moral requirements go—so far as is necessary to make faith firm and hope sure and love active—it goes no way at all to satisfy our speculative curiosity or to put us at the divine point of view.

Let me briefly suggest two fields of speculation, out of many which might be mentioned, on which no progress of knowledge is likely to throw any light. The first is, the relation of the time-process, and the contingency involved in the reality of free wills, to the Eternal Being and His absolute knowledge. All experience and all revelation imply the reality of the time-process. It seems to me idle to discuss it. Also this world is a scene in which, if we can at all discern by thinking or accept in faith the reality of a divine purpose, this divine purpose is being thwarted by multitudinous rebellious wills; even if no contingency is admitted as to its ultimate realization, yet contingency must be admitted as to its realization here and now, or in this or that individual. God appears not as losing his ultimate control, but as limiting himself in this present world-order by the grant of freedom to man, and perhaps to a vaster world of spirits. God must (so to speak), while sustaining free spirits in being, stand far enough off them to leave them their relative freedom. If they will to rebel, God must so far " deliver his strength into captivity and his glory into the adversary's hand." [1] Time and contingency are indubitable facts of experience.

But more than this : it appears to our logic that, strain as it will, it cannot reconcile human freedom, however limited, with absolute divine fore-knowledge. It cannot be true, *as far as logic can see,* that God knows exactly what I am going to do, and that yet I am free to choose. Nothing, it seems to me, is more wearisome or profitless than the endless pages which have been written about predestination and free-will.

Surely it has become evident that, though we

[1] Ps. lxxviii. 61.

have good grounds for postulating the Eternal behind the Temporal—both eternal will and eternal knowledge—yet that neither scientific nor philosophical insight can get anywhere near to the attainment of the eternal or divine point of view, the consciousness of past and present and future as one eternal now. And, if we accept the reality of revelation, there too it is plain that God has no intention of lifting us any nearer to that point of view. It assures us that we are indeed responsible and free, and it puts us into the hands of a God who loves and knows us, and is guiding the universe to its destined and glorious end ; but there it stops. The absolute reality we cannot know. The divine point of view we cannot attain.

A similar incapacity appears in our relation to the problem of pain, though not for the same reason. The problem of physical pain is (especially to some imaginations—not generally those of the sufferers themselves) a burden which they cannot bear. I need not attempt to repaint the picture of the waste and torture evident in the process of nature as it has been so often and so vividly portrayed. But I must briefly enumerate the reductions and qualifications which need to be made on such estimates.

(1) We must recognize the even gross element of exaggeration in some of these pictures, particularly as regards the pain of animals, outside the area of human cruelty and carelessness. The abundant happiness of animal life is ignored. (2) We must recognize how vast a proportion of the whole amount of recognizable suffering in

the world has been due directly or indirectly to human selfishness, pride and lust. (3) We must acknowledge that the world is a system of coherent parts, and that the alleged cruelties of the system may be, and indeed appear to be, inevitable conditions, at least in great part, of any world of system and gradual development; whereas, if there were no such " cosmos," existence would be unendurable. (4) We must own the vast difference made to the problem, so far as pain affects man himself, when our eyes are opened to the truth embodied in the Cross of Christ, that all that is most noble and that approaches perfection in humanity is seen in obvious experience to be the fruit of sacrifice —of pain willingly endured; while for the disastrous effects of pain unwillingly endured we must hold the rebel will responsible. (5) We must recognize that Christ was very far from acquiescing in the suffering and disease which He saw around Him. He saw in it, at least in great part, a monstrous invasion of the world of God by a hostile power. " An enemy hath done this "; " Satan hath bound this woman." When Jesus so urgently insisted upon the need of faith, He did not mean resignation, but a persistent importunity which could change things, which could " remove mountains," which could win what would seem impossible victories. This was to be quite consistent with the ultimate willingness to endure whatever finally it did not appear to be the Father's will to remove. But He certainly meant His Church to be a fellowship of men bent on

" rebellion " [1] against   a   world   of   needless
suffering. (6) We must remember that the picture
of suffering in this world is altogether altered
in its perspective for one who believes that this
world is only the vestibule of the true life, the
place for soul-making and kingdom-building.

Nevertheless, when all these considerations
are given their full force, there still remains a
problem of pain—of pain, too, which we at least
cannot conceive to serve any useful purpose at
all.   So much is this the case, that if we were left
merely to the observation of nature, including
human nature, as it stands, in forming our conclusions as to the character of God—I do not
say we should conclude that the Creator of the
universe could not be purely good, for there are
considerations which tend to show that He must
be so.   I mean, that the highest reaches of
human character, which are the highest products
of nature, are purely good, or are tending in
that direction ; and it is hard to doubt that in
these highest products of nature we have the
fullest and best image of the Creator.   I would
not say, then, that if we were left merely to the
observation of nature in drawing our conclusion
about the character of God we should decide
against His being purely good.   But I think we
should remain in what must be an awful state
of doubt.   What weighs down the balance of

[1] I am referring to Dr. D. S. Cairns's *The Faith that Rebels*,
an admirable stimulus to Christian thought.   On the whole
subject of pain I would still refer to I. R. Illingworth's " Problem
of Pain " in *Lux Mundi*, and to James Hinton's *The Mystery of
Pain*.   No better helps to right thought on the subject have
since appeared.

the scales decidedly on the side of pure goodness is the evidence—to me the satisfying evidence —that we are not left merely to our observation of nature in drawing our conclusion, but that God has been, in some measure everywhere, and especially along the line of Israel's prophets, and finally in His Son, revealing Himself—finally translating all the dark and incomprehensible mystery of His nature into the intelligible lineaments of the human character of Jesus of Nazareth. The pure love of God—of which His wrath upon evil is only an element—the pure goodness of God which is expressed in the term, " our Father which is in heaven," is the centre of Christ's whole teaching, and He speaks continually as the Son of the Father, who alone knows Him and can with full authority reveal Him as He is.

It is on Christ's assurance that the best of men and women have lived in the conviction that God is purely good, and have found it true in their own experience that " all things work together for good to those who love God " and take Him at His word. If from time to time He seems a hard taskmaster, " reaping where he had not sown and gathering where he had not strawed," they have accepted Him as such, and have been content for the time with unintelligent slavery (as we find St. Paul glorying in being " the slave of Jesus Christ "); but while thus submitting to be slaves, they have found themselves sons, basking in the light of the Father's face, only temporarily obscured. There remains, however, an unsolved mystery in nature which

22

it does not seem that in our present condition there is any likelihood of our clearing up. It is the arrogance of reason to resent this sort of limitation. It is the reasonableness of reason to accept ignorance, inevitable ignorance, as a condition of our present imperfect condition. I could easily go on giving examples of ignorance which there is no hope of remedying. If the believer in the divine self-revelation takes full account of what he has come to know, in virtue of what he recognizes as the word of God, he finds that, abundant as is the light granted him to walk by through a dark world, yet it leaves a large part of the field of vision still in obscurity. Revelation is certainly not satisfying to the speculative curiosity.[1]

This condition of illumination, which is only partial, or knowledge which is also inevitable ignorance, is expressed in two current phrases. The first is that of the *relativity* [2] of human knowledge. We may justly repudiate the ultimate scepticism which doubts the capacity of man to attain any knowledge of the universe as it really is ; but we cannot justly doubt that it is not at best a full knowledge. The best knowledge we can gain, in whatever department of life, while it is sufficient, or may hope to become sufficient, for practical purposes, is never absolute knowledge, or knowledge such as we must ascribe to the Perfect Mind. There are tremendous problems towards which our only reasonable

---

[1] See above, pp. 187-8, on " the life beyond."

[2] I am using the word, not in the special sense given it in Prof. Einstein's theory, but in its older and more general sense.

attitude is, and in our present state will remain, a deliberate agnosticism. Our knowledge is relative, on all showing, to our present state, which can only be described as glorious if it is viewed as the prologue to something only dimly to be anticipated in the hereafter.

The other current phrase which sums up the situation is that all departments of human knowledge are " abstract." We investigate reality in a certain aspect by abstracting from the whole what concerns our particular enquiry. Scientific men to-day show a general agreement that the physical sciences, even taken all together, are abstract. There are aspects of reality with which they are not concerned. Their business is not the truth about the universe as a whole, but the special truth about it which concerns physics or chemistry or biology.[1] Certainly the moralist or theologian or artist must make the same confession. But the difficulty arises when any attempt is made to harmonize all the special sciences in one comprehensive theory.

As was said, the great attempt to form a " Weltanschaung," or general conception of the universe, can never be abandoned; but it will never be attained by the arrogance of specialists in any one abstract science or group of sciences seeking to dominate the whole field. And even the more modest minds, which are content to take the findings of different departments from those who in these departments command the

[1] In Eddington's *Nature of the Physical World*, pp. 257 ff., there is a luminous passage on the abstractness of physical knowledge; cf. p. 327.

most respect, will be always found acknowledging
that the vision of the whole in any adequate sense
is something very far above their attainments.
" Relativity " and " abstractness " remain the
dominant characteristics of human knowledge,
properly so called.

§ 5

The ideal of " reasonableness " is then a
reasonable faith, which welcomes all the light it
can get from any quarter, which is enthusiastic
for the liberty of enquiring in all directions,
which could not tolerate the rejection of anything
that can make a valid claim to be called knowledge, on account of moral or religious scruples
or prejudices, but yet recognizes faith as the very
foundation of reason and the central light of the
soul.   And this reasonable faith finds its fullest
satisfaction in the acceptance of Jesus Christ as
the very word of God incarnate.   This is my
witness and my contention.   But those of us
who are most assured in this faith must recognize
how easily faith passes into fanaticism and
obscurantism, or, short of that, how easily it
passes into credulity.   The firmest believer can
feel how great is the debt he has owed to sceptics,
who have forced him to an anxious examination
of the grounds of his belief and a careful " proving " and purging of its contents.

For myself, the noblest sceptic whom I have
had the right to call a friend was Henry Sidgwick,
and I want to say a word about his scepticism
as it is revealed in the fascinating volume of his

memoirs [1]—especially in his letters. His scepticism, the frankest and most persistent determination to shrink from no really evidenced conclusion, never allowed him to doubt that the moral
idea—the idea of the good life and of the " cate-
gorical imperative of duty "—was an ultimate and
unanalysable idea which was of the very substance
of the soul. Nor could he fail to recognize that
this idea seems to postulate God and immortality.
Thus he was always searching for " proof " (by
the way of " spiritualism " and by all other
methods) of the objective reality of immortality
and God, but always failing to find it. And without demonstrative proof he held himself bound
to refuse his assent. He hoped but could not
believe. Surely, if " the pure in heart shall see
God," Henry Sidgwick sees Him at last—but
never was it so in this life.

This demand, then, for demonstrative evidence
which his scrupulous intellect insisted upon—
is it not, in fact, an excessive demand ? Has
not science itself been compelled to recognize
that it is an excessive demand, which, rigorously
insisted upon, destroys the very bases of knowledge altogether ? Must it not be admitted that
faith is at the very foundation of reason and its
constant accompaniment ? It is faith by which
we grasp an order in nature. It is faith by which
we welcome the absolute validity of moral values.
It is the same faith by which we recognize God
and accept His self-revelation. The spirit of
venture—the venture which goes beyond the

[1] *Henry Sidgwick, A Memoir*, by A. S. and E. M. S. (Macmillan,
1906).

demonstrative evidence—something of the nature of Pascal's famous " wager "—you cannot get rid of in the intellectual any more than in the practical life of man.[1] It has been the aim of these lectures to encourage this venture of faith as the highest kind of rationality.

The world is a dark place in many aspects, and life remains a perplexing experience ; but man has got quite enough light to live by, even gloriously and thankfully, if we will walk by reason, recognizing that faith is a primary and constant constituent of reason ; and that faith in a divine helper and friend, if it never ceases to be faith, and therefore a venture and an experiment, is an experiment which, for the best of mankind, has become, and for each of us may become, also an experience and a practical certitude, as sure as the evidence of the senses, and destined to pass into open vision.

[1] Cf. H. S. Holland's *Logic and Life*, Sermon II, " The Venture of Reason."

INDEX OF NAMES

Printed in Great Britain by
Hazell, Watson & Viney. Ltd., London and Aylesbury.

282